T0323052

THE BOOK OF ABBA

THE BOOK OF ABBA

MELANCHOLY UNDERCOVER

JAN GRADVALL

TRANSLATED BY
SARAH CLYNE SUNDBERG

faber

First published in 2024
by Faber & Faber Ltd
The Bindery, 51 Hatton Garden
London EC1N 8HN

First published in Swedish in 2023
by Albert Bonniers Förlag
as *Vemod Undercover: Boken om Abba*

Typeset by Sam Matthews
Printed and bound by CPI Group (UK) Ltd, Croydon, CR0 4YY

A CIP record for this book
is available from the British Library

ISBN 978–0–571–39098–4

Printed and bound in the UK on FSC® certified paper in line with our continuing
commitment to ethical business practices, sustainability and the environment.
For further information see faber.co.uk/environmental-policy

2 4 6 8 10 9 7 5 3 1

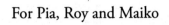

For Pia, Roy and Maiko

We have a story, and it survived.

Abba, 'I Still Have Faith in You' (2021)

CONTENTS

THE BOOK OF ABBA

THE DAY BEFORE YOU CAME

B enny Andersson is lying on the floor at Polar Studios, listening to all that remains of Abba. His eyes are closed. Everyone else has left. The song that he has just finished recording and which he is now listening to on his headphones is the chilling and portentous 'The Day Before You Came', a synthesiser ballad that is almost six minutes long. For thirty-nine years everyone assumed that this would be Abba's last recording.

Pop singles are supposed to be short and distinct, three minutes or so. Few other pop groups with Abba's track record would consider releasing a single almost twice that length, with no real chorus. The music in 'The Day Before You Came', recorded at the end of the summer of 1982, is from Benny's Yamaha GX-1, a polyphonic synthesiser with three keyboards and a built-in drum machine.

Benny's very first instrument was the accordion, and melancholy melodies, typical of Swedish accordion music, can be found throughout his compositions. With its black and white keys, his synthesiser is also an accordion of sorts, albeit one that has been beamed in from the bridge in *Star Trek*.

Outside observers may be tempted to speculate on the meaning of 'The Day Before You Came'.

For Benny, who wrote the music, the song might be about Frida. For Björn, who wrote the lyrics, it might be about Agnetha. For Agnetha, who is singing the song, it might be about Björn. The relationships and divorces of the four Abbas had been serialised in the tabloids. For much of that year Frida was recording her solo album, so she only contributed wordless backing vocals, but perhaps for her it was about her collaboration with Phil Collins, her new producer whose work epitomised 'divorcecore'.

Abba never officially split. After their eighth studio album, *The Visitors*, released in 1981, and the two singles, 'The Day Before You Came' and 'Under Attack' of the following year, the group took an ever-extending break that would span almost four decades.

'Honestly, I just wanted to take a two-year break,' Benny says. 'Try something new. Write a musical. I truly believed we would make a comeback after that. I didn't feel done at all.'

Frida maintains that it was 'the boys' desire to move on' that led to the dissolution of Abba in the early 1980s (the Abbas have always called each other 'the boys' and 'the girls'); that and the strain of working with someone who was once your lover and spouse. 'Of course that affected the decision. One is only human after all. It was a difficult departure. I would hazard a guess that we might have kept going for another couple of years at least, if it weren't for the divorces. As it was, we all felt an overwhelming sense of grief, more than anything.'

If 'The Winner Takes It All' from Abba's penultimate album *Super Trouper* offers some insight into the divorce between Agnetha and Björn, 'When All Is Said and Done' from the last album – *The Visitors* – is the corresponding song about the divorce between Frida and Benny, even though the lyrics, as always, are written by Björn.

In a 1982 interview in *Rolling Stone*, Pete Townshend of the Who said that 'Abba was one of the first . . . bands to deal with . . .

middle-aged problems in their songwriting. And [their songs were] quite obviously [about] what was going on among them.'[1]

When 'The Day Before You Came' was recorded it was as if the divorce of the entire band had been set to music. Their long-time sound engineer Michael B. Tretow says: 'There was a sense of finality in the air when the song was recorded.'

Everything had changed among the Abbas. Björn had remarried. His wedding to Lena Källersjö took place in utmost secrecy at famous restaurateur Carl Jan Granqvist's Grythyttan on 6 January 1981. Yet, the moment they left the manor house, journalists from all over the world began to call.

Agnetha was busy with her acting debut. In the film *Raskenstam* she plays a fisherman's daughter who is seduced by Gustaf Raskenstam, a notorious charlatan who romanced and swindled over 130 women during the Second World War.

Her co-star, Gunnar Hellström, directed the movie. He was an experienced and handsome actor who had gone to Hollywood to direct TV shows such as *Gunsmoke*, *Bonanza* and *Dallas*.

The Swedish press went to great lengths to generate headlines. The gossip magazine *Hänt i Veckan* wrote triumphantly: 'Pregnant Agnetha from Abba alone again.' The photo was taken on set. Of course, Agnetha wasn't pregnant, she was just playing a character who was.

'*Svensk Damtidning* decided to announce "the romance of the year" between me and Gunnar Hellström,' writes Agnetha in her autobiography *As I Am*. 'The first-page headline read "Abba Agnetha Swindled". With a still from the set of me with a giant pregnant belly.'

The gossip mill ran so hot that Agnetha wrote an op-ed in the respected Swedish daily, *Dagens Nyheter*, about how consequences were too lenient for those who published what they knew to be lies and profited from it. Legal consequences and fines were more or less unheard of, typically there was just a slap on the wrist from the Swedish Press Council. 'Why would the tabloids care about a few lines in some daily paper about a certain publication being denounced by the Swedish Press Council?' she wrote.

Five weeks after Björn had remarried, the private lives of the Abbas made world news again. When Frida was on her way to buy milk at the supermarket on 12 February 1981, she encountered headlines loudly declaring that she and Benny had divorced. She recalls turning around on the spot and not feeling able to show herself outside for a week. Once their divorce was final, Benny moved out of their joint home, taking nothing with him but two ashtrays and all the paintings.

All of this was in the air when Benny was at Polar Studios writing and recording 'The Day Before You Came'. The working title of the composition was 'Den lidande fågeln' ('The suffering bird'). Bird references are a recurring theme in Benny Andersson's work as a composer.

In 1978, Abba's manager Stikkan Anderson took over an old cinema where he commissioned the construction of the private recording studio that Benny had long dreamed of. The building that housed Polar Studios, the stately, fifty-eight-metre-tall Sportpalatset ('Palace of Sports'), is characterised by birds and the study of birds. It stands on the island of Kungsholmen, at the foot of Sankt Eriksbron, a bridge that leads from there to the Stockholm borough of Vasastan.

The property was built between 1929 and 1930, in the midst of the financial crisis, to house various sporting activities. It went into foreclosure prior to completion. Inside there was a swimming pool, tennis courts, gyms and the Rivoli cinema. Sportpalatset ('The Palace of Sports') also contains more than fifty apartments. At the very top of the building there is a three-storey apartment with a magnificent view of Stockholm. In 1933 Bruno Liljefors moved into this apartment and lived there during his final years. Liljefors, born in 1860, is one of the most prominent Swedish painters of all time, known primarily for his renderings of Swedish nature and animals.

He called the penthouse 'my little eagle's nest'. He left the windows open all year round, so that birds could fly in for him to paint. He fed the birds bucketfuls of meat and fish. Occasionally the birds would drop their food on to pedestrians below. Some birds built their nests inside the apartment. The entire apartment had to be decontaminated after Liljefors died in 1939. And the birds kept showing up, long after his death. If you looked out of the window of Polar Studios they were always there.

Karlbergskanalen flows below the building and the studio; this canal is one of the places in Stockholm where the seasons are the most noticeable. Trees reach across the water. In the springtime, leaves green with chlorophyl are reflected on the surface; in the summer the canal fills up with kayaks and motorboats; in the autumn, thousands of tourists, as well as Stockholmers, flock to the Sankt Eriksbron bridge to take selfies, capturing the red and yellow falling leaves. In the wintertime the canal freezes over and footprints of brave flâneurs can be seen on the snow. On New Year's Eve, the bridge is packed with people who know that this is the perfect spot to view the fireworks over Stockholm.

'The Day Before You Came' was recorded during the last week of 'sommarlov', a school holiday that lasts ten weeks over summer, but the mood inside the studio, as well as of the music, is more akin to that of the frozen canal in winter. The fragile, frosty sound brings to mind Yoko Ono's equally haunting 'Walking On Thin Ice', recorded by John Lennon in December 1980, the day before he was killed, and released in February the following year.

Once Benny finished the music, the original plan was to replace the drum machine with a human drummer. Percussionist Åke Sundqvist happened to be in Studio A at Polar and was called up to Studio B where Benny, Björn and Michael B. Tretow were working.

Åke Sundqvist did layering with a hi-hat, snares and bass drums, but in the end they decided to keep the sound from the drum-machine sketch, amplifying the icy feeling. 'The only other instrumentation on the song is some beats from percussionist Åke Sundqvist's snare drum,' Benny recalls.

Benny's Yamaha GX-1 had been an investment for Polar Studios when they opened in 1978. At the time the studio boasted the most state-of-the-art recording equipment in the world. The ambition was to draw the greatest international artists to the foot of Sankt Eriksbron.

Led Zeppelin heeded the call and recorded their eighth and last album, *In Through the Out Door*, at Polar Studios in 1979. On the tracks, bassist John Paul Jones can be heard playing the synthesiser that inspired Benny's choice of instrument on 'The Day Before You Came'.

These days Polar Studios is sometimes mentioned as the studio where Abba recorded all their masterpieces, but that is not entirely true. The purpose of the studio was for Abba to finally have unlimited recording time to themselves; in reality the studio was usually rented out to others. When 'The Day Before You Came' was created, the larger Studio A was being used by the West German singer Peter Griffin.

The majority of Abba's most successful songs were actually recorded in simpler studios under time constraints. When Abba began recording at the Metronome Studio on Karlbergsvägen in Vasastan, later renamed Atlantis, they only had access to one recording day a week.

The solution that enabled them to finish albums came from another Bruno, Bruno Glenmark, a musician married to the Swedish pop star Ann-Louise Hanson.

'Parallel to their other studio work, Abba recorded music in our house in Stocksund from 1973 and for a few years after,' says Bruno Glenmark. 'We got rid of our laundry room and the children's playroom and built a studio there instead. When Björn arrived in the mornings, the first thing he would say was "Where are grandma's buns?" Ann-Louise's mother used to bake buns which he loved. When they were headed to the Eurovision Song Contest in Brighton to perform "Waterloo", Agnetha asked if we could record it on video as she didn't have a video recorder of her own. So, when they came back after their victory, we all watched the video at our house.'

The Glenmark children, whose room lay above the laundry-room studio, remember how Abba would play the same song over and over again, well past their bedtime.

Abba would come to the studio with complete melodies. During the first years, Björn and Benny would sit together in a small boathouse in the Stockholm archipelago and write using a piano and a guitar. Over the years, their process became Benny writing the music on his own, after which he and Björn would go to a studio with musicians and produce the song together. The next step was that Björn brought a cassette tape home to write the lyrics. The entire music production would be done before lyrics were even considered.

They rarely discussed the subject of the lyrics; Benny says that Björn would intuitively capture the mood of his melodies.

Björn maintains that any autobiographical interpretations of his lyrics are misguided. He doesn't write about himself; rather he writes about people and relationships, which is one reason Abba's songs work so well in musicals. His lyrics, aside from the simplicity of the first years, are about everyday dramas with fully fleshed-out characters. When Björn went home to write the lyrics for Benny's 'The Day Before You Came', he began to write about a woman who accounts for an ordinary day in her uneventful life. She recounts what happened the day before her life changed due to an emotionally tumultuous encounter.

'I already knew that the melody was such – from a technical point of view – that the lyrics had to be constructed so that they would lead up to the "day before you came" place in the melody,' says Björn in *Bright Lights, Dark Shadows* by Carl Magnus Palm. 'Then, when I got the idea for a theme, I wrote down all the everyday incidents and things I could think of that would happen to someone leading a routine kind of life. It was very difficult from a grammatical point of view to get it all to fit together, because it would all have to be logical, there was no place for hitches.'

'I really like this song,' Benny tells me. 'It feels extremely sad when you listen to it. The recording is also sad, but the lyrics aren't really sad at all, which is an example of Björn's genius. If you read them, it's just someone recounting what she did on a certain day: she took the subway to work, ate lunch, came home, watched TV, read a book. It is only when the lyrics are combined with the music that you understand that something has happened to shake her up. The lyrics are very clever.'

When the woman in the lyrics comes home from work she watches TV. 'There's not, I think, a single episode of *Dallas* that I didn't see.'

The fact that Björn opts to use *Dallas* in particular – a series worked on by Gunnar Hellström, who at the time was working with Björn's ex-wife Agnetha – in lyrics that are to be sung by her, is a detail that the tabloids missed entirely.

Dallas, a series about a family that had made a fortune in oil, was by far the most popular TV show in Sweden in the 1980s. In the United States, *Dallas* had begun its run in April 1978. Swedish authorities restricted commercial television at the time, so until the late 1980s the only broadcasts available were from two public service channels, the contents of which were selected for their educational and edifying qualities. Celebrations of American capitalism were not in line with the unwritten rules of Swedish public broadcasting. Swedish viewers would have to wait nearly three years before *Dallas* was finally bought and broadcast in January 1981. The series quickly became deeply beloved and had nearly 4 million viewers in a country that at that time had 8.2 million inhabitants.

After the lonely woman in 'The Day Before You Came' has eaten her Chinese takeaway in front of the TV, she reads a book in bed before falling asleep. The author, who is named, is the American feminist Marilyn French. Her books *The Women's Room* and *The Bleeding Heart* had recently been published in Swedish.

The British synth-pop duo Blancmange released a popular cover of 'The Day Before You Came' in 1984, but thought the spectacle of a 'lanky' Northern man singing these lyrics would be even funnier if they swapped out Marilyn French for the romantic novelist Barbara Cartland.[2]

When 'The Day Before You Came' appeared on the soundtrack of *Here We Go Again*, the 2018 follow-up to the Abba movie *Mamma Mia*, the references were updated and re-established: the song is now sung by Meryl Streep; *Dallas* is the Netflix remake of *House of Cards*; the book she reads is by Margaret Atwood, author of *The Handmaid's Tale*, which had gained renewed relevance as a dystopian future vision when it became a TV series.

Agnetha's confounding restraint in singing 'The Day Before You Came' makes the listener stop and notice each turn of phrase. What is going on there? Agnetha has a voice that could cut through glass and concrete, but here she is holding back. Thus she is transformed from 'Agnetha from Abba' to the woman in the lyrics.

Benny and Björn wrote Abba's songs, but when asked about the hallmark of Abba's sound they both agree: it is 'the girls'' voices. Agnetha and Frida were part of shaping musical arrangements so complex that you will continue to find new details even after having heard a song hundreds of times.

One explanation for Agnetha's ability to vary her voice is that she often sat down when she recorded her lyrics.

'Initially the explanation was simple; we spent such an enormous amount of time in the studio,' she says. 'So I sat down because I was too tired to stand. Then I discovered that sitting affects how I sing. I sit close to the mic so as not to hunch over. That way I can hold back when the lyrics require it. That amplifies the sense that I'm not just singing, I'm narrating the lyrics.'

A couple of years earlier when Agnetha recorded the lyrics for

'Thank You for the Music', she went so far as to lie down in the studio.

'We tried different versions but couldn't get it quite right. There is a recording where I sing it like Doris Day. When we recorded again I was expecting Christian [Agnetha's and Björn's second child] and was at risk of premature labour. I was under doctor's orders to be on bed rest and to take it easy. But this was Abba, the world was waiting for a new album. We solved it by bringing a sort of lounge chair into the studio. So I sang lying down in that chair and that is the take that ended up on the album.'

Benny has likened Agnetha's singing style on 'The Day Before You Came' to a dimmer light switch, dialled down to the lowest setting. The song is structured as a solo performance by Agnetha, but Frida's discreet backing vocals are crucial to the mood of the song. While Benny is building a cathedral of synthesiser loops, Frida steps into the instrumental portion and harmonises in a high note reminiscent of a classical choral work. Frida is standing in the middle of the cathedral, singing, projecting up towards the ceiling.

Abba's sound was constantly changing and evolving. After a disco phase, the group was hugely influenced by the new synth pop that emerged in the UK and spread across Europe in the early 1980s; it was a genre created largely by visionary non-musicians who used sequencers to create noises and sounds that repeated automatically, doing away with the need to play every last note. Benny did not use a sequencer, but sound engineer Michael B. Tretow thought it would be cool if this synth ballad were to *sound* like sequencer-produced music, so he hand-cut the synth sounds played by Benny to achieve the desired, programmed, mechanical sound.

This way of gazing into the computerised and digital future – in an era that was still analogue – also characterises other recordings from the era. At the same time as Benny and Michael B. Tretow were working in Polar Studios, the finishing touches were being put to Michael Jackson's album *Thriller* on the other side of the Atlantic. Producer Quincy Jones, whose wife was Swedish, and sound engineer Bruce Swedien who was of Swedish descent and called 'Swede' by Quincy, created the music of the future on that record, working with old-fashioned studio musicians.

In 1981, when pioneering synth group Kraftwerk made their album *Computer World*, with a vision of a future in which personal computers defined daily life, they had no computers of their own. Instead, they borrowed an early personal computer, the Hazeltine 1500, for their cover image.

'The Day Before You Came' was released as a single in October 1982. It was the last song that Abba recorded, but it was their penultimate single. 'Under Attack' was released in December. Then it was over.

'The Day Before You Came' was not very successful. The single reached number 1 in the Finnish charts and number 3 in Sweden – two nations accustomed to darkness – but in the UK the single ground to a halt at number 32 and in Australia it only made it to number 48 – and these were the two countries in which Abba had seen their biggest popularity. For Abba, this strengthened the impression that their glory days were over.

But the song's popularity grew in the years that followed. In 2010, when the British TV channel ITV held a poll on Abba's best song, 'The Day Before You Came' came in third.

Many musicians have testified to the influence the song has had on them. When the single was released, the Pet Shop Boys had just formed. On their 1986 debut album *Please*, the duo's way of combining melancholy synthesiser melodies with detailed observations on daily life and subdued singing can be traced to 'The Day Before You Came'.

When Benny Andersson played 'The Day Before You Came' alone at a grand piano on his 2017 album of instrumental solo keyboard recordings, *Piano*, he reclaims the mood of the original title, 'The Suffering Bird'.

The piece that was regarded as Abba's swan song for almost four decades epitomises what the group did throughout their career.

'Even the happier songs are melancholic at their core,' Benny says. 'What we did was melancholy, undercover.'

A+B, B+A

A gnetha and Björn first met at a concert in a park in Ingared in the province of Västergötland in May 1968. She was eighteen, he was twenty-three. Both were already pop stars.

Three charts reflected the most popular music in Sweden in the 1960s and 1970s: Tio i topp, Svensktoppen and Kvällstoppen. Tio i topp was Sveriges Radio's first music chart. A jury would select new candidates every Saturday. Then young people would vote during a live show using so-called *mentometer* buttons. The two bands with the highest number of top hits on Tio i topp during the 1960s were the Beatles – and Benny's band, the Hep Stars.

Svensktoppen, which still exists, had a more middle-aged audience and was also determined by listener votes. For four decades, the rule was that songs on this chart had to be in Swedish. During the 1960s, Svensktoppen was dominated by Björn's band the Hootenanny Singers, as well as by artists who sang songs translated into Swedish by Stikkan Anderson, who would go on to become Abba's manager.

The rankings on Kvällstoppen on the other hand were based solely on sales. Confusingly, singles and full-length albums all shared the same list. Ninety-five per cent of the chart-toppers were singles. In 1969, the Beatles' *Abbey Road* became the first full-length album to make it to the top. On 27 February 1968 the number 1 song on Kvällstoppen was 'Jag var så kär' ('I was so in love'), written by eighteen-year-old debut artist Agnetha Fältskog – it sold an astonishing 80,000 copies. The song also stayed on Svensktoppen for twelve weeks, where it peaked at number 3, in competition with the Hootenanny Singers, who had three songs on Svensktoppen: 'Mårten Gås' ('St Martin's Day', three weeks), 'Så länge du älskar är du ung' ('As long as you love you are young', eleven weeks) and 'Så lunka vi såsmåningom' ('Eventually we wandered', four weeks).

That first meeting between Björn Ulvaeus from Västervik and Agnetha Fältskog from Jönköping got off to a poor start. Agnetha had had big success as a solo artist but still sang with a *dansband*.* Her band was late to that evening's gig at the outdoor performance venue Ingareds Folkpark, so the main act, the Hootenanny Singers, had to cover for them by coming on earlier. When Agnetha arrived in their shared dressing room, they shouted 'Get out of here, *dansband* singer!'

Björn was nicer than his bandmates. He had long admired Agnetha from afar.

'It's fascinating, I actually fell in love when I heard her song "Jag var så kär" on the radio,' he says. 'There was a powerful attraction in that voice. Now there I was in the park listening to her, standing a bit to the side. I don't think she even saw me. Then we met and she asked about my latest record. But I didn't have one on me.'

In the past year Björn had released a few singles under his own name. The following day, he bought his own debut single, 'Raring', or 'Sweetie', in a record store and mailed it to Agnetha. What he

---

* See the chapter on *dansband* for a fuller explanation of this uniquely Nordic phenomenon.

did not know was that Agnetha was about to get engaged to Dieter Zimmerman, who had produced her German record.

That relationship imploded a year later and Björn and Agnetha's paths crossed again, this time because of a TV show with the name *Räkna de lyckliga stunderna blott* ('Only count the happy moments'). In one scene, Björn was supposed to stand on a fishing boat, lifting girls aboard. There's no mistaking the joy in Björn's eyes when it's Agnetha's turn.

At the end of the show, everyone was supposed to hold hands and Björn made sure to end up next to Agnetha. She was dressed in a thin summer dress and afterwards he offered to keep her warm. Agnetha: 'Next day it was still cold on the dock and Björn continued to keep me warm.'

Benny and Frida's first encounter passed without event for either of them. It happened during the Swedish Eurovision heats in March 1969.

Their careers at that time were heading in completely different directions. Frida had won a talent show in 1967 in which the first prize was recording a single to be released by EMI. That became her debut single 'En ledig dag' ('A day off'). She got the chance to perform the song on *Hylands hörna*, Sweden's most popular TV show by far. That particular night happened to be a TV event of truly epic proportions, designed to entice Swedes to stay at home during the big shift to driving on the right – the authorities did not want any cars on the road during the shift. Anyone with a TV watched the broadcast.

The Hep Stars were the biggest band in Sweden during the 1960s, but subsequently ran afoul of the tax authorities: nobody in charge of the group's finances had thought to pay any taxes whatsoever during their successful years. The band's finances fell completely into disarray in 1967 when they shot a disastrous feature film in Kenya, *Habari safari*. In a documentary about the band, the singer Svenne Hedlund and drummer Chrille Pettersson call their trip to Africa 'the world's most expensive holiday'.[3]

In 1969, Benny opted to leave the Hep Stars to work on his collaboration with Björn, whom he had got to know when their respective bands were touring.

He also wrote songs with other people. He co-wrote 'Hej clown' ('Hey clown') with singer-songwriter Lasse Berghagen, for actor Jan Malmsjö, complete with a children's chorus; it is reminiscent of Scott Walker's recordings from the same time.

The 1969 Eurovision heats ended with Anni-Frid Lyngstad taking fourth place with 'Härlig är vår jord' ('Our earth is wonderful') and Benny Andersson in second place as the composer of 'Hej clown'. Both would later recall exchanging a quick hello backstage afterwards, nothing more.

A few days later, they ran into each other again at Kockska Krogen, a restaurant in Malmö. At this point Frida was touring with boogie-woogie pianist Charlie Norman. Benny was offered a seat at their table. Afterwards, Frida followed Benny to his hotel. According to reliable sources, they just talked and drank coffee with aquavit until seven in the morning.

They met again at the end of that month, this time on the jury for the radio show *Midnight hour*. Frida says, 'I thought Benny was super sexy. He had a big personality and was a very exciting man. But the love took a pretty long time to grow.'

Benny was twenty-two, Frida was twenty-three, but they both

had an uncommon amount of life experience for their age. Both became parents in their teens, and by the time they met had two children each from their previous relationships. Benny felt bad for Frida, since she lived so far outside of Stockholm, so he let her borrow his apartment.

'One day I cautiously asked him if it wasn't time for me to pack my bags and move back to Bro,' Frida says. 'He didn't think so.'

FRIDA

When Frida was going through pictures for *Abba: The Official Photo Book*, in 2014, she found an image of herself sitting in front of a mirror. 'Agnetha and I did most of our make-up ourselves. It became a sort of meditation, a way of preparing to meet the audience. Each stroke of the make-up brush transformed me from private Frida to stage Frida. I was ready to step into the limelight and give it my all.'

Abba's unique sound hinges in large part on Frida often being at the very limit of what her voice can handle and having to adopt a style of singing outside her natural range. But then, her entire life has been characterised by metamorphoses.

The Abba sound arises when Agnetha and Frida sing together, in the meeting of a soprano and a mezzo-soprano, a light voice and a somewhat darker one. Björn and Benny discovered that the unison singing was at its most powerful when the key was just a bit too high for Frida, so that she has to audibly fight to raise herself to Agnetha's level. The fusion between Agnetha's effortless and crystal-clear voice and Frida's sweat, muscle and soul creates an indestructible alloy.

Anni-Frid Synni Lyngstad was born on 15 November 1945 in Ballangen, Norway, close to Narvik, above the Arctic Circle. An initial metamorphosis was necessary immediately after her birth. Anni-Frid was conceived towards the end of the Second World War, when Norway was occupied by Hitler and Narvik was one of the most important ports in Europe. Her mother was Synni Lyngstad, a nineteen-year-old Norwegian girl. Her father was the seven years older Alfred Haase, a sergeant in the German Nazi army.

Frida was a lovechild, but there is also a political dimension: during the war, German soldiers were encouraged to have children with Norwegian women. But by the time Frida was born, the war was over and so-called 'German babies' were targets for acts of retribution.

In 1935 the SS chief Heinrich Himmler had created the breeding programme *Lebensborn*, as a way of securing German world domination in the long term. In France, the number of children born as the result of relationships between French women and German soldiers is estimated to be 200,000.[4] The French–Japanese cinematic masterpiece *Hiroshima mon amour*, written by author Marguerite Duras, tells one such story. However, Adolf Hitler disapproved of soldiers having relations with 'women of a different race' and thus discouraged this development in Latin countries like France.

Not so in the occupied Nordic nations, the population of which was considered perfect for 'breeding'. In terms of administration, Norway was tied more closely to the Third Reich than Denmark, which was at the time still formally under self-rule.

Historian Folke Schimanski has written about *Lebensborn* in Norway. The idea that the programme would have consisted of actual stud farms is a myth disseminated by pulp novels with pornographic elements. Schimanski rejects this idea, saying that women were not actively recruited to be impregnated; the children were the result of romantic relationships.

The first *Lebensborn* home outside of Germany opened in Norway in August 1941. In total, nine such homes were established in Norway, four of which had maternity wards. The homes were not intended to bring soldiers and Norwegian women together, rather they existed to care for mothers who had become pregnant through romantic relations with Germans.

During the occupation of Norway, several hundred thousand German soldiers were stationed in the country – one German soldier for every eight Norwegian citizens. Most Norwegians despised the Germans and wanted nothing to do with them. Frida's maternal grandparents, Simon and Anni, were active in local politics and leaned left politically; they were strong opponents of the Nazis, even though they had to keep their views secret. Simon passed away from cancer in February 1941 and Anni was left to support her children alone, among them her youngest daughter Synni, who would become Frida's mother.

In *Frida beyond Abba* by Remko van Drongelen, the book that most elaborately describes Frida's childhood and family history, Synni is described by her sister as calm, quiet, beautiful and known for her singing voice.

In the autumn of 1943, twenty-four-year-old Wehrmacht sergeant Alfred Haase arrived from Karlsruhe. He was tasked with organising the construction of defensive fortifications around the fjord and taking care of the German recruits arriving by train through Sweden. The way the war was going, a German victory no longer looked like a given. The German army suffered enormous losses in the Soviet Union, which shared a northern border with Norway.

After his first, long, Arctic winter, Alfred Haase spotted the teenage Synni Lyngstad in 1944. The German, who in photos has a moustache and wears his hair styled like Clark Gable, made sure to pass the Lyngstad house every morning. Synni could often be seen in the garden, where she sang as she tended to the fruit trees and flowers. Frida's biographer Remko van Drongelen draws no parallels to *The Sound of Music*, but it is hard not to think of the scenes with the young man in uniform who falls in love with Liesl Von Trapp and then betrays her and her family to the Nazis.

Alfred began to court Synni. He neglected to mention that he already had a wife back home in Germany, Anna, and a newborn daughter, Karin. Synni spoke pretty good German. At the time, schoolchildren in the Nordic countries studied German as their second language, rather than English. When Synni told her sister that she was seeing a nice German man who played the accordion, she was immediately counselled to end the relationship. The rest of her family also tried to change her mind. But Synni was in love.

She and Alfred took long walks in the countryside and made plans for where they would go after the war, when they could travel again. Their flirtation grew into a full-fledged love affair. They stopped sneaking around and began to appear in public as a couple. People started to talk behind their backs.

In 1944 it finally happened: the Soviet army managed to cross the Norwegian border; the fortunes of war had changed. Alfred was immediately transferred to the naval base in Bogenviken, west of Narvik.

In January, Norwegian troops, flown in from Great Britain and Sweden, started to fight back against the Germans, who were now being attacked from two sides in the north. Alfred's platoon was ordered to prepare for evacuation. On his last evening in Norway, he managed to bike all the way to the Lyngstad house and spent the night there for the first and last time. They got to say goodbye. At this point, Alfred had told Synni about his wife and child at home, but it had not stopped them from continuing their relationship.

At four in the morning, Alfred biked back to his platoon to be evacuated.

When Germany capitulated on 8 May 1945, Synni could no longer conceal her growing belly. Everyone in the area knew what had happened and who the father was. When Synni showed herself in town people hurled epithets and spat at her.

All around Norway, as in the rest of Europe, the celebration of peace soon turned into anger at what had taken place during the occupation. Women who had been in romantic relationships with German soldiers were labelled 'horizontal collaborators'. Many were harassed, had their hair forcibly shaved and some had swastikas painted on to their faces. In Norway they were called *tyskertøser*. Pregnant Synni and her mother, Anni, were accused of being collaborators and forced to clean buildings in which the Germans had lived.

After Frida was born, Synni thought everything would work out. She waited hopefully for Alfred to return. But as she walked around with her stroller and experienced harassment directed at her child, who was called 'German baby' and 'Nazi spawn', grandma Anni realised that the situation was untenable.

They decided that Anni and Frida would go to neighbouring Sweden. Synni had found work at a hotel in southern Norway where nobody knew about her past. The plan was for Synni to make money and then join them in Sweden. By travelling alone, she managed to avoid having a 'T' for *tyskertøs* stamped in her identity papers. Many women in her situation were stripped of their citizenship and forced to move to Germany.

Getting to Sweden was complicated for Anni and Frida. The

port in Narvik was blocked by capsized and destroyed vessels. After more than a week of travel by train and bus, grandma Anni and nine-month-old Frida arrived at a farm in the province of Jämtland in northern Sweden, where Anni was hired as a housekeeper for a widower.

Synni also managed to get to Sweden in the end and found work on a farm in neighbouring Härjedalen. Now both Frida's grandmother and mother had an income and the three generations of Lyngstad women were close to being reunited. But it was not to be. Working alone as immigrant women in the homes of older men cannot have been easy. Both Anni and Synni changed jobs often, constantly moving around, and were never to meet again.

In the summer of 1947, Synni began to develop kidney problems. She checked into a hospital. When her condition worsened, she asked her mother to take care of Frida if she didn't make it. On 28 September 1947, Synni died from kidney failure – before Frida had even turned two.

Frida's grandmother shouldered a heavy double responsibility: caring for a young child while making sure she maintained an income. After moving between various addresses in different towns, Anni and Frida put down roots in Torshälla outside Eskilstuna in January 1949, where the steel industry needed workers. Anni got an apartment, a small one-bedroom with no bathroom. She worked non-stop, took on extra work as a housekeeper and dishwasher at the restaurant Stadshuskällaren and worked as a seamstress at night. Frida started daycare on the other side of town. At first, her grandmother would take her, but soon she learned to walk there on her own.

'During long winter evenings my grandmother would sing Norwegian and Swedish folk songs in front of the fireplace,' Frida recalls. 'She encouraged me to sing as well. I discovered that I could and that I liked it.'

Displays of physical affection for her grandchild did not come easily to Anni; there were no hugs or kisses. When Frida saw her classmates get picked up by their parents, she realised for the first time how different her own situation was. 'We were two lonely people together,' she says. When Frida asked about her father, she was told that he was probably dead.

In the summers, they would go back to Ballangen in Norway, where Frida could spend time with Synni's sisters. Frida's aunt, Olive, has said that Frida was always singing, and never off key. Her favourite singer was Alf Prøysen, a Norwegian poet and writer of schlager lyrics, whose books about Mrs Pepperpot were popular in Sweden.

Every Saturday, Norwegian radio broadcast a show that played children's songs. Frida told me: 'When I think back on role models and what has inspired me, I realise that programme played an important part in my becoming a singer.'

Classmates describe Frida as introverted, and she agrees. 'I recall being a very shy and well-behaved little girl, with poor self-esteem,' she says. She withdrew, dreamed big dreams and went to the library to borrow as many as fifteen books at a time, which she would then read voraciously all weekend. She read, drew, sang and enjoyed gymnastics and sports. At nine she became a member of her school choir.

When she was around ten years old, Frida gained access to a piano and began to write her own songs. Her idol was Alice Babs, a virtuoso Swedish jazz singer with a wide vocal range of over three octaves; she recorded children's songs as well as collaborations with Duke Ellington.

In May of 1956, the annual Children's Day festival was arranged in Frida's home town of Torshälla. Stars such as Charlie Norman and rock 'n' roll pioneer Owe Thörnqvist were invited to perform. Frida was asked to sing in the parade that filed through town in front of tens of thousands of spectators. At the end of the parade, she was crowned princess of Children's Day. There are photos of her in a white dress, holding a bouquet of flowers. She has a crown on her head and her smile reveals how nervous she is.

The uniquely Swedish phenomenon of *dansband*, literally 'dance band', had begun to establish itself in the 1950s. Travelling bands, often with hyphenated names based on the founder's first name, traversed the country in minibuses and played any kind of popular music that couples could dance to – rock 'n' roll, schlager and swing. American soldiers lingering in Europe after the end of the war had introduced new styles of music and dancing.

Frida had started going out with friends on the weekends, but was not primarily interested in dancing. She gathered her courage and went up to the bands to ask them if she could sing a song or two with them. 'I'd take the chance any time I saw the opportunity.' Among those who remember the young girl with the powerful voice was Rock-Nisse, the town of Eskilstuna's own rock 'n' roll big shot: 'She showed so much promise that she was even allowed on stage.'

The cinema Saga on Storgatan in Torshälla became the big dream factory in Frida's life. Matinees on Sundays cost pennies. 'Movies defined my youth,' Frida says. *Jailhouse Rock* starring Elvis

Presley opened in Sweden in March 1958. Since the film contained four-letter words and a love scene, Swedish authorities rated it not suitable for young audiences, which meant people under fifteen could not see it, but Frida, barely thirteen at the time, still managed to sneak in. 'It had everything I could dream of: music, dancing, love, joy, people. I probably got my love of deep soulful voices from Elvis in that movie.'

It was also at this age that Frida became Frida. Her friends came up with the name, which sounded a bit cooler than her birth name Anni-Frid.

At thirteen Frida began to sing in a *dansband*. In Remko van Drongelen's biography, the band leader Evald Ek is quoted as saying, 'She was incredibly easy to rehearse with. She would hear a song once, cram the lyrics and then she'd know it. She sang songs that a thirteen-year-old should not be able to sing.'

Frida participated in local singing contests and often won them. Her grandmother did not mind her interest in singing as long as she got good grades in school, but things turned sour when Frida started to pay more attention to her career as an artist than to her studies. Late nights singing in a band got in the way of doing homework and she was rarely on time for school.

When Frida turned fourteen, she became the permanent vocalist for Bengt Sandlund's big band. She fell in love with the band's eighteen-year-old trombone player, Ragnar Fredriksson, who worked as a carpet salesman for a day job.

Frida: 'A four-year age difference is a lot in your teens. But we fell in love and I got pregnant at seventeen.' This was almost the same age her mother had been when she got pregnant. 'It wasn't a problem for me, but it was for a lot of other people.'

Even in her teens Frida had acquired a level of experience as a performing artist that it might take others half a career to achieve. By the early 1960s she was a professional singer and knew what she wanted to do with her life. At twenty-one she had her second child, but kept touring.

Much later, in early 1977, when Frida was more than thirty years old and Abba was one of the biggest bands in the world, her father suddenly got in touch.

Her family had always assumed that Alfred Haase, who had never contacted Synni during or after her pregnancy, had died at the end of the war. But a German girl, the daughter of Frida's half-brother, happened to read an interview with Frida and suspected that the unknown German father might be her grandfather, a hunch that turned out to be correct.

A meeting was arranged in West Germany. The German magazine *Pop Foto* was there. A joke Frida made, that her dad, who turned up in a suit, was not a particularly hip dresser, was turned into a headline: 'My father ought to dress a bit more trendy.'

In *Abba: The Official Photo Book* there is a picture of Frida walking under an umbrella with her father, Alfred.

Frida: 'I thought he was a nice man, but it still mostly felt strange to me. I was thirty-two years old and had a family and children of my own. Besides, I spoke no German at the time, though I got help from my aunt who had met Alfred during the occupation. Obviously we didn't develop the kind of connection we might have if we had known each other my entire life.'

RAGGARE

Watching raggare cruise around small Swedish towns in their American cars, dressed in clothes inspired by 1950s Americana, waving American flags, you'd be forgiven for assuming the subculture has a real counterpart in the United States. You'd be wrong. Raggare are unique to the Nordic countries.

The emergence of the Swedish culture of raggare might be likened to how pizza was imported and appropriated into Swedish culture. If a small town in Sweden only has one restaurant, that restaurant is surely a pizzeria.

Pizza arrived in Sweden at the end of the 1940s, with the wave of Italian guest workers who had come to Sweden for factory work and missed the food of their homeland. The fact that native Swedes also fell in love with pizza was not part of the plan, nor was it uncontroversial. The national organisation of farmers warned that '*palt* [Swedish dumplings] will soon be forgotten' and *Svenska Dagbladet* wrote of 'the foreign pancake that presents as pizza'.

In the decades since, any Italian influence on Swedish pizza has waned steadily. Pizzeria owners in Sweden today come from Syria, Lebanon, Iraq, Iran, Turkey, Palestine, Kosovo and Croatia. Making pizza is an entry point into the job market for new immigrants.

Common toppings on a Swedish pizza – now a concept in its own right – include everything from pork chop, banana, curry, beef tenderloin, chicken, goat's cheese and Béarnaise sauce, to kebab and kebab sauce. When the football player Tomas Brolin was fresh off the plane as a new recruit of Italian Parma in the 1990s he asked for pineapple on his pizza which led to impassioned debates in the Italian press about lack of respect for the local culture.

The way in which the American influences that seeded raggare culture were similarly Swedified owes a lot to the most popular band among raggare in the 1960s – none other than the Hep Stars.

Raggare are sometimes said to be a sort of Swedish take on Teddy boys or rockers, but they have very little in common with these groups, other than their taste in music and wearing their hair slicked back with plenty of grease. The Teddy boy, and Teddy girl, subculture emerged in Britain in the 1950s; they would dance to American rhythm and blues and rock 'n' roll, but they dressed like Edwardian dandies in long coats and brothel creepers with very high rubber soles.

By contrast there is nothing glamorous about Swedish, or Finnish, raggare. Swedish raggare dress in jeans, which they rarely wash, denim jackets with cut-off sleeves and T-shirts. Their trousers often hang so low that the cleft between the buttocks is visible.

Rockers, members of another British subculture that emerged in the 1950s, have grime in common with their Swedish counterparts. Grease-stained clothes are a plus. The term greaser, which was used for rockers, would work for raggare too. Rockers and raggare are united by their love of leather jackets and American boots. But one crucial difference is that where rockers rode motorbikes, raggare drive cars.

Young Swedes knew nothing of the battles between rockers and mods in England in the early 1960s. Swedish daily papers did not cover youth culture in those days; the phrase wasn't even in use. Swedish youth did not get to see rockers and mods duke it out on the beach in Brighton and determine who had the better outfits, until the film version of the Who's rock opera *Quadrophenia* ran in cinemas in 1979.

It was also at this point that Swedish youth realised that we had completely misunderstood the concept of 'mods' for over a decade. In Sweden during the 1960s the word was not used to describe minimalist modernists who listened to jazz and soul, rather it was a general term for youth who had given up on Brylcreem and taken on the trend of long messy hair for boys and girls. The people called mods in Sweden wore Afghan coats, knit sweaters, jeans and sneakers or sandals and listened to hippie music with long guitar solos. Stefan Jarl's 1968 documentary film, *De kallar oss mods* ('They call us mods'), is about young, sartorially hopeless drug addicts floating around the centre of Stockholm.

Through the record covers of late 1970s bands like the Jam and the wave of neo-mod groups, mods became associated with skinny suits, Vespas and target symbols in Sweden too. But confusion still arises any time Kenta and Stoffe, the iconic main characters in *De kallar oss mods* enter the conversation.

The members of the Hep Stars were not raggare. They dressed in a pop style, had long fringes, and aimed to look like Brian Jones of the Rolling Stones. But musically speaking they had their roots in American rock 'n' roll. Due to early gigs at cafés popular with raggare the Hep Stars built a loyal fanbase within the subculture. Crucially to raggare, it became clear that some of the members of the Hep Stars were as obsessed with cars as they were.

Music and clothes were and still are important to raggare, but most of the culture revolves around vintage American cars. Cruising around with your arm hanging out of the car window has become as Swedish as keyed fiddles and birdwatching. Raggare follow the seasons. Cars are garaged in October when snow, sand and salt could ruin the paint, and raggare go into hibernation. A sure sign of spring in Swedish towns is when the asphalt has been cleaned up after the winter and raggare begin to cruise again.

'I have always liked cars,' Benny says. 'During my time in the Hep Stars I had three different cars before I even got my licence. A black Mustang 65, a white Thunderbird 66 and a Buick Riviera 66.' Note: this was *before* Benny got his licence. 'But I swear, I was law-abiding! However I did often practise driving with friends.'

You knew when the Hep Stars were arriving in your town. The band's entrance was like a petrol-fuelled version of cowboys riding in. At the front, the band themselves and their entourage were driving three Mustangs, later updated to three Thunderbirds. Behind them a van followed, carrying equipment and instruments.

When the band came to the Jönköping and Huskvarna area, Agnetha Fältskog was one of the young fans greeting them. 'I was such a big fan of Hep Stars that I even went to their hotel once when they played in Huskvarna,' she says. 'I stood there in my green parka and asked for autographs. They wrote straight on my jacket. But not Benny. I didn't see him at all.'

Benny was seventeen years old when he became a member of the Hep Stars in the autumn of 1964. He'd had to grow up fast: he became a father at sixteen. By the time he was eighteen he had two children.

Benny was not one of the group's original members. He was recruited to replace the original keyboardist, Hans 'Hazze' Östlund, who would go on to become a sound engineer in Solna. Hazze's son, whose name is also Hans Östlund, later started the Nomads, who became a name worldwide on the reawakened underground garage rock scene.

The Hep Stars' tour director Lennart 'Felle' Fernholm would introduce the show by calling out the names of the band members as if they were at a circus, 'Chrille! Janne! Lelle! Benny! Svenne!' Then it would all break loose with a force that raggare loved.

The Hep Stars singer, Svenne Hedlund, writes in his autobiography that their new keyboardist immediately adapted to the stage energy of the rest of the band. After a few songs Benny took off his tie and used it to adjust the volume on his electric organ. Further into the concert he tipped the organ over and played it as if it were an accordion.

The band's greatest moment was the 1965 live album *Hep Stars on Stage*, which captured the feel of their live shows. Per Gessle of Roxette has named it the best Swedish album ever.

The song that elevated the Hep Stars from a band beloved by raggare and young girls to Sweden's biggest band in every category was 'Cadillac'.

The first person to growl, 'My baby drove off in a brand new Cadillac,' was Vince Taylor in 1959. Taylor was a charismatic English rock 'n' roll legend who turned bitter when he never achieved the success he desired. The final straw came at a concert in France in 1964 when he stepped on stage dressed in a white frock, under the influence of chemical substances, and declared: 'I am the resurrection! I am Jesus Christ!' Vince Taylor became part of David Bowie's inspiration for the self-destructive rock star character Ziggy Stardust in the 1970s.

But the Hep Stars had never heard of Vince Taylor. Svenne Hedlund heard the song on a radio show that played music from the countries neighbouring Sweden. The English band the Renegades never broke through in their home country, but they found their audience in Finland, the other big Nordic raggare nation, where they were regarded as being nearly Finnish. The Renegades took 'Brand New Cadillac' and trimmed it down, thus increasing its brutal efficiency. All that remained of the original lyrics was two verses, repeated over and over again. The title was short and sweet: 'Cadillac'. The song topped the charts in Finland.

Hep Stars stole the entire arrangement from the Renegades, but increased the tempo even further. 'You might have nodded off to the Renegades' version,' says Hep Stars member Lelle Hegland in the book *Benny's Road to Abba* by Carl Magnus Palm.

Finnish influences showed up in a number of places in the Hep Stars repertoire. One of the band's most popular and high-powered songs, also on their live album, was 'Farmer John'. The original is a 1959 rhythm and blues number by the duo Don and Dewey, which was picked up in 1964 by the Mexican-American garage rock band the Premiers. But the Hep Stars heard it through the Finnish group Andy and the Islanders; Antti Einiö sang it with a pronunciation that is very obviously that of someone who has never set foot in either the United States or the UK. In the 1970s, another Finnish band, a trio in denim vests, were inspired by the Hep Stars' early years: the band intentionally misspelled Hurricanes and called themselves the Hurriganes, and became as beloved in Sweden as they were in Finland.

The Hep Stars' 'Cadillac' reached a Swedish audience through the TV show *Drop in*, the first pop programme to air on Swedish television. The second episode, which was broadcast on 3 November

1963, is inscribed in both Swedish and international pop history: it was here that the Beatles made their first TV appearance abroad after their breakthrough.

When the Hep Stars appeared on the show on 23 March 1965, it was still the most important showcase for pop bands in Sweden. The Hep Stars brought all of their stage equipment, including loudspeakers and amplifiers. The TV producer was confused: 'But we're using a backing track?'

The Hep Stars knew what they were doing. Jumping off speakers and amplifiers was a crucial part of their stage show. Their performance of 'Cadillac' made a huge impression on every young Swede watching. And *everyone* really was watching. There was only one TV channel in Sweden at this time.

Bands all over Scandinavia began to play 'Cadillac' after the Hep Stars' immense success with it on TV: the Pussycats in Norway, the Defenders in Denmark, the Shanes in Sweden.

While the Hep Stars continued to cruise from town to town in their raggare caravan, the group was criticised for not writing their own songs. Even their manager Åke Gerhard admitted in an interview that they couldn't just take material from other artists for ever.

Their break turned out to come via Benny, now nineteen years old, whose significance for the band's musical output had before this been considered minor. Benny wrote 'No Response', a song that clocked in at a mere one minute and thirty-five seconds. That was enough for ten weeks on Tio i topp during the autumn of 1965.

Almost a year passed without any follow-up compositions from the Hep Stars. Everyone assumed that 'No Response' had been a one-off. In the interim Benny had fallen in love with a Norwegian girl, Ann, and suddenly had a melody in his head. While the other band members played poker in their hotel room, Benny managed to convince the receptionist to let him play the grand piano in the hotel restaurant despite the late hour.

In the book *Benny's Road To Abba* Svenne Hedlund says: 'After half an hour Benny came up and told us he had finished the melody, but that we needed to wait until he'd written the lyrics. Fifteen, twenty minutes later he came back: "I'm done now! do you want to hear it?" We told him "no", since we were playing poker. Benny also loved playing poker, so that's what we did for the rest of the night.'

When the rest of the Hep Stars finally felt like listening to Benny Andersson's second composition for the band they heard a seed of greatness. The song was called 'Sunny Girl'.

Benny fine-tuned the composition, added a verse and when it was released as a single in 1966 he could add a first pop masterpiece to his CV, even as the lyrics are a classic example of tourist English. The lyrics 'she's domestic, she is property' turned out to mean something entirely different than what he imagined. He was trying to describe the girl in the song as 'proper'.

The ballad 'Sunny Girl' marked the end of the Hep Stars' time as a band for raggare. When their recording of the Dutch-Swedish troubadour Cornelis Vreeswijk's translation of the American peace song 'Last Night I Had the Strangest Dream' was released later that year the Hep Stars suddenly became a favourite of *Svensktoppen* listeners.

The only time the phenomenon of raggare was discussed outside the Nordic countries was during the first punk wave.

Punk came early to Sweden. When the Sex Pistols were banned

from the BBC's airwaves in the UK, their manager Malcolm McLaren booked them on a Swedish tour in July 1977. The Sex Pistols played discotheques in small towns like Linköping, Växjö, Jönköping and Halmstad, gigs that sent ripples of creativity through the world of Swedish music.

Marie Fredriksson and Per Gessle of Roxette met for the first time the summer that the Sex Pistols came to their home town of Halmstad and played at the tiny venue Discotheque Stranden. The club had a maximum capacity of 125 people.

Marie Fredriksson and her friends were going, but turned around when they saw the chaos and heavy police presence outside. Per Gessle and his friend Mats 'MP' Persson stayed home, where they rehearsed Dr Feelgood covers and sent tapes to Swedish rock journalists in the hopes of being discovered.

Meanwhile the raggare decided they hated punks and attacked them with beer cans. The Sex Pistols' guitarist Steve Jones testified in the British press that they'd been attacked by 'regeri'.

Swedish punk band Rude Kids punched back at the raggare with the song 'Raggare Is a Bunch of Motherfuckers', which the iconic raggare Eddie Meduza countered with his 1979 song 'Punkjävlar' ('Punk bastards').

Another English punk band that found themselves attacked by Swedish raggare was the Stranglers. The group claimed they would not return for any more gigs and released a single in which they described Sweden as a cold Eastern bloc nation, 'Sweden (All Quiet on the Eastern Front)'. Once again Rude Kids replied with a single of their own, 'Stranglers (If It Is So Quiet, Why Don't You Play?)'. Rude Kids were celebrated in the UK, but their career was cut short when their singer Böna was killed in a car crash in 1983.

Neither raggare nor punks stopped to consider that they actually had a considerable amount in common. Both cast themselves in opposition to the hippie era. Both played simple rock songs at a furious tempo. Eddie Cochran and Gene Vincent were their fashion icons.

The Clash closed the loop when they too recorded 'Cadillac', although they covered the original version 'Brand New Cadillac' by Vince Taylor. The British punks had no clue that Benny had started his career in a raggare band called the Hep Stars, although many of them secretly loved Abba. Glen Matlock of the Sex Pistols nicked the riff for their classic single 'Pretty Vacant' from Abba's 'SOS'. When Abba played Wembley in 1979, Joe Strummer of the Clash and punk singer Ian Dury showed up backstage to say hi.

On *London Calling*, the masterful 1979 album by the Clash, there is also 'Spanish Bombs', with a melody that, to put it mildly, borrows a lot from Benny and Abba.

DANSBAND

The difficulty in explaining the Swedish *dansband* phenomenon to the rest of the world is apparent even in the name. The concept cannot be translated, no matter how international music press have tried using the literal translation 'dance bands', which gives the wrong associations entirely and does not convey anything of a culture that is as unique to the Nordic countries as raggare.

Dansband culture was crucial to Abba's evolution. Agnetha was thirteen years old when she began singing in a *dansband* (she lied about her age and said that she was sixteen). Frida also performed with a *dansband* at the tender age of thirteen.

When Björn and Benny toured with the Hootenanny Singers and the Hep Stars respectively in the 1960s they shared venues with the Streaplers and Sven-Ingvars, two pop bands that would soon recast themselves as two of the biggest *dansbands* in Sweden, active for decades to come.

Up until 1975, Abba is not referring to disco dancing when they sing the word 'dance', but rather to the dancing of *dansbanor* – open-air dance venues – and dance restaurants. The song 'Dance (while the Music Still Goes On)' on their 1974 album *Waterloo*, stands out in the Abba catalogue for being structured as a duet between Björn and Agnetha.

When Björn sings the refrain 'Baby, give me one more dance, while the music still goes on,' this is about organised dancing at ballrooms where one asks a partner to dance one song at a time. Here the question, 'May I have another dance?' should be taken literally, without sexual overtones. The line about letting a dance be 'our last goodbye' is understandable in the context of ballroom dancing, but confusing in a disco context. How can one say good-bye with a dance?

In the elongated and sparsely populated country of Sweden, petrol stations have been equally important to record stores in terms of selling music. If you stopped at a petrol station in Sweden in the 1970s and into the 1980s, you could see from the cassette tapes by the counter that the top sellers were Abba and various *dansbands*. Bands like Vikingarna, Flamingokvintetten and Thorleifs could sell hundreds of thousands of copies.

As far as Abba and *dansbands* went the influences flowed both ways. Abba's song 'I Do, I Do, I Do, I Do, I Do' from 1975 sounds like a *dansband* song. Jazz saxophonist Ulf Andersson did overdub upon overdub in the studio until it sounded as if there were half a dozen saxophones in the performing ensemble, precisely the sound favoured by *dansband*. 'They knew exactly what they wanted,' he says.

Subsequently, Ulf Andersson moonlighted for decades touring with an Abba cover band to supplement his jazz career. Whenever 'I Do, I Do, I Do, I Do, I Do' came up on the set list it was his time to shine at the front of the stage.

The saxophone became a signature instrument for *dansband* as the accordion was phased out in the 1960s. Lars O. Carlsson who produced legendary *dansband* Vikingarna, was a saxophonist himself and liked to emphasise the instrument in the mix. No band, other than possibly Thorleifs, had a fuller saxophone sound than

Ingmar Nordströms, where all six members of the band brandish saxophones on album covers and publicity photos.

The *dansband* scene became known for album series: the same title, numbered consecutively. Vikingarna did *Kramgoa låtar* numbered 1–20 between 1975 and 1992. Ingmar Nordströms' album series was called *Sax Party*.

On the 1974 album *Sax Party 1*, among other original compositions by organist Bert Månson like 'Partajlåten (På partaj)' there is also an instrumental cover of Abba's 'Honey Honey'. On *Sax Party 2* from 1975, Ingmar Nordströms do their take on the then brand-new 'I Do, I Do, I Do, I Do, I Do' in an instrumental version where the saxophones also play the lyrical melody – a veritable sax party, as it were. When Ingmar Nordströms play Fats Domino's 'Blueberry Hill' on their 1981 album *Sax Party 8*, they point to the true pioneer of the multi-harmony sax sound.

The extreme clothes and rituals of the Nordic *dansband* culture are probably as notable to the outside world as the costumes and songs of indigenous populations of Papua New Guinea.

American photographer Peter Beste has made a name for himself documenting extreme music cultures. After making a book about the rap scene in Houston, marked by abuse of cough medicine and the brandishing of guns, he went to Norway and made a book about the country's infamous early black metal scene, where members of these bands have burned down churches and committed murder. During his travels in Norway he encountered *dansband* for the first time.

'Ivar Peersen of the band Enslaved was the first person to tell me about *dansband*,' Peter Beste told Swedish music journalist

Per Sinding-Larsen. 'He said that there is a depraved side and a hedonistic madness to *dansband*. Qualities black metal bands often claim to have but do not necessarily actually possess.'[5]

Peter Beste's photo book *Dans med meg* ('Dance with me'), with photos from outdoor dance venues in Norway and Sweden, shows a blue-collar scene with a strong sense of community, partying in parking lots, tattoos, sweat and sex.

To leaf through the album covers of *dansbands* from the 1970s is to enter a parallel universe.

All band members are dressed in matching outfits. Eldorados from Eskilstuna wear medieval puffed sleeves with shiny golden trousers stuffed into platform shoes. Kjell-Åkes from Skara wear bib overalls in primary colours with matching scarves.

Bib overalls were big for a while: Svänzåns from Sundsvall had white ones, and clogs with a stars-and-stripes pattern, one of many examples of how *dansband* culture rubs up against raggare culture.

Other examples of *dansband* outfits are satin or velour jackets and white suits that look like something Elvis's Las Vegas stylist might come up with, if he was on acid and had no budget. Like the *dansbands*, Abba didn't dress in expensive clothes from exclusive international fashion brands in Milan or Paris, but rather in creations made by people from their circle of friends who happened to own a sewing machine.

The reason for the fantasy outfits of the *dansband* scene was practical as well as rational. In a country with the highest taxes in the world the term 'tax-deductible' was a lodestar for every Swede. Swedish tax law declared that stage clothes for a touring band were tax deductible only if they could not be worn in civilian life.

If you attempted to shop at your local supermarket dressed as the members in Gert Jonnys, you would quickly be escorted off the premises. If the clothes indicated that you worked together, that was yet another reason for a tax deduction to be approved.

According to a tradition that has followed *dansbands* from their origins in big bands they were often named for the leader, ideally a double name with a possessive 's' at the end: Berth Idoffs, Curt Haagers, Thor Görans, Thorleifs, Bernt Enghardts. For the audience this kind of name was an immediate indication of the sound of the music.

When Lasse Stefanz, one of the absolutely biggest bands in the genre began spelling their name with a 'z' they set off a new trend that many followed: Fernandoz, Jannez, Dolbyz, Larz-Kristerz. It all began by chance. When Lasse Stefanz were going to play the Sommarlust park in Kristianstad they ran out of letters for the marquee. The name requires four 's' but the organiser only had three. The park director took matters into his own hands and decided to put a 'z' at the end: Lasse Stefanz. Swedes thought it genius.

Despite *dansband* music being incredibly popular for more than half a century it has rarely been granted much space in broadcast media.

P4 is the public radio station in Sweden tasked with playing popular music for a broad adult audience. Statistics from February 2007 revealed that of the 17,121 songs played on P4 during two randomly selected months, only twenty-five were *dansband* songs.

Protests gathered under the banner 'The *Dansband* Rebellion'. All of the most important *dansband* artists in Sweden, including composers and booking companies, signed a joint discrimination complaint against P4: 'Public service means meeting listener wishes and demands. The employees at SR are hired by their listeners. Withholding music from a popular genre is in direct violation of their professional duty and we demand change.'

Dansband fan Silja Sahlgren-Fodstad wrote a comment on the website of Finnish public service company Yle: 'The adult radio stations assume that it is fine to play AC/DC's "Highway to Hell" to accompany our lunchtime coffee, but seem to think that, for instance, Vikingarna's version of "Leende guldbruna ögon" would cause an uproar among listeners.'

In a manner comparable to the famous Filipino cover bands that flawlessly mastered every song at the top of the charts, *dansbands* found and find their repertoire in every genre. Any kind of chart music can be picked up and transformed to fit the *dansband* sound and tempo, this is also an indirect audience demand. When you 'go out dancing' you want to hear the latest songs, regardless of if you heard them in the cinema, or at the Melodifestival.

Dansbands, and the dancers who love them, have also always been open to all forms of folk music. The roots in Swedish fiddler culture are obvious. In 1963 the biggest hit in Sweden, in the midst of the first big pop-music wave was the deeply folksy 'Spel-Olles gånglåt' by Trio me' Bumba. When the entertainment booking company Telstar asked Trio me' Bumba if they would consider a new band from Liverpool tagging along as their opening act they said yes. During the tour Paul McCartney used to stand backstage during Trio me' Bumba's set and help the singer with his costume change during an Elvis parody number.

Country music is the non-Scandinavian music tradition that has the most in common with Swedish *dansband*. The honky-tonks of the American South, where live bands provide the dance music, are not too different from Swedish dance establishments. In both cases the main focus musically is on rhythm; it is crucial that the music is truly danceable. Swedish *dansband* music is set to a steady 4/4 tempo. *Bugg*, a swing dance derivative, and foxtrot are the most common dances. Many Swedish artists, such as Kikki Danielsson, have oscillated between *dansband* and country music. The singer in Lasse Stefanz likes to wear a cowboy hat.

There are also parallels between Swedish *dansband* and American country musicians when it comes to their lyrics. Common themes are love, home towns, friendship, ageing, nature (with references to trees and birds) and nostalgia for childhood summers. 'The good old days', whatever that means, are a pervasive theme.

On the dance floor men and women become equals: either sex can ask a partner to dance. The expression 'båda ska vara med på noterna' (roughly, but not literally, translatable as 'it takes two to tango') becomes symbolic as well as literal. The book *Livets band: Den svenska dansbandskulturens historia* by Leif Eriksson outlines geographical differences and how they have changed over the decades. 'In the south of Sweden it was exclusively gentlemen until three or four songs at the end, at which point the ladies got their turn. In Norrland men and women took turns, with three invitations at a time. Egalitarian dancing became more common in the 1980s and an increasing number of organisers let go of all rules in this regard.'

Who invites whom to dance, gentlemen or ladies, can be indicated by a sign up on stage. Today many rules have fallen by the wayside, but, as Eriksson says, the last dance is emotionally significant – a dance for committed couples, and those hoping to commit.

When Abba released their comeback album *Voyage* in 2021, they emphasised through their choice of sound that Abba was not interested in getting in on any contemporary trends. In the same moment that Benny's rolling *dansband* piano shows up in 'Just a Notion' you know where the group is heading. Agnetha and Frida take the lead. The sign up by the stage reads: *Ladies*.

THE MANAGER

Stig Anderson, always called Stikkan Anderson, has the most misspelled name in the history of the Swedish press.

Swedish music would not be the same without him. He is a key figure in the story of Abba. Yet people can't seem to get the spelling of his name right. Since his life's work never goes out of style, from Abba to the Polar Music Prize, it can be seen misspelled monthly in the biggest Swedish newspapers. If you are feeling good about having managed the odd spelling of his nickname, typically spelled 'Stickan', you'll be so pleased with yourself that you will forget that his last name is not spelled with the customary double 's'.

One might say that misreadings are typical of the overall view of Stikkan Anderson and his work.

Stikkan Anderson is in some sense the archetypal music manager. A man with a self-assured smile, dressed in a fur coat, cigar in hand, who never misses a chance to mention how much money he is making. (It is unclear if he actually ever wore a fur coat, and he didn't smoke cigars, although he did chain-smoke cigarettes, but the general perception of him still looks something like that.)

His image contributed to the controversy that often surrounded him. When Stikkan Anderson's name was mentioned in the papers and on Swedish television, or radio, from the 1960s onward the context was almost always critical. Nobody spoke favourably of him, or mentioned his deep knowledge of music.

*

Stikkan Anderson was born in 1931 in the small town of Hova in Västergötland. His mother was a hairdresser and a washerwoman; his father was unknown. Stikkan used to call himself a bastard.

Ten years after Stikkan Anderson's death, his daughter, Marie Ledin, received a letter from a retired bank clerk from Hova, whose grandmother had been best friends with Stikkan's mother Ester. The letter-writer claimed to know that Stikkan's father was a womaniser from Blekinge by the name of Oskar Sjölander, saying that late in life grandma Ester had told Stikkan who his father was, but that at that point Stikkan had no interest in meeting him.

To make ends meet, when he was a child Stikkan's mother took on every kind of extra work she could find. She was at the very bottom of the social ladder in Hova, ironing shirts and starching collars for whomever could pay. Her son learned the importance of making use of every opportunity to make a dime. At this time schools did not have central heating, so as a boy Stikkan would bring home extra pennies by arriving at school before anyone else each morning and kindling the fire in the classroom stoves.

Stikkan would also distribute electricity bills to people in the area by bike and chalk the football field. He used the money he made to buy phonograph records, a passion that was ignited the day his mother came home with a portable gramophone. Their copy of 'Zeppelinarvalsen' had a scratch at the beginning which caused the needle to skip straight to the refrain. This had a profound effect on Stikkan's own songwriting – he went straight for the hook.

The fact that Stikkan Anderson went on to become a multimillionaire did not change his attitude to money. Not a paperclip was wasted at the Polar Music offices. Photocopies did not go in the bin;

each A4 sheet was divided into four parts and reused as notepaper. Marie Ledin: 'You would put a paperclip on the sheet and write the note.'

When he himself was travelling on business, or when the Anderson family was travelling and stayed at luxury hotels, Stikkan would bring his own coffee-maker. 'Hotel coffee is so expensive.' When the time came to install a swimming pool in their garden in Stockholm, Stikkan dug it himself, together with his wife's brothers.

As a teenager Stikkan Anderson loved music and entertainment. Along with his friends he would appear in various amateur revues in the area. He played acoustic guitar in local quartets, performing American standards like 'When You're Smiling'.

He also loved to solve crossword puzzles and continued to do so throughout his life. Every day Stikkan and his wife Gudrun would work together on solving the puzzle in *Svenska Dagbladet*. In his later years the solving of crosswords was purely a hobby, but when he was young that too was a way of making money. When the couple won fifty kronor solving the *Dagens Nyheter* crossword in the 1950s, their cash prize went straight to rent.

The solving of crossword puzzles is also key to Stikkan Anderson's prowess as a songwriter. Listening to his lyrics today, the joy of expression and richness of his language are striking. The most important thing in a song lyric is how well the words work together – much like in a crossword puzzle.

Stikkan's output as a songwriter is nearly unparalleled. During the twenty-five years or so that Stikkan Anderson was active he published 767 song lyrics. He bought the rights to songs that he heard on Radio Luxembourg and then wrote Swedish lyrics for them. Typically he could manage at least two in an evening. Marie

Ledin recalls how he would sit in his office and listen to imported records. 'He would play the song until he knew it by heart. Then he would write the lyrics.'

In the 1960s Stikkan Anderson met a Belgian man who taught him the basics of publishing. Together they travelled to the United States where they met publishers and songwriters, and picked out songs for which they bought the European market publishing rights. In New York they also went to Harlem jazz clubs. Stikkan would come to be best known for his Swedish pop chart-toppers and Abba, but jazz was always his passion.

Stikkan Anderson founded Sweden Music, one of Sweden's first independent record companies – ironically every bit as independent as the left-wing anti-commercial stalwarts MNW and Nacksving. When Sweden Music and Polar Records were finally sold to multinational PolyGram in the 1980s, their combined catalogues included more than 100,000 titles.

The fact that Stikkan had written the lyrics for half the songs on the Svensktoppen chart some weeks – his record was seven out of ten – was not celebrated as an accomplishment, but used against him by his colleagues. *Dansband* music and schlager were considered low status. Stikkan Anderson countered with attitude.

Lars Forssell, poet and member of the Swedish Academy, as well as the writer of immortal song lyrics such as 'Sommar'n som aldrig säger nej' ('The summer that never says no') with the line 'Dina bröst är som svalor som häckar' ('Your breasts are like nesting swallows'), said: 'Stikkan Anderson is dangerous and writes shit lyrics. The ideas he disseminates are repulsive to me.' Tommy Körberg, later the foremost singer of music written by Björn and

Benny post-Abba, said: 'Stikkan Anderson represents unscrupulous speculation.'[6]

Outwardly Stikkan Anderson never admitted that this hurt him. In a 1970 interview he said: 'Of course what I write is shit.' But at home he hung a framed letter of encouragement from the lyricist, composer and folklorist Ulf Peder Olrog. Stikkan had presented Olrog with his very first composition, 'Tivedshambo'. Thanks to Olrog's support he found the courage to keep going. In the letter Olrog encourages Stikkan to start reading Swedish poetry.

Stikkan Anderson wrote tongue-in-cheek everyday poetry within the constraints of the three-minute pop song. Listen to Monica Zetterlund's recording of 'Gröna små äpplen'. On one level it is a straight translation of the original 'Little Green Apples', but it is also a love letter to Stikkan's own wife, Gudrun.

Stikkan's reworking of 'Sadie (the Cleaning Lady)' is transformed into ironic kitchen-sink realism in Siw Malmkvist's signature number 'Mamma är lik sin mamma' ('Mum is like her mum'). Stikkan himself has said that he had a lot of fun writing the following lines:

Och så ska man då va' älskarinna
ha krafter var
när ens karl
läst 'Jag, en kvinna'

Som en dröm
ljuv och öm
fastän sliten

(And then to be the temptress
in the bedroom
when your man
has read *I, a Woman*

Like a dream
sweet and tender
though worn to the bone)

Back then they were perfectly of their time, but the lyrics require some explanation today: *I, A Woman* is the title of a Danish book that became a much-talked-about and notorious Swedish sex film by the same name.

The same mix of humour, desire and dreams from the post-war social democratic state can be found in Brita Borg's 'Ljuva sextital' ('Sweet sixties'). In the book *Svensktoppen i våra hjärtan*, Stikkan Anderson himself describes how the song was conceived: 'In 1969 Björn and Benny were in the studio and sent a tape over by messenger with a song that they wanted me to write the lyrics for. I was in a hurry because I was getting ready for a night on the town.'

The result was a Swedish classic.

Björn and Benny had considered recording 'Ljuva sextital' themselves. But their producer at the time, Bengt Bernhag, a colleague of Stikkan at Polar, said, 'The lyrics are too comical for you.' Instead the song ended up with the variety performer and actress Brita Borg who recorded an unforgettable version.

When Stikkan Anderson finally won a *Grammis* award for songwriter of the year, he won 'for the tenderness of "Gröna små äpplen", the humour in "Mamma är lik sin mamma", and the ironic nostalgia of "Ljuva sextital".'[7]

During his years as a publisher and songwriter Stikkan was always looking for new collaborators. He discovered Björn's abilities in 1963 during a talent show arranged by Sveriges Radio.

Mackie's Skiffle Group, the first group Björn Ulvaeus started to play with, shifted gears from skiffle to folk and became West Bay Singers, an allusion to their home town of Västervik. When they won the contest Stikkan Anderson and Bengt Bernhag were in the audience and signed them to their new company Polar Music. They also convinced the band to change their name to the Hootenanny Singers and start singing in Swedish.

Stikkan Anderson had taken Ulf Peder Olrog's advice and read Swedish poetry to enrich his writing. On their debut album, the Hootenanny Singers included a recording of Dan Andersson's poem 'Jag väntar vid min mila' ('I am waiting by my charcoal pile'), set to music, which bored its way straight into the Swedish soul.

The Hootenanny Singers became one of Sweden's most popular groups. It is hard to beat their record of playing 168 gigs at public parks in one summer. At times they would play four shows in one day.

As the Hootenanny Singers made their way through Sweden, the even more popular, and wilder, group the Hep Stars did the same. Björn and Benny met for the first time on the evening of 5 June 1966.

The Hootenanny Singers met their rivals by the side of the road and invited them to an afterparty by shouting 'Party in Linköping!'

The Hep Stars were late; they had misheard the invitation and drove to Lidköping, three hours in the wrong direction. The night ended with Björn and Benny sitting on a bench outside of Rally

Hotel in Linköping playing songs by the Beatles. Today there is a memorial bench there, to commemorate their meeting.

Starting with 'Ljuva sextital' Björn, Benny and Stikkan Anderson began to collaborate on writing songs for other artists; a sort of Swedish equivalent of the songwriters working in the Brill Building in New York City. Björn and Benny wrote the music together. The lyrics were written by Björn with occasional input from Stikkan who was good at coming up with catchy titles and the right phrasing. Meanwhile Stikkan Anderson built his company and created a stable of artists.

Then Björn got together with Agnetha, and Benny with Anni-Frid. Marie Ledin writes: 'Dad probably didn't know much about the boys' girlfriends initially. He is said to have grumbled that there were too many uninvited guests running in and out of his offices.'

In 1970 Björn and Benny put out an album together: *Lycka* ('Happiness'), the first and only one that they made as a duo under their own names. The album was released on Polar Music and produced in collaboration with Bengt Bernhag.

When they needed backing vocals for 'Hej gamle man!' ('Hey old man'), a song about the Salvation Army, they asked their girlfriends. When Stikkan heard the results he exclaimed: 'My god! What a workplace choir!'

That is the first recording including all four members of the band that was to become Abba.

Björn and Agnetha got married in the church in Verum in northern Skåne. The priest misheard them and thought the happy couple were 'atheists' rather than 'artists'. Everyone who was there describes their wedding as joyous and romantic, with the bride and groom in a horse-drawn carriage.

Marie Ledin was fourteen years old and drank wine for the first time ever. 'That night all three of us slept in the same room, Mom, Dad and I. Early the next morning I was woken up by the news that Bengt Bernhag was dead.'

Bengt Bernhag, who had been very close with Stikkan and Björn, took his own life on the wedding night. He suffered from recurring bouts of depression and made previous suicide attempts. 'That was the first time I saw Dad cry,' Marie Ledin recalls.

Stikkan had known Bengt Bernhag since his teens. To Björn, who had a complicated relationship with his own father, Bengt Bernhag was a mentor.

In 1986, when Stikkan Anderson was a guest on the TV show *Här är ditt liv*, a Swedish version of the British format *This Is Your Life*, the name Bengt Bernhag is mentioned three times during the cavalcade of guests and memories. But neither the host Lasse Holmqvist nor anyone else says one word about what happened to Stikkan's most important friend and colleague.

When Stikkan enters the TV studio, Lasse Holmqvist feels the need to explain to viewers why one of Stikkan's eyes is red and swollen. Stikkan, fifty-five years old at the time, says that he accidentally fell earlier in the day. The previous year, his family asked him to undergo treatment for alcoholism, but Stikkan's answer was: 'I don't want any goddamn treatment!'

He processed Bengt Bernhag's suicide by not talking about it at all and throwing himself into work with renewed fervour.

Stikkan Anderson's international breakthrough came in 1974 when he wrote the lyrics for 'Waterloo'. But if the rules for

Melodifestivalen, the annual Swedish contest that determines what song will represent the country in the Eurovision Song Contest, had been different he, Björn and Benny might have won the previous year as well as the year before that.

One night, while he was driving home in his car, Stikkan Anderson heard a song on the radio, sent to the youth desk by a fifteen-year-old girl from Halmstad. The song itself was not what piqued his interest, it was her voice. Stikkan Anderson called everyone he knew in Halmstad to track down the singer – Lena Andersson. A couple of days later they had signed a contract.

Lena Andersson was called 'the girl with a voice like silver bells'. Stikkan Anderson bought the rights for Buffy Sainte-Marie's 'I'm Gonna Be a Country Girl Again' that became 'Är det konstigt att man längtar bort någon gång?' ('Is it so strange to want away sometimes?') The song rose straight to number 1 on the Svensktoppen chart. Her debut album from 1971 was titled *Lena, 15*.

The following year Björn, Benny and Stikkan wrote Lena Andersson a song for Melodifestivalen. In those days the viewers didn't vote, a so-called expert jury did, a concept that Stikkan Anderson hated. Lena Andersson's contribution 'Säj det med en sång' ('Say it with a song') came third. When the Swedish public had their say, after the festival, the song went to number 1 on the Svensktoppen chart.

Lena Andersson signed to Polar Music. Not long after that Stikkan Anderson signed a contract with another fifteen-year-old super talent, Ted Gärdestad. Lena Andersson sang backing vocals on Gärdestad's 1972 debut album *Undringar*, together with Agnetha and Anni-Frid. The album was produced by Björn and Benny. On Ted Gärdestad's first four albums it is the Abbas who are working in the background.

In 1973 the quartet entered Melodifestivalen as Björn & Benny, Agnetha & Anni-Frid with the song that introduced the Abba sound: 'Ring ring (bara du slog en signal)', written by Stikkan, Björn and Benny. When the expert jury chose Malta's 'Sommar'n som aldrig säger nej', the phones rang off the hook at the Sveriges Radio complaint hotline. The tabloids ran the headline 'The Wrong Song Won!'

'Ring ring (bara du slog en signal)' went to number 1 on Kvällstoppen instead, the album made it to number 2 and the English single version came in at number 3 (shortened to 'Ring Ring', with lyrics by chronically smiling megastar Neil Sedaka).

When Abba entered the contest again the following year, the rules had changed. For the first time the jury groups consisted of regular listeners. If it weren't for that, who knows if 'Waterloo' would have won?

Stikkan knew exactly what to do after the Eurovision win. Through his contacts with music publishers he had made sure to put into place a complete business plan, as well as contracts signed with record companies in each country.

Björn has said that Stikkan Anderson was the first person to have even the faintest sense of the possibility of a major breakthrough for a Swedish pop band. 'Stikkan was the first to believe we could make it big out in the world.'

When Abba achieved that goal and became one of the biggest bands in the world, Stikkan Anderson stopped working as a songwriter and became their full-time manager. Among the last Abba lyrics that Stikkan had a hand in creating were 'Knowing Me, Knowing You', 'Dancing Queen', and 'The Name of the Game' – not a bad finale.

The last year in which relations between Stikkan Anderson and Abba were still good was 1981. He turned fifty years old that January. At seven in the morning the group surprised him in his home. Agnetha and Frida, fronting a chorus line, rang his doorbell to sing 'Ljuva sextital'. Björn and Benny stepped in off his balcony to sing 'Happy Birthday'. The next day the whole thing was documented in the evening paper *Expressen*, in a special appendix, *Stikkan-Expressen*.

For his birthday Abba made a record, the rarest one in their entire catalogue, *Hovas vittne* ('Hova's witness'), released as a twelve-inch single on red vinyl, pressed in 200 copies. It has fetched upwards of 50,000 kronor (about £3,600) at auctions.

The titular Hova is the town in which Stikkan was born and raised. In the lyrics Stikkan is called 'a country bumpkin with rhythm'. The lyrics are full of inside references to his life and to the way he believed a song should sound. Agnetha and Frida sing: 'The bridge, Stikkan, it's worth it this time, even though you think this song is too long. The bridge, Stikkan, we wrote this thinking you'd like it if we raised it by half a note.'

The fissure that emerged between Stikkan and Abba soon thereafter had to do with attitudes to money. Stikkan's way of dealing with the constant criticism that he was subject to in Sweden was to hit back equally hard, which indirectly affected Abba and the group's music.

'The Rolling Stones' manager never spoke of how much his band made, but ours did,' Björn says. Stikkan dealt in everything from oil to bikes; this, too, became associated with Abba.

By the time the recording of *Här är ditt liv* rolled around on 18 January 1986, relations were in a deep freeze. Watching the show today feels like watching television from 1956. The pace is incredibly slow. The host, Lasse Holmqvist is uninquisitive and misses chances to ask obvious follow-up questions. There is nothing about the mood or the guests to indicate that Stikkan has led a glamorous life and travelled the world. The whole thing feels more like the retirement ceremony for the director of a handball team.

There was no way Abba could refuse to participate, but they aren't in the studio either. Does Abba even exist at this point? It has been almost four years since Benny put the final touches to their swan song 'The Day Before You Came', alone in the studio, as the only remaining member of the band. Agnetha and Frida are trying their luck at solo careers, Björn and Benny are working on the musical *Chess*, which has yet to open.

Abba participates in a pre-recorded segment in which they perform 'Tivedshambo', Stikkan Anderson's first hit from 1951. Björn plays the guitar, Benny the accordion. They look like they always do in their blazers. Agnetha looks like an international pop star in brilliant red. Frida wears elegant hunting attire and looks more like royalty than a singer. It will be decades before Abba appears together in public again.

But then, towards the end of the ninety-minute show it turns out that two of the Abbas have travelled from Stockholm to Malmö after all, where *Här är ditt liv* is broadcast live. It appears to be unplanned. 'We didn't know that you'd show up until a few hours ago,' Lasse Holmqvist says.

Once Björn and Benny sit down in the studio, the atmosphere is tense. Björn is diplomatically polite. After Lasse Holmqvist says something about how much Stikkan has meant for Abba, Benny interjects, 'We are probably the preconditions for one another.

Stikkan was important for us when we started out. But if it hadn't been for us, Stikkan would not have been here now.'

Marie Ledin writes that her father was greedy when it came to attention. 'After all those years Dad was still vain. He wanted to keep eyes on himself, one way or another. It was hard for him that Björn and Benny wanted to move on on their own. He acted like the curious, prying, worried father of teenagers that he already was with me and my brothers. Butted in too much. Became less helpful and more of a burden.'

The final collision came in 1988 when the large American record company RCA put in an offer on Sweden Music and Abba's entire catalogue.

Some historical perspective is in order when writing about old deals in the record industry. Up until the early 2000s very few artists managed to steer clear of bad decisions in terms of contracts and rights. In the 1960s nobody could have predicted that a consumable product like pop music might have lasting, or even appreciating, value. Nobody predicted that other music formats such as cassette tapes, CDs, VHSs, DVDs, minidiscs, mp3 and streaming, would succeed LPs, EPs and reel-to-reel tapes, making it possible to sell the same songs, over and over again.

The Beatles broke up after Brian Epstein, their Stikkan Anderson, died of an overdose in August 1967. Brian Epstein had managed the band's finances. In his absence a rift emerged between John, George and Ringo on one side and Paul on the other. John, George and Ringo argued that the Beatles should begin working with Allen Klein, a powerful American businessman who, it was later revealed, defrauded all of his clients. Paul, influenced by conversations with his wife Linda's lawyer father, opposed the decision. The Beatles split up shortly afterwards. The band members lost their catalogue. Much later, John Lennon would admit that Paul McCartney had been right.

When RCA made their offer, Stikkan was the sole owner of Abba's catalogue. After Abba's last two singles flopped commercially, Abba had disappeared off the media's radar. As late as 1988 nobody could have predicted Abba's powerful 1990s revival. Björn and Benny thought the old pop band was dead and gone and sold their shares to Stikkan when Björn moved to London.

When Stikkan wanted to sell the catalogue to an American company, RCA, Benny vehemently opposed it. Benny wanted to buy back the rights himself. Under no circumstances did he want to see the songs in the hands of a foreign company. Stikkan maintained that Benny didn't fully grasp the amount of money involved. 'You don't have that kind of money at all. How could you possibly buy out Abba's entire production?' In the end, Stikkan decided not to sell to RCA. Those who knew him think he did so out of respect for Benny.

But the following year a new offer appeared from a different company, PolyGram, who raised the bid to the then-astronomical 189 million kronor. Stikkan called the Abbas and said: 'I simply have to say yes; this offer is far too good to refuse.'

Marie Ledin: 'And this is when, in the wake of a conflict between two people who had long been like father and son, the real disaster occurred.'

Benny was furious and got the other Abbas on his side. Contracts were examined, financial advisors found mentions of royalties that could be interpreted in various ways, the tension kept ratcheting up, both parties were ready to go to court, until PolyGram finally intervened and convinced them to settle.

At that point it was already too late and the parties never got over the conflict. The chasm between Stikkan and Abba still remained when Stikkan Anderson died on 12 September 1997 at sixty-six years old, his body ravaged by alcohol abuse.

In the end, PolyGram paid 189 million kronor for the sale, equivalent to 415 million (around £30 million) today. When artists of Abba's status have sold their catalogues in the 2020s the sums involved have been ten or twenty times that number. It is clear now that the real winner in the battle over Abba's songs was PolyGram.

Stikkan Anderson didn't always spell his name that way. He was born Stig Erik Leopold Andersson and initially went by Stickan.

He started spelling his name 'Stikkan', inspired by actor Akke Carlsson – known for playing iconic comedy character Åsa-Nisse, and an early business partner of Stikkan's – as well as TV entertainer Pekka Langer.

These two dignitaries were at a level that the young Stikkan aspired to one day reach.

WATERLOO

Abba had the perfect song for success in the Eurovision Song Contest 1974. Their first attempt, the previous year, failed. They competed under the cumbersome name Björn & Benny, Agnetha & Anni-Frid. The name of the song was 'Ring ring (bara du slog en signal)' and their attempt ground to a halt at third place in the Swedish Melodifestival.

The following year Benny, Björn and Stikkan Anderson wrote a song that had all the right elements to win the entire thing. It was a ballad, uncommonly catchy, in the style of the dramatic songs that had won Luxembourg the title two years running. Since the competition was dominated by solo artists, the focus lay on Agnetha's solo. The name of the song was 'Hasta Mañana'.

In her book *My Dad's Name Was Stikkan*, his daughter Marie Ledin explains: 'I have heard Dad standing in a hotel reception on the Canary Islands with his fist full of pesetas shouting the lyrics for "Hasta Mañana" into the phone to [his secretary] poor Görel Hanser in Stockholm: "No, it's H-A-S-T-A. Hasta mañana! It means 'see you tomorrow'! Don't you know any damn Spanish?!"'

But Abba and Stikkan changed their minds. Instead of the Eurovision-perfect song they decided to take a wild chance. They retracted 'Hasta Mañana' and bet on a loud pop song in an upbeat tempo that didn't sound like anything in the history of the Eurovision.

'I don't know what the others were thinking, but I never thought we'd win,' says Björn. 'But if we have a song that stands out, and also look weird when we perform it, people will remember us even if we end up placing seventh or ninth. The object of the exercise was to make the Eurovision broadcast our launch pad into the world. That was why it was strategically correct to take a chance with "Waterloo". Who knows, "Hasta Mañana" may also have won, but it didn't set itself apart.'

All of Europe gathered in front of their TV sets on 6 April 1974. Actually, not all of Europe. France dropped out of the event at the last moment when President George Pompidou died unexpectedly just four days prior. It was deemed unsuitable to send the singer Dani to Brighton to sing 'La vie à vingt-cinq ans'. For the same reason, French singer Anne-Marie David, who had won for Luxembourg the previous year and was scheduled to hand out the prizes in Brighton, didn't make it either. Instead the prize was handed out by EBU president Charles Curran, the head of the BBC, a corporation known for producing comedy series such as *Dad's Army*.

Italy was competing, but decided not to broadcast the festival. The nation was in the midst of intense electoral debates over whether or not to ban divorce. Artist Gigliola Cinquetti's song 'Si', where she repeats the word 'yes' in the lyrics, could possibly be interpreted as a hidden message to sway the election. The song was not played on the radio until after the referendum on 12 May, when 59 per cent of Italians voted to continue to allow divorce.

The Eurovision Song Contest was held in Brighton Dome; TV personality Katie Boyle hosted it for the fourth time. Each nation's entry was presented alongside a sort of visual postcard, a montage of archival footage. Greece participated for the first time.

When it is time for Sweden's entry, the BBC commentator bloviates over the tourist images about a country 'full of blonde Vikings'. During the presentation of the members of the band Agnetha is called Anna. Björn is Born.

The conductor Sven-Olof Walldoff takes his place in front of the orchestra dressed as Napoleon and the BBC's commentator nearly shouts: 'It's Napoleon! No wonder the song is called "Waterloo".'

Next the Eurovision Song Contest is shaken to its very core and a new chapter of pop history begins. Agnetha and Frida dash down off a step – in platforms and high-heeled boots – and start singing in their surreally synchronous harmonising, 'My, my! At Waterloo, Napoleon did surrender. Oh yeah! And I have met my destiny in quite a similar way.' Benny plays in the highly expressive style of a classical concert pianist; his forceful striking of the keys releasing cascades of sparkling notes that the world will soon come to know as a cornerstone of the Abba sound.

Even their stage costumes, created by designer Inger Svenneke, are louder and more sparkly than anything anyone has ever dared attempt in the history of the competition. Frida, the one in the group with the best fashion sense, had seen a jacket in the window of a Stockholm boutique with the very 1970s name Green Clouds and Blue Grass.

'The jacket had chains and sequins and looked so cool,' she said. 'First I brought Agnetha there and then the others and asked what they thought. That jacket became the prototype for the "Waterloo" outfits.'

Agnetha: 'I spent hours in the make-up lounge gluing teeny-tiny stars to my face.'

When the song is over, the BBC commentator sounds as if he is standing hunched over the microphone when he exclaims: 'Sweden! They have never won it, but they surely have to be amongst the reckoning with that one.'

Benny: 'There's something about a competition. It does something to you. Standing there, knowing that there are sixteen others who can also sing and want to win just as badly as you do brings on the adrenaline. But I like it. The competitive aspect is the entire substance of Eurovision, I think, that is what makes it interesting. When we heard the other entries I was worried about the Dutch group Mouth & MacNeal and their song "I See a Star". That was a good song.'

Did you talk to other artists backstage?

'We hung out with Olivia Newton-John a bit. Nice lady. We went on to meet her several times over the years.'

British-Australian Olivia Newton-John competed for the UK that year. Four years later she got the part of Sandy in *Grease* and became a megastar. Marie Osmond was the first to be offered the part, but said no when she realised that the Sandy character underwent a transformation into a rebel. She couldn't jeopardise her homespun image.

A few years later Olivia Newton-John would lead her own TV variety special, *Olivia!*, with guests such as Andy Gibb, younger brother of the members of the Bee Gees – and Abba. In one incredible scene, all six of them are sitting in a circle and sing songs by the Beach Boys. Björn and Andy Gibb play acoustic guitars, Benny plays the piano, Frida the tambourine, Agnetha the congas and Olivia Newton-John the snare drum. It is rare to see something so charming and unrehearsed in such a big TV production. The unique sextet performs 'Help Me, Rhonda' and 'Barbara Ann', followed by Frida singing some opera at Andy Gibb's request.

When the voting in the 1974 Eurovision Song Contest started, no country was in a clear lead. The UK, the number-one pop nation, marked their territory by giving Abba zero points. Greece, Belgium, Monaco and Italy also gave Sweden zero points. The only ones to give Sweden full marks were Finland and Switzerland.

The big favourite ahead of the contest and throughout the broadcast was Dutch duo Mouth & MacNeal, who Benny predicted would win and who already had an international career. Their 1971 single 'How Do You Do' sold a million copies and had made it to the top ten on the American Billboard chart.

But their popularity didn't take them all the way. Abba won! *Sweden won!* The fact that Sweden won the competition was more unexpected in the 1970s than Azerbaijan winning in 2011. Sweden was not on the pop-cultural map. It was considered completely unthinkable that Sweden might be able to defeat the countries that typically set the tone in the Eurovision Song Contest.

When the final result was announced and the bombastic intro to 'Waterloo' once again echoed through the speakers, Frida lit a victory cigar. Maggie MacNeal of Mouth & MacNeal recalled that after the vote was over, Agnetha hugged her and said, 'I'm so sorry.'

When the composers and songwriters were called back on stage to be congratulated as winners Björn had to kick himself free from a zealous security guard who grabbed him by the legs. 'That guy took one look at my platform shoes and said, "No, no, that's just for the songwriters!" In those days only the creators were supposed to receive the accolades. The guard couldn't fathom that someone who wrote songs could be dressed as strangely as I was. So it was the biggest moment of my career up until that point and I was in a fight with a guard.'

Musically speaking, 'Waterloo' was revolutionary. The Eurovision Song Contest was transformed overnight from an old-fashioned schlager festival into a pop festival. In the following years all of Europe tried to find their own Abba. The UK won in 1976 with Brotherhood of Man, two women and two men who looked and sounded like Abba.

The Abbas soon came to learn that it was one thing to win the Eurovision Song Contest. Becoming international pop stars was something else entirely.

The single 'Waterloo' reached number 1 on the sales charts in the UK. The British public clearly didn't agree with the expert jury. The runner-up, Gigliola Cinquetti's 'Si', as well as third-place-finisher Mouth & MacNeal's 'I See a Star', also became top ten hits in the UK.

Additionally 'Waterloo' made it to the top five in large parts of Europe and became a top ten hit in the United States. Then things ground to a halt. Being from Sweden was still a big liability when it came to making it in pop music. Ever since 1972 Björn and Benny had diligently been sending their singles to international record companies. 'They didn't even listen to them, since we were from Sweden,' Björn says.

While Abba was trying to make it internationally, producer Bengt Palmers and singer Björn Skifs' group Blåblus were doing the same with their version of 'Hooked on a Feeling', originally recorded by B.J. Thomas. Bengt Palmers' productions had a more 'international' sound than those of other Swedes from that era, and after 'Hooked on a Feeling' made number 1 in Sweden in 1973 Bengt Palmers realised it might have a chance. 'I felt if there was ever a song that could make it on to the Billboard chart, it was this recording.' But they got a no from Capitol Records, which was connected to Swedish EMI.

'So I started sending it to American record companies myself,' says Bengt Palmers. 'In those days you wrote up a cover letter on a typewriter, put the single in an envelope and put a stamp on it.'

Nothing happened.

'Finally we got a telex that read "Not suitable for our territory." The people who bothered to answer all used the exact same phrase when they said no. "Not suitable for our territory."'

Bengt Palmers did not give up. 'I had a fat yearbook from *Billboard* magazine with addresses for every record company in the United States. I went through the list – A&M, Bell, Capricorn – and sent the single to every last one of them.' Finally something happened. An A & R guy at CBS liked what he heard and wanted to release the single.

But when CBS requested formal approval from Capitol, which owned the rights, Capitol suddenly changed their mind. 'I think their guy was scared shitless that he would be fired if it became a hit for another company,' says Bengt Palmers.

So in the end Capitol released 'Hooked on a Feeling'. Internationally, Björn Skifs' group went by the name Blue Swede, a name inspired by the Stockholm nightclub Alexandra where the upstairs walls were covered in blue velvet. The song was a huge hit on the American airwaves.

The same week that Abba won in Brighton, Blue Swede became

the first Swedish band to reach number 1 on the Billboard chart with 'Hooked on a Feeling'. It was an amazing breakthrough for Swedish music. But Swedish papers barely covered pop culture and pop music and the event passed unnoticed by most.

For the rest of that year Blue Swede did better in the United States than Abba. Their follow-up 'Never My Love' rose to seventh place on Billboard. The narrative has Abba becoming world-famous with 'Waterloo', but actually Abba had to overcome significant hurdles to convince the world that they were more than a one-hit wonder. Their follow-up numbers 'So Long' and 'I Do, I Do, I Do, I Do, I Do' flopped in the UK. The Abbas were dejected when they went home to their semi-detached homes in the Stockholm suburb of Vallentuna, where the couples lived close to each other. Soon Björn and Benny headed out to Viggsö, an island in the archipelago, and wrote new songs in their little boathouse.

After the doldrums that followed their victory in Brighton the Abbas were made aware of what an enormous amount of work it would take for them to conquer the world. Worldwide touring was impossible for a group in which half the members were parents of young children.

Instead, they made four so-called promotional films ahead of their new album, *Abba*. The idea was to have something to send to all the TV channels around the world that Abba would not have time to visit. The concept of a music video had yet to be invented in 1975, but that was exactly what Abba had made.

The four songs selected for this purpose were 'I Do, I Do, I Do, I Do, I Do', 'Mamma Mia', 'SOS' and 'Bang-A-Boomerang'. These were directed by Lasse Hallström, who had already made a name for himself in Sweden at the time and would become world-famous ten years later with *My Life as a Dog*. These four Abba videos were playful, unpretentious and thoroughly Swedish in a way that was reminiscent of the films Lasse Hallström made with comedians Brasse Brännström and Magnus Härenstam.

Abba did not appear as untouchable superstars in these films. The home-grown feeling was not a strategic plan, but contributed to Abba's aura of accessibility. The films did the job in Australia. After 'I Do, I Do, I Do, I Do, I Do' had been broadcast on Australian TV the song made number 1 in the charts. Australia was the first place to experience 'Abbamania'.

When the indisputable pop masterpiece 'SOS' was released as the fourth single after 'Waterloo', the UK woke up as well. Then came 'Mamma Mia'.

Benny: 'In 1975 we figured out how to do it. "Mamma Mia" was the first song where we really went hard with the arrangement. Almost all our songs after that had that type of arrangement. All the instruments on the recordings add something that deviates from the basic melody. Listen to the marimba, listen to the guitar on "Mamma Mia". They play their own defined lines, something entirely different from the basic melody. We worked on that forever. Added lots of detail.'

Agnetha: 'The time when we were at home in Stockholm, working in the studio was my happiest time with Abba.'

LEFT TURN

In 1955 Sweden held a referendum about switching from driving on the left to driving on the right-hand side of the road. It went the way referendums tend to: those who wanted to keep left-hand traffic won by a landslide, 82.9 per cent. Prime Minister Tage Erlander cleared his throat and reminded Swedes that the referendum was merely intended to guide the decision. Eight years later he overrode the will of the people and gavelled a yes to right-hand traffic.

Those knowledgeable in matters of traffic planning were eager to transition. As opposed to Britain, where cars are built to drive on the left, Swedes drove cars built for right-hand traffic. When passing, one had to swerve far into the oncoming lane to see if the coast was clear, ideally aided by one's passenger, who had a better vantage point. Before right-hand traffic was introduced in the autumn of 1967, Sweden saw thousands of traffic fatalities each year, compared to about 200 today.

For several years a campaign was mounted to get Swedes used to the idea of driving on the right; informational films produced by the national commission for right-hand traffic were screened in schools and at workplaces. A stamp was also published with an image of a highway and the date of the transition: 3/9/1967.

Several pop songs vied for the position of most popular song about right-hand traffic. The very popular Thore Skogman's ''67 håller vi till höger' lost out to Telstars and Rock-Boris' 'Håll dej till höger Svensson' ('Keep to the right, Svensson'), which became one of the biggest hits that year. Telstars and Rock-Boris would later be the touring backing band for the earliest version of Abba, before they'd even found a name.

Shortly after the transition to right-hand traffic, the entire Swedish public discourse took a sharp left turn. Thus the adage 'Keep to the right, Svensson' was replaced by 'Keep to the left, Svensson'. In 1968 a wave of leftist fervour swept the world, marked by protest and rebellion among students and intellectuals. The street riots in Paris in May are perhaps the most famous event of that turbulent year. But in no other Western country did the new left establish itself as deeply, or gain as much cultural sway, as it did in Sweden.

Of importance in this context are two music festivals at Gärdet, a large open field in Stockholm formerly used for military exercises. The first Gärdet festival, which took place in June 1970, was inspired by the hippie festivals in Woodstock and Monterey in the United States and was chaotic in terms of organisation, with bands that were 'progressive' mainly in the musical sense: Träd, Gräs och Stenar, Solen Skiner, Love Explosion and Gunder Hägg.

The second festival, in August of the same year, was more professional in terms of planning and also presented bands with an overtly leftist political agenda, such as NJA-gruppen, Södra Bergens Balalaikor and Det Europeiska Missnöjets Grunder. This is the festival documented in the famous double LP *Festen på Gärdet*.

'For me the Swedish *musikrörelsen* emerged between the first and the second Gärdet festival,' says Leif Nylén in Håkan Lahger's book *Proggen*. Leif Nylén was an art critic, author and drummer in Blå Tåget, for which he wrote 'Den enda handen vet vad den andra gör', which would become better known as 'Staten & kapitalet' when punk band Ebba Grön recorded their version in 1980.

'Planning the second festival it was clear that there were a bunch of bands and musicians and that tons of people would show up,' Nylén continues. 'That wasn't a given ahead of the first festival. At that point there was a feeling that this was a musical movement that could challenge commercial music and build something of its own.'

The left-wing movement commonly known as *Svenska musikrörelsen* (literally, 'the Swedish music movement', but also called the alternative movement or the progressive movement, and widely referred to as progg or proggen), was run by people who turned out to be very good at coordinating and organising, which is not typically a hallmark of musical movements. In his book *Schlagerkungens krig: Abba och Hoola Bandoola på Stikkan Andersons slagfält* (*The Schlager King's War: Abba and Hoola Bandoola Band on Stikkan Anderson's battlefield*), Klas Gustafson writes, 'It took six years, counting from the first festival on Gärdet, until the Swedish *musikrörelsen* controlled an entire chain of production: recording, manufacturing, distribution. Thus a *musikrörelsen* emerges that is unique in the world.'

The *musikrörelsen* also gained crucial influence over content on Swedish radio and TV.

Abba and Stikkan were cast as the main enemies of this movement, symbols of commercial music and culture. Abba's outspoken manager was an especially gratifying adversary, since he took the bait and constantly retaliated.

The image projected was one of capitalist pig Stikkan Anderson's war against the workers. In actuality the *musikrörelsen* was dominated by a university-educated middle class, while Stikkan himself came from a working-class background.

*

In 2013 the BBC produced *The Joy of Abba*, an ambitious documentary about Abba in which many British artists and music journalists participated. Björn was the only one of the Abbas who agreed to an interview. Some of the airtime is taken up by Mikael Wiehe of progg outfit Hoola Bandoola Band, as well as myself, trying to explain to English viewers how Swedes regarded Abba in the 1970s. How was it possible that Sweden's by far best and most popular band ever was lambasted by the media in their home country? It wasn't easy to convey the social and cultural climate in Sweden at the time to the BBC team.

In Sweden the debate about what actually happened still rages. There are those who claim that the left turn has been exaggerated after the fact. And then there are those who, to the contrary, claim that the extent of what went on has never been fully investigated.

To understand the currents that coursed through Sweden in the 1970s one needs to begin by understanding the contrast with what came before. Perhaps the best way of doing this is to watch TV.

Up until the end of 1969 there was only one TV channel in Sweden, run by Sveriges Television. In December that year a second channel was launched, TV2, at which point the first channel was named TV1. There was a lot of controversy surrounding TV1's newborn sibling, but the actual birth was as peaceful as one can imagine.

Opening night line-up for TV2, 5 December 1969:

6:00–18:00: Test talker
18:00: Test card
18:29: Head of Sveriges Radio Olof Rydbeck inaugurates TV2
18:30: *Babar*

*

The test talker who broadcast for twelve hours was Carl-Uno Sjöblom, a presenter known to the public from radio quiz shows. He had all the necessary attributes for a quiz show host: a cardigan, a well-ironed shirt and a bow tie, thinning hair and a dry sense of humour.

'According to Televerket's rules we could not broadcast moving images,' Carl-Uno Sjöblom is quoted as saying. 'Instead people had been told to send postcards. So, over stills of Haparanda, Borås, Eskilstuna, and other small Swedish towns, I talked to the listeners in the same way I had on the radio.'

Going forward, life was anything but peaceful for TV2. Only four days after the inauguration of the new channel a wildcat strike erupted among miners in Svappavaara, in the far north of Sweden, a conflict that spread to nearby mines in Kiruna and Malmberget within days.

The media attention was intense. There were daily reports in TV1's news programme *Aktuellt*, in TV2's new rival news show *Rapport*, in six broadcasts of radio's *Dagens Eko*, four regional news broadcasts, as well as the radio station P3's minute-long news broadcast. Every day. Additionally there were reports on the strike for various TV and radio shows focusing on current events, such as *Fokus, Direkt, Kontakt med arbetslivet, I kväll, Tvärs, Bakom rubrikerna* and *Tidsspegeln*.

The mountains Kiirunavaara and Luossavaara, which were also mining sites, lent their names to the company Luossavaara-Kiirunavaara Aktiebolag (LKAB), a state-owned mining conglomerate founded in 1890, which had been central to making Sweden a wealthy nation.

For the sixteen weeks – 121 days – of the LKAB strike and its aftermath, 640 news segments were broadcast on 521 programmes on Swedish public media. The advent of TV2 created a brand-new competitive situation within the public service sector. No editorial desk wanted to be accused of not being relevant. Above all, nobody wanted to be accused of the worst thing you could be in 1969 – *apolitical.*

The coverage of the strike led to heavy criticism of Sveriges Radio, the broadcasting group that encompassed both TV and radio, which had a monopoly on broadcasting in Sweden until the early 1990s. The LKAB leadership as well as the Swedish Employer Organisation and the Swedish government refused to comment, or delayed comment, on radio and TV. The same was true of LO, the Swedish Trade Union Confederation, which had a close relationship with the Swedish Social Democratic Party (SAP). Both of these were also targets of the wildcat strike. The new leftist movement in Sweden was far to the left of the social democratic establishment. The strikers themselves were more willing to do interviews with public service channels, as were their delegates and the chief of staff at LKAB.

Due to this imbalance there were complaints that Sveriges Radio was in breach of its mandate to be impartial. The company was said to be 'controlling' the strike and the brunt of the criticism was levelled at the newcomer, TV2.

The channel's news programme *Rapport* hired the socially conscious writer Sara Lidman to do a report on the miners' strike: on site, she was greeted by a team of striking miners. Soon she was speaking at strike meetings and ended up donating her fee for the project to the strike fund.

Rapport never broadcast Sara Lidman's reportage, but the damage was done. The news programme was accused of being leftist and

TV2 was deemed a leftist channel, a mark that would take decades to fully wash out.

The leftist tilt to broadcasting was not limited to news coverage. The Mascots was one of many Swedish pop groups influenced by the Merseybeat sound, of which the Beatles was the prime example. The Mascots had hits in Sweden with songs like 'Baby, Baby' and 'Words Enough to Tell You'. In August 1969 they played their last gig as pop artists and reformed as a musical political theatre group, which first went by the name NJA-gruppen and later Fria Proteatern. On 25 February 1970, TV2, in collaboration with the Royal Dramatic Theatre, broadcast the group's controversial theatre play about Norrbottens Järnverk AB, a steel company in Luleå. The play generally went by the name *NJA-pjäsen* and has been described as 'a very tendentious piece of agitprop about industrial working conditions'.

In the midst of the unusually cut-throat contractual negotiations of 1970–1, TV2 broadcast the satirical revue *Har du hört vad som hänt?* ('Did you hear what happened?') The revue contained a sketch where the inception of Saltsjöbadsavtalet – the 1938 agreement between trade unions and employers that has come to be known as 'the Swedish model' – is portrayed as a betrayal of the working class. The actual signing is depicted as a drunken party during which LO chairman August Lindberg, who was in fact a lifelong teetotaller, almost signs a cheque rather than the actual agreement.

An interesting detail that shines a light on how media debates work: while only about 3 per cent of the population watched the revue, an audience four times that size watched the debate that followed on the programme *Kvällsöppet*.

One of the talking heads in TV2 at this time, Anders Egerö, appeared on screen introducing the evening's segments with long hair and an unkempt beard, wearing a T-shirt and a long necklace. Such a style might have been surprising for a TV presenter any-where else in the world, but in Sweden we just shrugged. That was what you were supposed to look like.

So it was in this media climate that Abba won the Eurovision Song Contest, dressed in sparkling clothes. The victory was taken as a provocation by the Swedish new left and resistance was quickly mounted in various corners.

TV2's news programme covered the competition. First, Frida was asked a few general questions along the lines of 'how do you feel?' After that, the assigned reporter pointed the mic at Stikkan Anderson and asked, 'Why would one write a schlager about Waterloo?' Stikkan's answer explains the international perspective: 'The first thing one does is pick a title that one thinks everyone will understand. We did something similar last year, when we had a song called "Ring, ring", where the title would be the same in any language.'

After this the writer of the lyrics to Sweden's first ever victory in the Eurovision Song Contest gets an astounding follow-up response: 'Last year you made a pop song about calling someone on the phone. This year you made a pop song about how 40 million—' here the interviewer says the wrong number then corrects himself – '40,000 people died, to put it cynically.'

The direct action group Rädda Radion ('Save the Radio') was formed in 1973 aiming to start a debate about 'the commercialisation of Sveriges Radio'. Rädda Radion demanded that Sveriges Radio scrap their chart shows, since charts contributed to 'conserving musical tastes' in the interest of the multinational record companies' 'imperialist Coca Cola culture'.

As Abba took the charts by storm, the group sensed an opening. If Rädda Radion's words above make it sound like a marginal activist group, it is worth noting that their protests and lobbying were instrumental in closing down two out of three of P3's chart programmes, despite the fact that these were some of the most popular shows on the air in terms of listener numbers. On 29 June 1974, a little over two months after 'Waterloo', the final *Tio i topp* was aired. The next year the chart show *Kvällstoppen* also went off the air. The reason it was a target: *Kvällstoppen* was considered beneficial to commercially successful groups.

It is unclear how stopping these chart shows served democracy. Radio shows in which the entire Swedish population had a chance to influence which songs would be played, either by voting or by reflecting record sales, were now replaced by a selection made by a small handful of musical programmers employed by Sveriges Radio.

The activists wanted to liquidate Svensktoppen as well, as Leif Schulman tells us in an article on the website News55, ahead of the ninety-ninth anniversary of Sveriges Radio in 2015.[8] The action group had a lot of support for this goal from the editorial desks at the daily papers. A writer at the tabloid *Aftonbladet*, Schulman says, wrote a four-page complaint to the Swedish Broadcasting Authority in which he demanded *Svensktoppen* be taken off the air since the programme violated the agreement Sveriges Radio had with the state to provide 'good entertainment' as well as 'enlighten the public about current events'.

Leif Schulman recounts the events: 'Strangely the Swedish Broadcasting Authority took the complaint extremely seriously and this led to both the radio entertainment head Stig Olin as well as radio chief Otto Nordenskiöld being called in for questioning. In February 1976 it was decided: *Svensktoppen* would be allowed to live on. Two board members opposed the decision.'

The attempt to take the show off the air had failed, but the new left did manage to pass an amendment to the rules of *Svensktoppen* that dealt a direct blow to Stikkan Anderson's method of buying up the rights to foreign songs and writing Swedish lyrics for them. Stig Olin decided that, starting at the New Year 1974 – eight months after 'Waterloo' – songs played on *Svensktoppen* had to be composed by Swedish songwriters and must have Swedish lyrics.

The songs that had been the biggest hits on Svensktoppen during the 1960s were often pop and schlager songs that had been picked up from Italy, Germany, Britain or the United States and translated into Swedish. Anna-Lena Löfgren's 'Lyckliga gatan' ('Happy Street') for instance was the tune of the Italian song 'Il ragazzo della via Gluck' ('The boy from Gluck Street'); Britt Lindeborg's lyrics changed the song to address the demolition of the Hagalund neighbourhood. Françoise Hardy also recorded a version of the same song in French.

In the autumn of 2020, schlager queen Anita Lindblom died at the age of eighty-two. In Sweden, her major hit 'Sånt är livet', with lyrics by Stikkan Anderson, is even more famous than she is. The punk icon Joakim Thåström of Ebba Grön said to *Dagens Nyheter*, '"Sånt är livet" is one of the best Swedish songs of all time, even better than the American original.' The American original is 'You Can Have Her', written by Bill Cook and recorded by Roy Hamilton. Stikkan Anderson's Swedish lyrics have depth, humour and complexity far superior to the bland English version.

*

So by the new year the party was over, and with it, it was presumed, Stikkan's dominance on Svensktoppen. *Musikens makt*, the music magazine of the new left wrote, 'Hats off to old Olin!'

However, the music that did take over on Svensktoppen now that covers of foreign songs were banned was not made by leftist artists such as Nynningen and Södra Bergens Balalaikor, as the activists had imagined, but by *dansbands*. A young record company man from Skara, Bert Karlsson, was waiting in the wings. In 1972 he formed the record company Mariann Grammofon. He turned out to be a talent scout with an extraordinary understanding of what would be popular, especially in rural areas. 'I know what people like,' as he put it.

Björn: 'You need to remember that the progg wave in Sweden was bigger with the media than it was with the public. In the media it was inflated into a huge deal. But if you look at record sales during that time, you will get an entirely different picture of what music resonated deeply with the public. Namely us, and *dansbands*.'

The infrastructure built by the Swedish *musikrörelsen* in the 1970s included record companies and music forums, or music houses, that became important concert venues. An interesting PhD thesis in musicology by David Thyrén, *Musikhus i centrum*, gives an account of two of them: Uppsala Musikforum and Sprängkullen in Gothenburg. As nonprofit organisations, both were politically independent, but they had ties to political parties on the very far left. Uppsala Musikforum had connections with SKP (Sveriges Kommunistiska Parti), Sprängkullen initially had links to KFML(r), which stands for Kommunistiska Förbundet Marxist-Leninisterna, or the Communist Union of Marxist-Leninists. The letter (r) in parenthesis stands for 'revolutionary'.

There were many political parties on the left vying for voters in Sweden in the 1970s. To the left of the Social Democrats there was the parliamentary communist party VPK (Vänsterpartiet Kommunisterna), which later dropped 'kommunisterna' and now goes by just Vänsterpartiet, literally 'the leftist party'. Even further to the left were the extra-parliamentary splinter parties like SKP and KFML(r). After the advent of the socialist revolution that party was working for, there would be a period during which there was no democracy, but rather 'the revolutionary dictatorship of the people'. An extreme party in every sense of the word, which gained influence because some of the best-beloved actors and musicians in Sweden supported it openly for a time, among them Sven Wollter, Fred Åkerström, Lasse Brandeby and Kent Andersson.

In the magazine *Musikens makt* the debate raged for and against turning the *musikrörelsen* into party politics. In the December issue of *Musikens makt* in 1973 the artist Channa Bankier and the drummer from the band Träd, Gräs och Stenar, Thomas Mera Gartz, wrote an op-ed in which they warned of leftist sectarianism and argued in favour of the forces inherent in rock music: 'The heavy rhythm, the high energy, the power to draw forth instinctive liberation.'

Within SKP, rock music was considered to be an expression of American cultural imperialism and the party took a dim view of music performed with electronic instruments. KFML accused rock music of embodying bourgeois decadence. KFML(r) follower Christian Diesen answered the op-ed in a later issue saying 'the revolution does not need a rock gala'. Sprängkullen boycotted musicians who had anything at all to do with Abba.

*

Saxophonist, clarinettist and flautist Ulf Andersson – the one playing the *dansband* sax on 'I Do, I Do, I Do, I Do, I Do' – has musical skills that make him unique in the history of Swedish music. Aside from Abba, he played with trombonist Eje Thelin, singer Monica Zetterlund, and the fusion group EGBA, among others.

When I met with him in the autumn of 2021, not quite two years before he passed away, he had just recorded an excellent jazz album with his own quintet, *Turdus merula*. The title means blackbird in Latin. 'I always hear blackbirds sing when I walk to my studio in the Stockholm suburb of Kärrtorp.' The interest in birdsong was something he shared with Benny.

During a tour with EGBA in the 1970s they had a gig booked at Sprängkullen in Gothenburg. When the band started to unload their instruments, a person told them, 'You can't come in here.' Ulf and the others in the band said, 'Yes, we have a gig here tonight.' The person pointed at Ulf Andersson and said, 'That's not happening, that guy has played with Abba!'

Percussionist Ahmadu Jah moved from Sierra Leone to Stockholm in the 1960s and left a big impression on the Swedish music scene. Two of his daughters went on to become even more successful musicians in their own right, Neneh Cherry and Titiyo. When Ahmadu Jah died in 2018, Titiyo was interviewed on the radio and said that her father had been asked to play with Abba on their Australian tour. She loved Abba, but her father said no.

'My mum wouldn't let him,' said Titiyo. 'Her hatred of Abba was so strong.'[9] Titiyo's mother was the dance teacher and actor Maylen Bergström who moved in the nation's alternative circles.

In his thesis, David Thyrén takes a look at a 1975 article from *Dagens Nyheter* in which the writer Ingmar Glanzelius compares two completely different entertainment events on a Saturday night in Gothenburg. One was a Røde Mor performance at Sprängkullen. Røde Mor was one of the biggest bands in Denmark during the progg era, a band way out on the far-left fringe, with socially critical lyrics. The other was the first stop of the summer folkpark touring circuit for pop artists Ted Gärdestad and Harpo on the main stage of the amusement park Liseberg.

At Liseberg, Ingmar Glanzelius wrote, there were guards 'with military belts and walkie-talkies'. Some might consider this a pretty normal level of security for an amusement park that may see more than 50,000 visitors in a day. At Sprängkullen, on the other hand, things were copacetic and there were only a handful of guards, playing guitar and harmonicas and allegedly greeting visitors politely.

After this *Dagens Nyheter* gets to the heart of the matter. David Thyrén: 'His hypothesis in the article was that "pretty boy" Svensktoppen artist Ted Gärdestad was potentially far more dangerous than the socialist agitprop group Røde Mor. Glanzelius criticised Gärdestad, as well as Harpo, for being superficial and openly performing as idols aiming to manipulate the feelings of young girls in order to sell records.'

Ted Gärdestad, who was nineteen years old at the time of that concert, and Harpo, who was twenty-one, were among the most popular artists in Sweden. Ted Gärdestad made his first four albums in close collaboration with Abba and Stikkan Anderson. No music critic today would argue against songs like Ted Gärdestad's 'Sol, vind, och vatten' ('Sun, wind and water') and Harpo's 'Moviestar', on which Frida sings backing vocals, being some of the best and most timeless Swedish pop songs ever made.

The most dedicated audience members at Liseberg were teenage girls. Ingmar Glanzelius went on to describe – in Sweden's pre-eminent morning paper, no less – the teenagers' attempts at getting closer to their idols. 'As the tempo increases fifty or so girls are about to burst through the chain of guards in front of one side of the stage, and in some sense it was too bad that they did not manage to storm Gärdestad and pull down his pretty white trousers and force him to live up to his promises to all fifty of them at a rapid pace, so that he would finally understand what he has wrought.'

Abba's victory at the Eurovision Song Contest in 1974 meant that Sweden would host the next contest in 1975. The Swedish *musikrörelsen* used the entire year leading up to this to prepare a protest and managed to get the support of Sveriges Television.

At the same time as TV1 broadcast the Eurovision Song Contest from the Saint Erik Convention Centre, TV2 broadcast an alternative festival from a large circus tent at Storängsbotten.

The always luminous Karin Falk hosted the Eurovision Song Contest. The hosts for the alternative festival were the three children's TV characters Ville (Jörgen Lantz), Valle (Anders Linder) and Viktor (Hans Wigren). Normally they presented socially critical children's TV shows, often sniping at capitalism. This evening Viktor opened by saying, 'You cannot compete in music.' Big cheers from the audience. The artists performing that evening came from all five Nordic nations as well as from Greenland, Chile, England and the Netherlands.

When watching the alternative gala today, it is hard to categorise the segments as being of musical interest, or high quality. English rock musician Kevin Coyne plays a song. The most eye-catching member of his band is his guitarist Andy Summers, who would become a world star a couple of years later as part of the Police.

As the final act the fictive character Sillstryparn ('the herring strangler'), a lightly camouflaged Ulf Dageby from the progg band Nationalteatern, performs 'Doin' the omoralisk [immoral] schlager-festival', a rather catchy hate song directed at Abba and Stikkan Anderson. Ulf Dageby sings, 'And here comes Abba in plastic clothes, as dead as a can of pickled herring,' and goes on to describe Stikkan as 'a cynical pig' in the lyrics.

Sillstryparn's song got a lot of play on Sveriges Radio. The alternative schlager festival was considered a success and Sweden ended up not participating in the Eurovision Song Contest the following year. No Swedish entry was sent to The Hague in the Netherlands in 1976, despite viewer protests. This decision is especially interesting in light of the status that Melodifestivalen and the Eurovision Song Contest have achieved during the 2000s, as a sort of Swedish equivalent to the American Super Bowl. There is no other country in Europe today where the contest has the significance it does in Sweden.

In 2014 the Swedish Music Hall of Fame was started with the intent of spreading knowledge about the history of Swedish music. I was the chair for the first three years. The inaugural year saw both Abba and Nationalteatern among those inducted.

At the press conference Ulf Dageby said, 'One finds oneself in unlikely company, all of my music idols from my years as a barroom troubadour, Evert Taube, Cornelis [Vreeswijk]. And Jan Johansson, Benny and Abba, I am overwhelmed.'

Benny, standing next to him, added: 'It's nice that you are here Ulf, considering the amount of abuse directed at us from your general direction over the years. But on the other hand you were one of few who accomplished anything of note musically in the progg movement, you and Mikael Wiehe.'

Tommy Rander was one of the leading voices of the Swedish *musikrörelsen*. He was a founder of the magazine *Musikens makt* as well as the record company Nacksving and presented the radio show *Rundgång* on P3. As a writer at *Aftonbladet*, Rander canned Bob Dylan's 1975 divorce masterpiece *Blood on the Tracks* with the argument that Bob Dylan no longer was sufficiently political.

But by the time Rander hosted *Sommar* on Sveriges Radio in July 1998, even he had come around. The first song he played in his programme was 'Födelsedagsvals till Mona' ('Birthday waltz for Mona') by Benny Anderssons Orkester.

In 2000 Lukas Moodysson made the movie *Together* about a Swedish progg commune in 1975, a film that has been ranked by *Empire* as one of the best 500 movies ever made. In one scene the children of the commune sneak out to listen to forbidden music that expresses all of their longing for a better life. The cinema is filled with the music from Abba's 'SOS'.

TOURIST ENGLISH

English is believed to be the most widely spoken language in the world. Well, that is not entirely true. The language that is currently most widely spoken is *passable* English.

'Lingua franca' is the term for a language used in communication by people who don't speak each other's mother tongue. The de facto lingua franca on Planet Earth today is *tourist English*: English reduced to its bare essence, a stock cube containing the language's most commonly used phrases.

According to the *Oxford English Dictionary* slightly more than 171,000 English words are currently in use. Yet, as long as you know 3,000 words or so, you can be said to speak the language.

With tourist English, you don't even need that many words. Good grammar isn't necessary, either. Swedes and Italians and Greeks come up with conjugations and idioms all their own. But we do understand each other: 'You don't want milk in latte too hot, yes?'

'Perfect' English is a language that only those who are born in English-speaking nations understand. (And even they barely do. As a Swede, you don't need subtitles to understand the straightforward English in American shows, but you often do for British movies.) A display of linguistic virtuosity while writing a review on the Tripadvisor website would be a complete waste of resources.

The evolution of tourist English is central to understanding how Abba – from Sweden, a small country with fewer than 10 million inhabitants – could achieve international success. Pop music was one of the first cultural expressions to harness the inherent potential of tourist English.

In 1972 Italian artist Adriano Celentano released the single 'Prisencolinensinainciusol'. He performed the song together with his wife, actress and singer Claudia Mori. The lyrics are as impossible to decode as the name of the song. The word 'Prisencolinensinainciusol' doesn't exist; nor do any of the words that he sings.

Adriano Celentano is using a home-cooked made-up English, that sounds vaguely like actual English when heard in passing on the radio. Adriano Celentano is mimicking American folk singers such as Bob Dylan and Don McLean. He doesn't have the words, but he nails the accent. Don McLean's song 'Vincent' topped Italian charts at this time. Adriano Celentano wanted to find out if an Italian audience would listen to anything, as long as it sounded like English.

In Italy he was known as an actor, musician, jack of all trades and homegrown rock 'n' roll pioneer. Adriano Celentano shows up in Federico Fellini's classic 1960 film *La Dolce Vita* singing Little Richard's 'Ready Teddy' in a language that sounds like a phonetic transcription of English.

Decades later, when Adriano Celentano was interviewed about the song on the American radio station NPR – in Italian with an interpreter by his side – he clarified his intentions: 'I like American slang – which for a singer, is much easier to sing than Italian – I thought that I would write a song which would only have as its theme the inability to communicate. And to do this, I had to write a song where the lyrics didn't mean anything.'[10]

The experiment was successful. 'Prisencolinensinainciusol' was not received as a parody, but as a good song. It took a year, but 'Prisencolinensinainciusol' became a huge hit, not just in Italy, but also in other non-English-speaking nations and it landed on the top ten charts in Belgium, France, West Germany and the Netherlands. It even became popular in the United States where it made the Billboard Hot 100. Millions sang along to a song without real words.

A number of European artists began to release songs in an English that was hopeful and functional, though perhaps not eloquent. Daniel Vangarde, father of Thomas Bangalter of Daft Punk, was active in Parisian nightlife, where influences from African, Arab and Jamaican music were as central as those from American music. The world of disco was open to all, regardless of skin tone, nationality or sexual preference. Vangarde had a hand in a hit called 'Cuba', Latin disco, with the Gibson Brothers, three brothers who weren't Cuban in the slightest; they were Frenchmen, originally from Martinique. The refrain is in Spanish, the verses are in tourist English. It sounds like a slightly hoarse nightclub bouncer calling out the lyrics: 'You dance to the music like nobody does, the first time I saw you I knew it was love.' Europe loved it.

Filling a Mediterranean dance floor calls for a special sort of music, music that bypasses the brain and goes straight for the heart, the legs, the crotch. Daniel Vangarde put together the Great Disco Bouzouki Band which released songs with titles like 'Ouzo & Retsina', 'Greek Magic', and 'Do Re Mi Fa Soul'. Swedes heard this music and thought: 'This is genius. Let's do something like this.' Daniel Vangarde was also the man behind the French-Belgian-Swahili Euro dance hit 'Aieaoa' or 'Aie a Mwana'.

*

In the evenings the Abbas liked to frequent nightclubs and discotheques around Stockholm, preferably Alexandra, where on a good
night one might see Benny and Frida, as well as Björn Borg and
King Carl XVI Gustaf. Sometimes Benny would play the club's
grand piano; he also brought the demo version of 'Dancing Queen'
and asked the DJ to give the song a test spin. The photos for the
album cover of *Voulez-Vous* were taken at Alexandra.

Hasse Huss, a songwriter and anthropologist with a focus on
music, used to spin records at some of the most famous discotheques
in Stockholm. 'I have actually played all three versions of "Aieaoa",'
he says. 'They were all very popular in Stockholm. I played the original version at Cat Ballou in 1971, Black Blood's version at Alexandra
in 1975, and Bananarama's recording at Atlantic, 1981–2.'

In fact the original version of 'Aieaoa' was also issued in Sweden,
by Stikkan Anderson's record company Polar. Stikkan had music
industry contacts all over the world and was always sniffing out the
latest hits from the continent.

Stikkan and Björn knew that the most important thing about a
pop lyric is that it sounds good. Today Björn talks about 'the sound
of the lyric'. 'There are three aspects when you write a song. These
are: the melody, the lyric and how the lyric sounds. *The sound of the
lyric* is very, very important. Many just write song lyrics and forget
what the words sound like. For me it has always been very important to integrate that into the song.'

Swedish tastes in music were also influenced by holidays in southern Europe.

Due to Sweden's controversial policy of neutrality during the
Second World War, the Swedish economy flourished in the 1950s.

In 1951 the Swedish parliament passed a law mandating three weeks of holiday for all. A Swedish middle class emerged; one that could afford to travel.

Charter travel was invented: package deals during which unaccustomed travellers were taken care of by the company that arranged the trip. Everything was organised: flights, hotels, bus travel to and from the hotels, activities at the destination. Hog roasts where guests would eat a whole roasted pig and drink with abandon were a given.

On 23 April 1955 the first Swedish charter group landed on Majorca. The following year saw 10,000 Swedes go on a package holiday. By 1962 that number had increased exponentially to 132,000 and it continued to grow with each passing year. The most popular destinations were Majorca, the Canary Islands and Cyprus, but all of the Mediterranean appealed – locations with a warmer climate than Sweden.

Fritidsresor was one of the biggest Swedish charter agencies. The company soon introduced a new type of accommodation where hotels were supplemented with holiday rentals. If you can find a copy of Fritidsresor's catalogue for the 1970/71 season, with the headline 'Trips for autumn, winter and spring', you will spot some familiar faces on the cover. A photo of conventionally Swedish looking sunbathers with fledgling tans on a golden beach. Blue sky, an even bluer sea. In the background are small fishing boats and a white five-storey beach hotel. In the deckchairs in the foreground are Benny, with a paperback novel in his lap, and Frida. The child in front of them is Frida's three-year-old daughter, Lise-Lotte.

Behind Frida's shoulder you can see Agnetha in a white bikini, she is sitting on a beach blanket and has closed her eyes and turned her face to the sun. If you get out a magnifying glass you can also catch a glimpse of one of Björn's legs behind Frida's arm. Abba wasn't Abba yet, just four individuals who had all had songs on the Svensktoppen chart. The year was 1970, the month was April and in Sweden the skies were still grey and the streets covered in sleet.

The Abbas-to-be didn't have to pay for the eleven-day holiday in Famagusta, Cyprus. Part of their deal with Fritidsresor and the co-organiser, the supermarket magazine *ICA-Kuriren*, was that they would pose for pictures and perform at the hotel.

It is not widely known that the first audience to see the four of them on stage together was a battalion of UN peacekeepers. In the evenings the whole gang jammed and practised at their hotel, Twiga Towers. None of them can recall the set list at their very first show in April 1970. 'But it must have been a hodgepodge of Swedish songs,' Frida says. 'The show was about half an hour long. However I do remember that my chest got burned in the sun.'

What Björn and Agnetha remember is that they got engaged on the chartered plane on their way to Cyprus and that Björn lost his engagement ring on the beach. 'It was a bit too big and slipped off while I was swimming. I had time to think, "What the hell?" and then it was gone.'

Agnetha: 'I was extremely pissed off when I realised he'd lost it.'

The musical genre 'charter disco', transmitted in tourist English, spread across Europe. For European artists this presented a new opportunity. Artists from continental Europe had always been at a disadvantage compared to artists from England and America; the countries that had invented pop music and spoke perfect English to boot.

The Spanish vocal duo Baccara, with their unstoppable tourist English song 'Yes Sir, I Can Boogie' – a huge hit in Sweden – were discovered by a talent scout while performing flamenco for holiday-makers at a charter hotel on the Canary Islands. The songwriters and producers behind this disco song, in which Baccara promises, 'You try me once you'll beg for more,' were two German men.

Swedes and other Scandinavians had an advantage in this new world of pop as we generally spoke better English than the denizens of larger nations like France, Italy and Germany. On the continent, television shows and movies were overdubbed, but in Sweden everything was shown in the original language. For someone hailing from a geographically remote country with a language that nobody understands, it is absolutely essential to learn English as a second language from childhood.

Sweden was also the country that pressed for allowing contestants from non-English-speaking nations to sing in English in the Eurovision Song Contest. Between 1956 and 1965 there was no rule stating that artists had to sing in their national language, but everyone did anyway.

In 1965, Sweden tried to innovate. In order to focus on the song rather than the artist, all of the contributions to Melodifestivalen were performed by the same artist for the first and only time, the opera singer Ingvar Wixell. The winner was Ingvar Wixell with 'Annorstädes vals'. When he sang at the finals in Naples, the name of the song had been changed to 'Absent Friend', and the lyrics were in English. This was not popular with his competitors, who claimed that this was an unfair advantage as the English lyrics could be understood by more people.

New rules regarding language were introduced the next year:

contestants could only sing in their native language. The rule stayed in place until 1973. If Abba had not been allowed to sing 'Waterloo' in English they might not have won.

Up until this point Abba had sung in both English and Swedish, but after their victory they recorded only in English. After a few years of experimentation, with lyrics such as 'King Kong Song', Björn evolved into one of the pre-eminent narrators of marriage, relationships and adult life in all of pop music, perhaps in the entire world, although at times this was conveyed using rather questionable grammar.

Online discussions present examples of bad grammar in Abba songs that would never have passed muster if Abba was from the United States or England. The use of the word 'funny' is one example. In Swedish textbooks for English it was translated simply as *roligt* which can mean either 'fun' or 'humorous' in Swedish, thus losing the dimension of 'strange' or 'odd' that the word 'funny' can carry in English. Conversely, if something is *roligt* in English you would use the word 'fun'.

Thus lines like 'Money, money, money, must be funny, in a rich man's world' don't come across quite the way the writer intended. The same is true of Björn's own showstopper as a singer, 'Does Your Mother Know', in which he sings, 'Well you can dance with me honey, if you think it's funny.'

But it did sound good – the 'sound of the lyric' was right, and audiences from non-English-speaking countries had no problem with that. This was tourist English at its most effective. In a *New York Times* review of the 2008 movie *Mamma Mia!* film critic A. O. Scott writes of 'those lyrics in a language uncannily like English, those symmetrical Nordic voices'.[11] This was intended as devastating criticism, but it had Abba's fans nodding in agreement.

Abba also paved the way for the pop world of today, where artists like BTS can top the charts in the United States, even as they switch between Korean and English.

When rock 'n' roll emerged in the American South as the 1940s turned into the 1950s, the key drivers were Black artists like Little Richard rather than the white artists who are often lauded as the genre's creators. The musicians of this era made up words not found in any dictionary, not too different from Adriano Celentano. Little Richard's most genius line is 'A wop bop a loo bop a lop bam boom.'

One of the best books ever written about rock music is Nick Tosches' *Hellfire: The Jerry Lee Lewis Story*. The descriptions of speaking in tongues are among the book's strongest passages. Jerry Lee Lewis and his cousin Jimmy Swaggart, later a famous TV preacher, were hugely impressed by the itinerant evangelical preachers who could put their parents and neighbours in an ecstatic state. Speaking in tongues could be used as a road to ecstasy.

When I interviewed Nick Tosches in his Tribeca home in NYC, he said: 'I don't write this in the book, but the more I think about it I realise that rock 'n' roll is also a form of speaking in tongues. When I was little I never understood what Little Richard was singing about – nobody understood. It was like a new, universal language that could be understood by everyone across the whole world.'

BJÖRN

Björn Ulvaeus might be sitting in his kayak when he calls you. 'It's so tranquil here.' You may not hear the lapping of the water through the phone, but the tranquillity of the surroundings is evident in his voice.

On the face of it, Björn may appear to be the least complicated and most extroverted member of Abba. He is the tireless entrepreneur who initiates and leads projects such as the musical *Mamma Mia!* or the Abba museum in Stockholm. Over the years Björn is the one who has agreed to the most interviews, always with a smile, and has been the most publicly visible.

But there is a split between public Björn and private Björn, a split that has been there since he was a child. For most of his career, running has been his main way of letting off steam. Björn's refrain is that he doesn't remember much from his career, but he does remember his runs. 'Now, many years later I have almost no memory of the shows I did with Abba. It's all one big blur. I recall the runs I went on in the daytime much more clearly. That was my way of getting ready. I also tried to arrive at the stadium as late as possible. Otherwise I would just be there, pacing back and forth, waiting to go up on stage.'

In 1959 the British working-class writer Alan Sillitoe published the short-story collection *The Loneliness of the Long-Distance Runner*. Alan Sillitoe's depiction of lost young people has had a huge influence on a number of musicians. His debut novel *Saturday Night and Sunday Morning* from the previous year has inspired British bands like the Smiths, the Specials, and Arctic Monkeys. On the B-side of the vinyl version of the Smiths' classic 1986 album *The Queen Is Dead* a line from the film *Saturday Night and Sunday Morning* is inscribed along the edge of the label: 'Them was rotten days.'

The titular short story, as well as the movie adaptation, *The Loneliness of the Long-Distance Runner*, is about a teenager without any future prospects. In long-distance running he discovers a path to emotional liberation. For him, running is not about winning a race, it is about a personal, internal victory.

The lonely long-distance runner Björn Ulvaeus, who was eighteen when the film was in the cinemas, also uses running as a way to tap into his self-esteem. When he toured with Abba, Björn used to book a limo to drive ahead and show him where to run in foreign cities. He would go on ten-kilometre runs during which he would push himself to run faster at the end. In a 1979 interview with a Dutch journalist he said: 'After a run I feel completely clean, all the dirt has been cleansed from my pores. Besides, I believe jogging affects my musical abilities.'

One Abba song that has been born directly out of Björn's lonely long-distance running is 'Take a Chance on Me'. Benny had given Björn a cassette tape with one of their new songs, so that he could write the lyrics. When Björn went for a run and heard the sound of his feet against the trail he had a rhythm in his head that went: 'T-k-ch, t-k-ch, t-k-ch.' The sound eventually began to form into words: 'Take a chance, take a chance, take a chance.' Yet another Abba classic was born.

On 23 August 1980, when Abba was at its very peak, one month after 'The Winner Takes It All' had been released as a single, Björn secretly ran the Stockholm Marathon. The Stockholm Marathon archives have the only photo taken of Björn during the race. It is from the Västerbron Bridge. Björn scowls at the photographer – he has been revealed; his smile could be ironic, or perhaps he is just tired.

On his head, Björn is wearing the same kind of sweatband his namesake Björn Borg famously used to wear. He is dressed in a dark vest, the kind of tight running shorts that were typical of the time, and there is a watch on his wrist. The shoes are the then-rare model Nike Eagle, weighing in at a mere 149 grams, according to Stockholm Marathon's own documentation.

It was Björn's desire to lose weight that got him into running. When Björn hosted an episode of *Sommar i P1* in 2008 – a programme every bit as Swedish as Abba, which has been broadcast on Sveriges Radio since 1959 – he described how he reacted to photos of himself after winning the Eurovision Song Contest in Brighton.

'What I saw was far from how pop stars are supposed to look. Pop stars are supposed to be rail thin. You can't tour the world looking like this.'[12] Björn devised a diet, which consisted of eating beef tenderloin with homemade blue cheese dressing. Every day And he started running. 'I was blissfully unaware that my colleagues in England and the United States had a different way of staying slim: they used drugs.'

In *Sommar*, Björn Ulvaeus says that he has not written his memoirs and has never talked about his life. Then he proceeds to do exactly that. His story is vulnerable and personal, but the content wasn't picked up and made into headlines in the domestic press. The easy-going format, in which his talking is interspersed with his favourite songs like 'I'll Save the Last Dance for You' by Damita Jo and 'Love Hurts' by the Everly Brothers, may have obscured the extent of his earnestness for many listeners. Since *Sommar* is recorded in Swedish – there are no subtitles on the radio – it also passed unnoticed abroad. (In 2020 then-seventeen-year-old environmental activist Greta Thunberg made an exception and read her programme in English as well as Swedish.)

'If I wanted to write my memoirs I wouldn't be able to,' Björn says, with composure. 'I look at a photo of myself from when I was growing up and I see a young boy of thirteen or fourteen. I look at him and wonder what he thought when he looked in the mirror in the mornings. I know where that mirror was, on which wall, which street, in which town. But I don't know what the young boy thought and felt. The boy who was me is a stranger.'

Björn's episode of *Sommar* grows into an exploration of why he repressed his own memories as an adult. He looks up old friends, classmates, and asks them questions about himself. He knocks on the door of his first love in her house in Kalmar. He speaks with actors, doctors, psychologists; he goes to a hypnotist and a psychotherapist.

'I asked Benny what he remembers of winning with "Waterloo". He remembers everything. Why don't I?'

Björn teases out the difference between semantic memory and episodic memory.

'Semantic memory is the encyclopaedia of your brain. This is where we store facts such as the name of the town on the southern coast of England where we won, a town with many piers. The episodic memory consists of literal events. Moments of experience, a linking of the internal and the external. The core of the auto-biographical self.'

This is where his memory fails him. He has no sense of self; it follows that he has retained very few memories. When he asks a childhood friend he is told that he once played the lead in a play about Beppo the clown. He has no recollection of that. Nor of playing himself in *Abba: The Movie*. When he says *he played himself* he means exactly that.

The disconnect has been there his entire life. Self-confidence has come in flashes, only to disappear again. 'For me self-confidence is a perishable item.'

His visit to the hypnotist is slow going. Björn is starting to think that he may be the one in ten people who cannot fall into deep hypnosis. He is told that it tends to be easy for artistic people to fall into a trance. 'So what's the opposite of an artistic temperament? I don't think I want to know.'

But one exercise at the hypnotist does produce results. The hypnotist puts Björn in a variety of imaginary situations. Standing on a mountaintop, he meets an old man. 'What is the man saying?' asks the hypnotist. Björn then hears the old man say 'Vadan och varthän?' ('Wherefore and where to?')

Where does this come from? Two archaic Swedish words, rarely used in the 2000s. Why does he remember them? 'Vadan och varthän?' turns out to be a 1914 poem by national poet Viktor Rydberg that Björn might have heard as a child, in school perhaps. Of course, he does not remember it.

Björn refers to questions he has kept returning to his entire life:

'Why are we here? Where do we end up once we're dead?' Then he plays a recording of 'the best ballad I know': Judy Collins's version of Stephen Sondheim's devastating 'Send in the Clowns'.

He saves the big revelation for the end of the show: 'A poor sense of self makes it harder for you to recall episodic memories,' he says. 'Really nothing is more vital than our sense of self, the interplay between the child and the important people in that child's life. Today, when I see how much love my grandchildren receive I realise that my own idyllic childhood probably wasn't as idyllic as I've wanted to imagine. I did always go home from school for lunch. And my mother would serve me freshly made pancakes. But my parents lived in an unequal and very unhappy marriage. My dad likely felt like a failure, someone to whom fate had been unkind, compared to his brothers. This in turn caused him to try to escape reality. There were loud, bitter fights when he came home late at night. That must have been commonplace for me. I probably wasn't seen in the way that my grandchildren are seen.'

That is all that Björn says about his parents. He says there is no point in prying any further into his childhood and quotes the diaries of Sylvia Plath, where she writes of the importance of the present, reiterating that 'this is now, and now, and now'. Then he plays 'Strawberry Fields Forever' by the Beatles.

Björn Ulvaeus was born in Lundby, Gothenburg, 25 April 1945, at the end of the Second World War. During Björn's early childhood, his father, Gunnar, ran a boatbuilding company on the west coast.

'And then that business went to hell, I don't know why but I imagine he wasn't the best businessman,' Björn has told *Dagens Nyheter*. 'I think it was a big blow for him. It left him sort of adrift and he never managed to get his life back in order.'

For a while Gunnar worked as a cook on a boat on Göta Kanal, a canal that connects Lake Vänern with the North Sea. The family, including Björn and his sister, had to crowd in with Gunnar's mother in her small apartment.

Björn's family were Anderssons; his paternal grandfather and grandmother were named Erik Andersson and Hulda Höglund. When the couple had their first child, Esbjörn, in April 1908, the priest added 'out of wedlock' to the birth certificate after noting that the parents had married just four months earlier.

Many working-class Swedes changed their last names in the twentieth century. Changing your name to something more original than the common Svensson, Andersson, or Pettersson was a way to set yourself apart and raise your social status. My own father was born Sten Gustafsson and changed his name to Sten Gradvall. When Esbjörn left high school he changed his name to Ulfsäter. His younger brother Gunnar took the name Ulvaeus, a latinisation of that name.

Esbjörn was the most driven and successful of his five siblings. When he was only twenty-five years old he became a manager at a paper mill and was able to help his sibling get a job. Gunnar became the foreman at the mill in Vastervik, known as Småland's gate to the archipelago. When Björn was six years old, his family moved into a tenement in Västervik.

Björn got his first guitar at thirteen. 'An orchestra guitar like the one Tommy Steele had. The guitar was compensation for Dad forgetting to pay the registration fee for a bus trip to the Alps.'

His father drank. 'Everyone in my family drank too much.' This inheritance was also passed down to Björn.

The door to music was opened for Björn by his cousin Joen, Esbjörn's son, who was a year older than him. 'I looked up to him more than to anyone else,' Björn says in *Sommar*. 'Joen came home from a trip to London with his bags full of skiffle.'

They formed a skiffle band with a guitar, bass and washboard. They built the bass at the company woodworking shop in Västervik. 'Building a bass was easier than finding a bassist.' Resourceful Joen made sure that they also had a Dixie jazz band on the side. This was Mackie's Skiffle Group, which would eventually become the Hootenanny Singers.

Cousin Joen moved to Sigtuna and stopped playing music. Another person stepped in to fill the role of lodestar and driving force in Björn's life: Hansi Schwarz, who joined the group in 1961.

Hansi Schwarz was born in Munich in 1942. He came to Sweden aged three, when he was saved from the ruins of Germany by the 'white buses', a Swedish Red Cross operation launched in 1945 under the supervision of diplomat Folke Bernadotte. Prisoners were rescued from work camps and concentration camps and brought to Sweden in buses that had been painted white with red crosses on the roof. Later, his family would move back to Munich, but life there was not easy after the war. Hansi's mother arranged for her son to return to Sweden and start school in Västervik.

Hansi Schwarz was full of energy and ideas. And things moved fast – the Hootenanny Singers soon became one of the most popular bands in Sweden.

When Hansi Schwarz died in January 2013, Björn wrote an obituary in *Västerviks-Tidningen*, a local paper. In it Björn writes that he visited Hansi in the hospital a couple of days before he passed and 'squeezed his thin, bony hand'. In the Hootenanny Singers, where all four members sang and harmonised, Hansi Schwarz was known as the German thunder. 'He stood next to me and I had that voice in my ear for all those years, so I would know.'

'I wasn't prepared for the chill of loneliness I felt when I received notice of his death,' Björn writes and continues:

> Some people maintain an inner core their entire lives. Somehow they stay essentially the same as the world around them changes. [. . .] There was an essential Hansi who was always there throughout the years. We were different in that sense and he was always my rock. Most of us have people from our youth that we will return to with childish pride to show how good we are and how well we've done. For me Hansi was one of those people and he was probably the last.

The Hootenanny Singers' fourth album, *International*, released in 1965, contained the group's biggest hit to date, the evergreen 'Björkens visa' ('Song of the birch tree') but also the first seed of what was to come. While the three other members are dressed like folk musicians on the cover, Björn looks as if he aspires to be in the Beatles or the Stones.

On the album, the band also opens the door to the world by singing a few songs in German and a few in English. A blurb on the cover says of the song 'No Time', written by Björn: 'Englishmen and Americans bet it has a good chance of making it *over there.*' The Hep Stars would make their own recording of 'No Time' the following year.

Around this time Hansi Schwarz took over Visfestivalen i

Västervik, a music festival that he would continue to direct until his death. Under his leadership the festival would spend forty-five years inside the medieval ruins of Stegeholm.

The Hootenanny Singers' biggest hit was released on an album not long before the group ceased to exist. Despite the song never being released as a single, the Hootenanny Singers' recording of 'Omkring Tiggarn från Luossa' ('The Beggar of Luossa') on the compilation record *Våra vackraste visor 2* from 1972 became one of the biggest songs of all time in Sweden. It was on the Svensktoppen chart for fifty-two weeks from 26 November 1972 until 18 November 1973.

'Tiggarn från Luossa' was ranked number 1 in Svensktoppen's annual overview of the biggest hits of 1973. When the same overview was done in 1974, the top song was Abba's 'Waterloo'.

'Omkring tiggarn från Luossa' is a poem by Dan Andersson – yes, yet another Andersson – that was published in 1917 in his collection *Svarta Ballader*. Dan Andersson died three years later, only thirty-two years old, in a hotel room in Stockholm; he had travelled from his home province of Dalarna to seek work at the newspaper *Social-Demokraten*. A fumigation company by the name of Desinfektionsanstalten Cyan had smoked out bedbugs at the hotel using hydrogen cyanide, which lingered in the air and ultimately killed him.

The headline for Björn's obituary for Hansi in *Västerviks-Tidningen* reads 'Det är något bortom bergen', a line from that same poem. 'He stood by my side with his six-stringed tenor guitar,' writes Björn, 'and together we sang, "Det är något bortom bergen, bortom blommorna och sången."' ('There is something beyond the mountains, beyond the flowers and the singing.')

THE PERFECT SOUND

Album covers are about more than just the visuals. A good album cover brings the artist closer to the listener. No other cover in Abba's catalogue does a better job of this than 1976's *Arrival*, which mirrors the sound as well as where the group was at the time the record was released.

On the cover of their previous album, *Abba*, released in 1975, the group is sitting in the back seat of a borrowed Rolls-Royce Silver Wraith drinking champagne. Luxurious, yes, but hardly original: fancy cars with private drivers are a dime a dozen in rock, there are plenty of similar images in circulation. Plus, none of the Abbas were able to mask the uncertainty in their smiles. This isn't their world. The choice of clothes makes them look like they're playing dress-up.

Abba didn't own the vehicle on the cover of *Arrival* either, but they look like they do. By now they have upgraded to a helicopter, another level, a league of their own. The group is sitting in a Bell 47 with its characteristic soap-bubble canopy, the first helicopter in history to be designed for civilian use, by inventor Arthur M. Young in 1946.

The helicopter happens to be standing at Barkarby Airport outside of Stockholm, but nobody who bought the album knew that – the image is intended to give international associations. Abba was world-famous now.

All four of them sit side-by-side in the bench seat. Agnetha and Frida in the middle, with access to the controls, a reflection of the Abba sound – Abba wouldn't be Abba without them. Their gazes are relaxed, confident, almost a bit devious: they know something we don't. The photographer Ola Lager waited for the perfect golden-hour light. That aspiration to perfection characterises the entire album.

The cover for *Arrival* is also the first regular edition with the iconic Abba logotype, typeset in uppercase with the backs of the B's turned towards each other. The device had actually been used once before, on the French collection *Golden Double Album* issued earlier that year. Designer Rune Söderqvist chose the News Gothic font from the early 1900s. The logo was placed in a small font in the upper edge of the image alongside the title. That was enough to mark the arrival of a new era.

The helicopter takes off as soon as the first notes sound. No pop album has a more life-affirming opening than 'When I Kissed the Teacher'. What sounds like a dozen acoustic guitars stream out of the speakers. You don't quite know what you're hearing, but you don't want to leave this place. It sounds as if the sun had signed a record contract.

The voices come in, singing, 'Everybody screamed when I kissed the teacher.' My god. Then the harmonies. This is pop music in its purest form. When I was thirteen years old and heard it for the first time I felt there was no way it could possibly be any better.

I was wrong. Because then came the next track, 'Dancing Queen'.

One reason that Abba's music never ages, that new generations of listeners constantly come to it, is that the music is so well recorded. The sound is rich, yet distinctive. The arrangements, limited by the number of channels, are well thought out and chiselled, yet playful and full of surprises. A lot of pop music sounds dated after a decade or two, but fifty years after Abba's recordings there is nothing in terms of the sound that binds them to a certain time.

The sound that made Abba take off – and which had the group outdoing themselves on album after album – was largely down to Michael B. Tretow. Abba's albums were produced and arranged by Björn and Benny, but they worked closely with their sound engineer, Micke to his friends.

Benny: 'Micke was as important to us as George Martin was to the Beatles. In 2015 Micke gave me a stack of old tapes. Without telling us, he had let the tape run during our recording sessions. You can clearly hear how important he was. He was always a step ahead of us.'

The opening track on *Arrival* is a clear example of the genius of Michael B. Tretow.

'So many have tried to replicate the sound of the acoustic guitars on "When I Kissed the Teacher", and have asked us how we did it, but no one has succeeded,' says Benny.

Björn played the guitars himself, rather than one of Abba's usual studio guitarists. He does not recall what they did, but Michael B. Tretow does: 'I recorded two guitars, and increased the speed slightly on one of them. That is why the sound is so rich.'

They were always striving for perfection in the studio; it would take as long as it needed to. Michael B. Tretow: 'When I began working with Benny and Björn the studio hours were 10 a.m. to 3 a.m. After a couple of years I managed to shrink it down to 10 a.m. to 10 p.m.'

*

Michael B. Tretow was born in 1944 in Norrköping, a working-class town that in those days had similarities to Manchester, with a large textile industry and a good football team.

In his boyhood room at Kungsgatan 25, he began recording himself and local pop bands using two mono tape recorders. He gained a reputation as a sound maven and an inventor, a Swedish Joe Meek, even though nobody in Sweden knew who Joe Meek was. Michael B. Tretow took what was available to him and invented what wasn't; he built his own echo machines using piano wire.

After a while, he could afford to buy a Tandberg reel-to-reel tape recorder. His reputation spread and Norrköping's best pop bands came to his room to record: Scarlet Ribbons, the Mixers and the Tramps. Record company executives in Stockholm heard the Norrköping bands and when they asked which studio they had recorded at, they could hardly believe that these were home recordings.

Tretow also played guitar in bands, and the fact that one of his own pop groups called themselves the Crystals is evidence of how he idolised the American demon producer Phil Spector. Spector's sound was a clear influence on future Abba recordings such as 'Ring Ring'.

His other big inspiration was the blues; the immediacy of the music and the recordings had an indelible influence on him. 'I especially loved Snooks Eaglin. He was really good at playing accompaniment and the melody at the same time.' Snooks Eaglin was a New Orleans-based musician with 2,500 songs in his repertoire, earning himself the nickname 'the human jukebox'. This same kind of versatility characterises Tretow.

Michael B. Tretow also worked on compositions of his own in

his room, recordings where his playfulness was given full room to bloom and which he then sent to the revue master Povel Ramel's record company Knäppupp, known for humorous music. In 1966, Povel Ramel's son Mikael heard his talent and asked him to come up to Stockholm to record an EP, *4x Tretow*.

After completing his military service in the mid-1960s, Michael B. Tretow reached out to the studio head at Metronome in Stockholm – the studio where Abba would later record *Arrival*, among others – and asked for a job.

In 1967, his first year as sound engineer at the Metronome studio, Michael B. Tretow got to record the album *Bellman på vårt sätt* ('Bellman our way') with Björn's band the Hootenanny Singers. Björn brought along his new friend Benny, who played the piano on a couple of songs.

That was the first time the three of them recorded music in the same room, and it was the start of a collaboration that continued throughout Abba's career and beyond. Michael B. Tretow was the sound engineer on *Chess* as well as on several of Agnetha's solo albums. He suffered a stroke in the early 2000s, which consequently limited his ability to work.

In 2022 I did a filmed interview with Björn and Benny in the Metronome studio, which now goes by the name Atlantis. The assignment was from their record publisher, Universal Publishing, which wanted employees across the world to gain a better understanding of Abba's history.

Benny immediately stepped up to the large grand piano in the studio. 'It's still here!' He could not resist sitting down and playing the intros to 'Mamma Mia' and 'Dancing Queen', two of the recordings that were made on this very grand piano. 'There's something special about the sound of this one. A Bolin. I don't know what it is but it still sounds good.'

As we shot the film, Björn and Benny sat in the chairs by the old mixing table in the studio, which was also still in place. Right here, in one of these chairs, was where you would find Michael B. Tretow for ten years, listening intensely, up until Abba's own studio, Polar, was inaugurated in 1978.

Michael B. Tretow smoked a pipe. Björn recalls how Benny would subject him to the same prank over and over again. 'I would pull out the matchbox and then put it back together, upside down,' Benny says. 'When Micke opened it to light his pipe, all the matches would fall on to the floor. He fell for it every time.'

All three loved Kalle Sändare, a legendary Swedish comedian who documented crank calls on records, and they developed their own internal brand of humour. 'Micke was brilliant,' Björn says. 'If we did an eight-hour session we would spend at least two hours laughing. As if it were a playground. I can see now how important that was, it made for a creative and permissive working environment.'

There were a few things that Michael B. Tretow refused to compromise on. One of them was that he would not eat fast food. 'The rest of us might go to the hotdog stand across the street,' says Benny. 'But with Micke we always ate a proper lunch, at a restaurant, often on Rörstrandsgatan.'

Another guiding principle was that Michael B. Tretow hated cymbals. Cymbals were prohibited on most of Abba's recordings, a detail in the sound of the group that not everyone has noted. There were practical reasons for his hatred of cymbals: the cymbal sound 'leaks' during the recording and complicates the possibility of doing retakes. After an enthusiastic drummer had set up his drum kit Michael B. Tretow went over and unscrewed his cymbals. Perhaps the absence of cymbals contributes to Abba songs packing such a punch.

But 'Dancing Queen' was an exception to the cymbal rule. After the song was mixed and finished they felt something was missing and let drummer Roger Palm do an overdub with only a hi-hat – the percussive instrument that in effect consists of two cymbals on top of each other. Ola Brunkert plays the drums on all the other songs on the album. The fact that Roger Palm was called in to play on 'Dancing Queen' specifically is something he has been grateful for, as the royalty distribution to the musicians has continued to be calculated, year after year, for half a century.

'Dancing Queen' stands out in every way. Had Abba never recorded any other song, it would still have earned the group their place in musical history.

When the Beatles' album *Revolver* was re-released in 2022 with improved audio, American musician Questlove, known as the drummer and band leader in the hip-hop group the Roots, wrote an essay for release with the deluxe edition. Questlove writes that he has developed a theory after having studied the best albums of all time: as long as the artist has an unbeatable opening track, something to completely knock the listener out, the next song can be less important. Track two becomes something of a recovery for the artist.

The second track on Michael Jackson's *Thriller* is 'Baby Be Mine', one of only two tracks out of nine on that album not to be released as a single. Prince's *Purple Rain* has 'Take Me With U' as its second track, also not a key song on that album. What breaks that theory, Questlove writes, is *Revolver*, where the album explodes into sound with 'Taxman' and follows it up with 'Eleanor Rigby'.

The theory is pulverised by *Arrival* at the moment 'When I Kissed the Teacher' switches to 'Dancing Queen'.

'Dancing Queen', recorded in August 1975, was Abba's first attempt at disco. Things were a bit slow to begin with. Michael B. Tretow: 'Roger Palm plays four steady beats on the bass drum – what we today call *four on the floor* within dance music – I had a hard time with it back then. I was used to the Chuck Berry rhythm.'

To bring out the groove on 'Dancing Queen' they recorded a version on a click track, a series of audio cues that the musicians heard over their headphones as they recorded the song. The inspiration for the rhythm came from two sources. One was George McCrae's 'Rock Your Baby', one of the first disco recordings, a song that had been released the year before and which the members of Abba had heard many times at Alexandra. The other was the New Orleans rhythm on the 1972 album *Dr John's Gumbo*, which Roger Palm had been listening to.

These two templates were American, but when Abba plays disco there is an unmistakably European sound to it. The song opens with Benny running his finger over the keys on the Bolin grand piano, then the song starts – and it is always slower than you remember.

While Abba was recording in Stockholm, David Bowie was working with new music in France and West Germany, where he abandoned an American sound to explore a European one. In January 1977 he released *Low*, a collaboration with Brian Eno. At this time he also produced Iggy Pop's *The Idiot*, which was released in March. Elvis Costello writes in his autobiography *Unfaithful Music* that it was through intensive listening to these three northern

European albums – Abba's *Arrival*, David Bowie's *Low*, and Iggy Pop's *The Idiot* – that he found his musical way forward ahead of his third album *Armed Forces*. This is emphasised by the fact that Elvis Costello and his pianist Steve Nieve also stole the piano part from 'Dancing Queen' for 'Oliver's Army', which would become their greatest hit.

The working title for 'Dancing Queen' was 'Boogaloo'. When the recording was done Björn and Benny understood that they had created something special. They went home late that night to play it to their respective partners.

Frida: 'I cried when I heard it. I thought it was so incredibly beautiful.'

Agnetha was asleep when Björn came home and he didn't want to wake her. Instead Björn headed over to his sister's house nearby. 'I played it for her over and over. We couldn't believe how good it sounded.'

'Dancing Queen' dovetailed perfectly with the nascent disco wave – the movie *Saturday Night Fever* along with its soundtrack arrived a year later – but if you listen to the lyrics you realise that it isn't disco, or even soul or funk, that is being played on the dance floor that Abba describes in the song.

In the lyrics Agnetha and Frida sing, 'With a bit of rock music everything is fine.' The refrain refers to the jive. Nor did Björn and Stikkan have any concept of how the title 'Dancing Queen' would be interpreted and worshipped once the song hit the gay scene.

Few expressions are more telling of the creative process than, 'If you want something done, ask a busy person.' As every expression of that calibre it is ascribed to a variety of famous people through history, among them Benjamin Franklin and Lucille Ball.

Without romanticising stress, it is of course true that someone who maintains a hard pace gets more done. The advantage is that you don't have time to dither over decisions. There is no time for hesitation.

On one level, *Arrival* is Swedish perfection in a 33.09 minute play time.

Side A:
'When I Kissed the Teacher'
'Dancing Queen'
'My Love, My Life'
'Dum Dum Diddle'
'Knowing Me, Knowing You'

Side B:
'Money, Money, Money'
'That's Me'
'Why Did It Have to Be Me?'
'Tiger'
'Arrival'

Another classic might be added to this: 'Fernando', which was on the Australian and New Zealand edition of *Arrival* and was also added to the album when it was eventually issued on CD.

'Fernando' was originally a solo for Frida, recorded the previous year for her Swedish album *Frida ensam* ('Frida alone'). When Abba needed a new song in the spring of 1976, English lyrics were written for the song which placed the events in the Mexican revolution in the early twentieth century. 'Fernando' is one of few singles in musical history to have sold more than 10 million physical copies.

On one level Abba knew exactly what they were doing on *Arrival*, their first true masterpiece, on another level they had no clue. They had to make quick decisions and trust their intuition.

Björn: 'We were under a constant time crunch, working at the Metronome studio. In the beginning we only had one day a week to record with Abba. The rest of the weekdays we wrote and recorded for other musicians. The songs needed to be done in a day. By the end of the day a song had to be mixed and ready to be released.'

The album was created under the worst possible conditions timewise. Recordings began in August 1975, but had to be interrupted several times and could not be completed until a year later. After a slow period following the 1974 Eurovision victory, Abba's big breakthrough happened right as they were about to record *Arrival*. Abba travelled the world, miming to 'SOS' in TV shows. 'Mamma Mia' went to number 1 in the UK. West Germany wanted a TV special. 'Fernando' topped the Australian charts for fourteen weeks (beating the Beatles' record with 'Hey Jude'). When Abba went to Australia to record a TV special, 54 per cent of the population watched it, more than watched the moon landing in 1969.

Their studio work, meanwhile, was characterised by total freedom.

'Benny could do just about anything in the studio,' says Michael B. Tretow. 'He had a million ideas and was ready to try every last one of them. Björn and I had to rein him in.'

One example is a folk-inspired song with the working title 'Hamlet', or 'Dr Claus von Hamlet' after Kalle Sändare, that was recorded in forty different takes, with and without lyrics. It never made it on to any Abba record. 'Benny was obsessed with finishing it,' Michael B. Tretow says. Ten years later the composition finally surfaced as the core of the song 'Lottis schottis' ('Lotti's schottische') on Benny's 1987 solo folk album, *Klinga mina klockor* ('Ring my bells').

The work on *Arrival* dragged out. Recordings were completed the month before it was issued in October 1976.

But now came the reward.

In the UK, *Arrival* became the bestselling album in 1977, despite the fact that it was issued in October 1976. The album was also in the running to become the top-grossing album in 1976, but was beaten – by Abba's *Greatest Hits*. In Sweden *Arrival* sold 740,000 copies, which is the equivalent of 10 per cent of the population owning a copy.

Today the album is seen as one of the best in pop history. Benny concludes by calling it 'our best album – up to that point'.

SIDE-PITCHED

Every time 'Dancing Queen' plays, something happens to the room. The song takes over, transforms its surroundings. It doesn't matter that you've heard it a thousand times. It doesn't matter in what context you are hearing it: at a wedding or in your car. 'Dancing Queen' releases things you did not know needed releasing.

At thirteen, I was sitting in front of the TV when Abba performed the song for the first time. It was at a live TV gala in June 1976, in anticipation of the wedding of King Carl XVI Gustaf and the future Queen Silvia. Abba performed a completely new song that only us Swedes got to hear. It would be another two months before it was released on a record.

First I thought it was a song in celebration of the queen, only meant to be performed then and there, but something about the melody and arrangement moved me more deeply than I'd anticipated. When the song was over I immediately wanted to hear it again.

Andy Bell of synth-pop duo Erasure, who is one year younger than me, says, 'I remember when "Dancing Queen" was released. I was so moved by the song that every time it was on the radio, I ran with my radio to my bedroom, opened the windows and cranked the volume all the way up so that everyone on the street could hear it.'

Pulitzer-winning art critic Jerry Saltz has lauded 'Dancing Queen' as an important historical work of art. When I ask him why, he says, 'Because you cannot avoid smiling, or dancing, or singing along to it, or feeling good when you hear it.'

On a rainy weekday evening I go to see the musical *Mamma Mia!* in London's West End, a show that has been cranked out since 1999 and ought to feel routine. But when 'Dancing Queen' is played it happens again: during the cheers it is as if the roof of the theatre opens and the stars in the sky switch places with the sparkling eyes of the people in the audience. Nobody is thinking about their day, or about work, about yesterday or tomorrow. As long as the music plays, no evil exists in the world.

'Dancing Queen' is like the scene in Cormac McCarthy's post-apocalyptic and ruthlessly cruel 2006 novel *The Road* where the dad, in an ash-grey setting, finds a bright red can of Coca Cola. His son has never seen such a thing. The dad opens the can and lets his son taste a better world.

The 2008 film version of *Mamma Mia!* presents the best rendition of the effervescent joy of 'Dancing Queen'.

When the piano starts to play, Donna is sitting at a mirror, staring at her reflection. She is a single mother, a British woman who owns a hotel on a Greek island, and whose daughter is now getting married. Donna, played by Meryl Streep, looks at her image in the mirror and wonders what happened to her life. When her two friends who have come for the wedding, played by Christine Baranski and Julie Walters, try to cheer her up by singing 'Dancing Queen' using hair dryers, deodorants and whatever else they can grab to hand as microphones, Donna jumps into bed and pulls the covers over herself in embarrassment.

As a viewer you feel the same way. Everything in that scene – everything in the entire movie – is *too much*. You can barely bring yourself to watch. Or rather, you *want* to watch, you just hope no one will see you watching.

Things get even more cringeworthy when the three of them run out of the house and through the village, singing 'Dancing Queen' in unison. The almost painfully idyllic surroundings, with pine trees and a bright blue ocean, bring to mind an ad for Greek yoghurt. Men, wearing caps above their sunburned faces, ride donkeys. Weathered, strong women in headscarves carry bundles of sticks.

Transported by the music, the village women abandon their bundles and bread-baking and laundry hampers and become part of the dancing party train led by Meryl Streep. Here the film decouples itself from any real-world logic or sense in a way that brings to mind the classic 1950s musical *Seven Brides for Seven Brothers*.

All the women in the village, young and old, are now singing 'Dancing Queen' and dancing their way to the harbour together. Down at the dock, Benny makes a sudden cameo appearance, wearing a captain's hat. Of course, he is playing the piano. During the song's crescendo Donna throws herself into the water and then everyone else follows her in.

This scene has spawned a tourist industry. The exteriors of *Mamma Mia!* were shot on the islands of Skiathos and Skopelos in the Sporades archipelago. Tourists are still arriving today, especially Brits, buying tickets to party boats that glide out of the harbour at night, pumping non-stop Abba music. The film is also screened at outdoor cinemas several times a week. It is kept quiet that the sequel was shot in Croatia.

*

'Dancing Queen' becomes the embodiment of joy every time it is played. The bassline is especially full of life. On bass is Rutger Gunnarsson, an irreplaceable part of Abba's band and sound.

Abba knew exactly what they wanted in their recordings and hired the very best studio musicians to achieve it. But they were also open to last-minute changes in the studio, if someone had a better idea. Feeling always trumped technique. Michael B. Tretow once said that Abba never let precision get in the way of expression.

During their active period 1972–82, Abba was primarily considered a studio group, as opposed to a live band, but below the live clips of Abba's tours on YouTube today, there are scores of comments from younger listeners and musicians across the world who are amazed by their live sound and rhythm, Agnetha's and Frida's perfect voices (they always sing in tune, without any aids) and the level of musicianship. Bassist Rutger Gunnarsson is the one of their musicians who receives the most digital applause. There are discussion forums and comments with headlines like 'A forgotten bass genius', 'Top Abba basslines' and 'My mind is blown from this Abba bassline'.

Abba used many brilliant musicians: Ola Brunkert (drums), Lasse Wellander (guitar), Anders Eljas (keyboard), Janne Schaffer (guitar), Roger Palm (drums), Per Lindvall (drums), Mike Watson (bass), Malando Gassama (percussion) and many others.

But Rutger Gunnarsson played the same role in Abba's band as James Jamerson did in the Motown studio band: part of the sound would disappear were it not for the intuitive musicianship of these two bassists, feeling their way outside the frame.

Jazz musician James Jamerson played on almost everything Motown recorded in Detroit from 1963 to 1968, including twenty-three chart-toppers on the Billboard Hot 100 and fifty-six number 1s on the R&B chart. Berry Gordy, the Motown founder, made sure that everyone played according to the arrangement, but made an exception for James Jamerson and called him an 'incredible improviser'. The way in which James Jamerson plays on Motown classics like 'You Can't Hurry Love', 'I Heard it Through the Grapevine' and 'Reach Out I'll Be There' never ceases to amaze.

After Motown Records moved from Detroit to Los Angeles, Jamerson received fewer commissions, but his bass is the one heard on Marvin Gaye's 'What's Going On'. James Jamerson was so drunk that he was lying on the studio floor when he recorded it. Jamerson died at age forty-seven from the effects of his alcohol addiction.

There are clear parallels between Rutger Gunnarsson's and James Jamerson's styles of playing. Rutger Gunnarsson was inspired by soul and R&B. In a 2000 interview in *Bass Player* magazine, he says that his favourite musicians include Donald 'Duck' Dunn (studio bassist at Stax Records), Chuck Rainey (who has played on over a thousand albums, from Aretha Franklin to Steely Dan) and Joe Osborn (a member of the legendary session band the Wrecking Crew in Los Angeles and the A-Team in Nashville).

But Rutger Gunnarsson also says that he never thinks of the bass in first place, he sees himself as 'a utility bassist, not a flash guy', who submits himself to what the song needs rather than trying to impress: 'To me, music is about a melody line on top, the bassline as the fundament, and the other parts filling the gap in between. It all begins with a good melody and a strong bassline.'

Rutger Gunnarsson always downplayed his role. In an interview with Swedish Yle, the Swedish-speaking division of Finnish public service radio, he says that he was inducted into Abba's inner circle thanks to Benny's dog.

Benny was hosting a party at his house and his dog chewed up Rutger's shoes. Björn and Benny, who were working as a duo at the time, felt so bad for Rutger that they asked if he wanted to play bass on their records.

A more comprehensive explanation is that Rutger Gunnarsson was studying classical guitar at the Stockholm Royal School of Music in 1972 when somebody told him about an audition for the group that would later become Abba. The job included singing backing vocals. Rutger could read music and nailed the harmonising. 'They were so impressed that they gave me the job on the spot. They didn't even hear me play a single note on my bass.'

Rutger Gunnarsson also wrote arrangements for string instruments, including on 'The Winner Takes It All'. Besides Abba, he has put his golden touch as a bass player or composer to several of the biggest songs in Swedish pop history: 'Visa vid vindens ängar' by Mats Paulson, 'Öppna landskap' by Ulf Lundell, 'Sommaren är kort' by Tomas Ledin, 'Bra vibrationer' by Kikki Danielsson, 'Kärleken är evig' by Lena Philipsson.

One of Rutger Gunnarsson's most joyful moments as a musician is the disco bass on Ulf Lundell's '(Oh la la) Jag vill ha dej'. Ulf Lundell can be called the Swedish Bob Dylan *and* Bruce Springsteen. In the late 1970s and early 1980s Ulf Lundell and Abba moved in the same circles, as they were all shunned by the progg movement. Several Abba musicians play on Lundell's album *Nådens År* and Agnetha sings backing vocals on 'Snön faller och vi med den'. Ask Benny today about the best concerts he's ever seen; he will mention Ulf Lundell in the same breath as Crosby, Stills and Nash and Led Zeppelin.

Rutger Gunnarsson's musical knowledge and skills stretched far beyond just thinking about the bass part, and this influenced the way he played. Another example of this is Wilton Felder's bass playing – at once tight and completely free – on the Jackson 5's 'I Want You Back', a candidate for the grooviest pop song ever made. On the Internet there are recordings where only the bass has been laid bare and it is astonishing how the entire groove is still intact. Felder, like Gunnarsson, was multitalented, having started out as a tenor saxophonist for the Crusaders.

Rutger Gunnarsson, who was born in 1946 and died in 2015, spent his entire life in obscurity as far as media attention went, a common fate for studio musicians. One year before his death he was given the Studioräven award by Musikerförbundet, the Swedish musicians' union. There is a video recording of the award ceremony at Nalen in Stockholm. Per Herrey from the Eurovision Song Contest-winning trio Herreys presents the prize and reads the judges' decision.

The person stepping on to the stage to accept the award is not Rutger but one of his three children. Rickard Gunnarsson accepts the diploma, which depicts a fox in headphones, and a cheque for 50,000 kronor (about £3,600). He grabs the microphone and says, 'Dad can't be here today because he is undergoing in-patient treatment for his alcoholism. But he wishes he could be here and he will definitely be here next year.' The son reads a speech written by his dad. Rutger politely thanks the Musicians' Union, but spends most of his acceptance speech lauding the other winner of that year's Studioräven award, the backing vocalist Liza Öhman who also sang with Abba.

The journalist who worked more than anyone to highlight Rutger Gunnarsson's place in musical history during his lifetime was Kjell Ekholm at Swedish Yle and FST (Finnish Swedish-language television).

In 1994, Kjell Ekholm produced a series for FST about Abba's studio musicians and filmed Rutger Gunnarsson in his apartment. In a memorial text online Kjell Ekholm writes: 'Just inside his door there were tons of gold and diamond records that had probably been sitting there for a few years waiting to be hung on the wall.'[13]

Rutger opened the door to an attic space and pulled out the two white bass guitars with red plexiglas that he used on Abba's recordings, a Fender Precision and a Fender Jazz Bass.

The reporter had brought a copy of 'Dancing Queen' and asked if Rutger Gunnarsson might consider playing along to the song. 'So we put the record on and Rutger plays along from the first notes,' Kjell Ekholm writes. 'He probably hadn't played that song since he used to work with Abba, which was more than ten years ago at that point. But it just flowed out of him.'

That clip is on YouTube now and has more than two million views, full of comments from bassists all over the world. It is only ninety seconds, but Rutger Gunnarsson's music, and his smile as he plays, are unforgettable.

Thirteen years after Rutger Gunnarsson was filmed in his home, Benny called to offer a new Abba commission. They were recording a soundtrack for the movie *Mamma Mia!* They were making completely new recordings and Benny was gathering the troops again with Lasse Wellander on the guitar, Per Lindvall on drums and Rutger Gunnarsson on bass and flew them all out to London.

If you ask an Abba connoisseur, it is the new recording of 'Dancing Queen' – the one you hear in the movie scene on the Greek island

TOP The Hep Stars were the biggest rock band in Sweden in the sixties. Beloved by raggare, they travelled around the country in American cars and were known for their wild live shows. The most energetic member was the young keyboard player, Benny Andersson (*front row, right*).

BOTTOM Agnetha Fältskog started performing as teenager, while working as a switchboard operator. At sixteen, she became a permanent singer in Bernt Enghardts Orkester, who later shortened their name to Engharts, in the tradition of Swedish *dansband* names.

TOP Frida in 1969 with pianist and entertainer Charlie Norman. Frida toured the country with the *Charlie Norman Show* and then joined him in residency at the Hamburger Börs Dinner Show in Stockholm.

BOTTOM The Hootenanny Singers were a folk rock group in Sweden in the sixties and early seventies, with numerous national hits. Björn Ulvaeus (*left*) often took lead and became their biggest star.

Abba before they were called Abba, at Gärdet in Stockholm.
In the background is Kaknästornet, a telecommunications tower, which was
the tallest building in Sweden and a major hub for all the broacasts in radio
and television, crucial for Abba's success.

Abba winning the Eurovision Song Contest in Brighton in 1974 with their first international hit, 'Waterloo'. The quartet began with two relationships and ended in two divorces. The ups and downs were documented in their songs.

ABOVE

Abba with their manager and lyrics co-writer, Stig 'Stikkan' Anderson. He was crucial to the group's international career, but their relationship turned sour in the late seventies. The last Abba song for which Stikkan has a writing credit is 'The Name of the Game'.

RIGHT

Despite media speculation, the group never officially broke up, but Abba dissolved in 1982. Their last two singles, 'The Day Before You Came' and 'Under Attack', were commercial disappointments. Their performance on *The Late, Late Breakfast Show* in December 1982 was their last together.

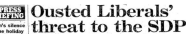

ABOVE

The premiere of the *Voyage* show in London All four members of Abba
were present – a rarity.

OPPOSITE TOP

The world premiere of the first *Mamma Mia!* movie in Stockholm in July 2008
at Rival, a cinema and hotel owned by Benny Andersson. Agnetha and Frida
with the stars of the movie: Amanda Seyfried, Meryl Streep, Christine Baranski.

OPPOSITE BOTTOM

In March 2010, Abba was inducted into the Rock and Roll Hall of Fame.
The group was represented at the ceremony by Frida and Benny, who gave
personal speeches, where they opened up more than in most interviews.

The specially built arena for the *Abba Voyage* show. The phenomenal success of the *Voyage* concert experience is a testament to the timeless nature of the band's music, and has showcased their genius to a whole new generation.

– that most clearly showcases the genius of Rutger Gunnarsson.

The actors Meryl Streep, Christine Baranski and Julie Walters sing, of course none of them are anywhere close to Agnetha and Frida's level, but that isn't the point. The musical foundation is joy.

'Listen to that track on the soundtrack that the original guys and Benny recorded in London,' says musical jack-of-all-trades Claes af Geijerstam, who was always somewhere in the vicinity of Abba. 'Goddamit it's good, it's so damn good. Benny's arrangement, Rutger's ideas, the sound, side-pitched.'

'Side-pitched' is a word that he coined to describe Abba's highly compressed sound.

Claes af Geijerstam emphasises how hard it is to play Abba's songs. Musicians in cover bands are shocked when they realise the virtuosity it takes to make the music sound so immediate, especially the bass and the piano.

'Rutger's bass-playing was so amazingly fluid and inventive. It's not just ground notes up and down in major and minor, he embroiders and does such clever stuff. I tear up hearing Rutger's last work on the soundtrack to *Mamma Mia!*'

GRACIAS POR LA MÚSICA

I t is New Year's Eve in Vietnam, 2015. The Vietnamese New Year, Tết, corresponds with the Chinese New Year and happens at the new moon during the period 21 January to 20 February. The full name of the holiday is Tết Nguyên Đán, meaning 'celebration of the first morning'. On her blog, travel journalist Tammy Lovett writes about a Tết celebration on Cát Bà Island in the Gulf of Tonkin: 'Ringing in the New Year isn't the same as it is back home. This is serious stuff; there are rules to follow if the year ahead is to be successful.'[14]

As New Year's fireworks light up the sky at midnight, Abba's 'Happy New Year' begins to play on all speakers. When the song has ended Tammy Lovett notes that it is played again. And again, and again. 'Happy New Year' is played for almost half an hour straight, as part of the New Year's celebration.

In the Vietnamese paper *VnExpress*, Martin Rama writes that the same thing happens every year, all over the country. Vietnamese people of all ages know the song and its lyrics by heart.[15] Rama notes it is the most loved song in Vietnam after 'Tiến Quân Ca', the national anthem.

'Tiến Quân Ca' is known in English as 'The Marching Army Song', or 'Song of the Advancing Soldiers' and only has two verses. In 1946 North Vietnam appropriated it as its national anthem. After the Vietnam War it became the national anthem of the new Socialist Republic of Vietnam, founded during the unification of North Vietnam and South Vietnam.

During the post-war period, Vietnam cut itself off from the rest of the world. The only links were to the brotherly socialist nations in the Soviet bloc. Foreigners were rare in Hanoi in the 1980s, but Vietnam maintained close ties with Sweden – both during and after the war. Sweden's Prime Minister Olof Palme was one of few in the Western world who dared to openly criticise the United States during the Vietnam War. On 10 January 1969, Sweden became the first Western nation to formally recognise North Vietnam. In the spring of 1975, during the fall of Saigon, the Swedish state signed a sixty-year lease for an embassy property in Hanoi.

Olof Palme was as critical of the Soviet Union as he was of the United States and continued to be engaged in international politics until he was assassinated in 1986. In 1975 Olof Palme was the first Western head of state to make an official visit to post-revolutionary Cuba.

Sweden assisted Vietnam through foreign aid. Bai Bang is fifty-six miles north-west of Hanoi. The area became the site of Sweden's largest aid project of all time, in the shape of a paper mill that was erected as part of the rebuilding of North Vietnam. The aid lasted from 1970, the middle of the war, until 1995.

The protracted and, for Swedish taxpayers, costly Bai Bang project became hotly debated in Sweden, but Vietnam has never forgotten it. The Swedes who built the mill brought Abba's music with them. Vietnamese authorities were suspicious of Western and American pop culture, but made an exception for Swedish culture. Sweden was regarded as a trustworthy ally.

'The official acceptance of Abba songs happened at a time when scarcity raged and there was very little to be celebrated in Vietnam,' writes Martin Rama. Cultural life was minimal, but 'Abba's songs were there to remind them that there was a prosperous and optimistic world outside of Vietnam'. And the song that represents these dreams, better than any others since it was issued in 1980, with lyrics like 'feeling lost and feeling blue', is 'Happy New Year'.

Christofer Fredriksson at the Swedish embassy in Hanoi corroborates that the nation's love for Abba is as big as it ever was. For obvious reasons, Vietnam continues to be wary of American artists. The most respected pop bands, besides Abba, are two disco groups formed in Germany: Boney M. and Modern Talking. Liz Mitchell of Boney M. has said that she, during travels in East and South East Asia has often heard people say, 'The three most important pop artists in the world are Abba, Boney M. and Michael Jackson.'

It is interesting that Abba, a group accused in their home country of glorifying capitalism, became the most popular pop group in several socialist nations.

Sweden's position as a neutral country, located between West and East, with a social democratic government and a globally engaged prime minister, made it possible for Eastern regimes to accept Abba.

The Cold War was raging in 1976. American and English pop artists rarely or never visited countries behind the Iron Curtain. It was difficult to find Western pop records in Eastern Europe.

That is why Abba's visit to Poland drew a lot of attention. The group participated in a live TV broadcast that was watched by most of the population. Ahead of the show they made a Polish music video for 'SOS'. Agnetha and Björn, who had young children at home, did not want to travel on the same plane for safety reasons. Agnetha flew to Warsaw a day ahead of the others, accompanied by her dad.

In the Polish video for 'SOS', cut under a time crunch, Agnetha stands alone on Plac Trzech Krzyży in Warsaw, miming. This is interspersed with footage of Frida, Björn and Benny on the plane to Poland, singing along. Judging from their faces, the duty-free cart definitely made a couple of stops by their seats.

Abba's visit led the Polish communist regime to spend the entire 1976 budget for Western pop music on pressing one single album edition: 800,000 copies of *Arrival*.

A book has been written on Abba's visit to Poland, *Abba w Polsche*, by Maciej Oranski. Abba followed up the TV show with visits to Warsaw nightclubs and a short sightseeing tour the next day. Agnetha says in the book that Poland was not a rich country, but that people were extremely friendly.

Even the USSR, which would never have accepted any American artist, approved Abba and pressed records on licence. Abba often topped the list that readers of the newspaper *Moskovsky Komsomolets* voted on. In *Schlagerkungens krig*, Klas Gustafson writes that 1977's *Abba: The Movie* played sold-out screenings at twenty-two cinemas across the Soviet Union.

The Soviet regime's attitude to Abba shifted when the group spoke out in support of the Solidarity trade union in Poland and the nascent democratic movement there, which threatened the stability of the entire Eastern bloc.

Abba's eighth album, *The Visitors*, released in November 1981, is marked by the Cold War and the oppressive regimes in the east, both in terms of lyrics and sound. Now the Soviet regime considered Abba a threat. Klas Gustafson writes, 'Records were recalled and movie screenings ceased. The newspaper *Komsomolskaya Pravda* wrote that Abba was a bad influence on Soviet youth and that the group's music was like "sweet, cheap candy".'

But the people of Russia never stopped loving Abba. The Abba museum opened in Stockholm in 2013; a striking percentage of its visitors come from the formerly communist nations in Eastern Europe.

In 2010 Ahmad Sarmast founded the Afghanistan National Institute of Music in Kabul, where children, especially young girls, could learn to play instruments. The repertoire consisted of both classical Western music as well as traditional Afghan folk music.

To punish him for this the Taliban attempted to assassinate him several times, and one time, during a concert, a suicide bomber nearly succeeded. In 2018 the institute was awarded the Polar Music Prize, created by Stikkan Anderson. Ahmad Sarmast received his prize from the Swedish king, side by side with the other award winners that year, American heavy metal pioneers Metallica.

Ahmad Sarmast was especially pleased with the Swedish connection. Ahead of the award ceremony I interviewed him in Davos where he was giving a speech at the World Economic Forum. 'I grew up with Abba,' he said. 'They were the most popular pop group in Afghanistan. Every Thursday there was a TV show, *Colour by Colour*, and on each programme they would play a song by Abba. When I studied in Moscow, Abba was also the most popular group at every dance party.'

When the Taliban took back power in Afghanistan in 2021, Ahmad Sarmast, along with Stikkan's daughter Marie Ledin, organised a risky rescue operation so that more than one hundred students and teachers from the school could escape Kabul and find a safe haven in Portugal.

When Abba released their comeback album *Voyage* in November 2021, the *New York Times* wrote an article in which readers from all over the world were encouraged to share their memories of the group.

Readers from ages twenty to seventy shared their stories. For obvious reasons most were from the United States, but a reader from Łódź, Poland also participated ('I recall Abba's concert on the Polish TV channel TVP2 in 1976') as did many with roots in Latin America.

Fernanda González Pèrez from Santiago, Chile, said that Abba's music reminded her of her grandmother. They used to dance and sing along to 'Chiquitita' in Spanish. When her grandmother passed away the previous year, Fernanda continued listening to Abba as a way of remembering her.

Laura Rentas from San Juan, Puerto Rico, said that her father gave her an Abba LP with the song 'Chiquitita' and that for her the song represented a safe and happy place where she felt loved and protected.

Chiquitita means 'little girl' in Spanish. Abba performed the song during *Music for UNICEF* at the UN headquarters in New York in 1979, a fundraising gala at which their friends in the Bee Gees as well as Andy Gibb and Olivia Newton-John also performed. Rod Stewart, Donna Summer and Earth, Wind & Fire also participated.

The gala started with everyone singing Abba's 'He Is Your Brother' together and ended with Jackie DeShannon's 'Put a Little Love in Your Heart'. A few artists didn't just participate in the gala, they also donated their royalties for the songs they performed, among them the Bee Gees with 'Too Much Heaven' and Abba with 'Chiquitita'.

Abba donated 50 per cent of all future royalties for that song to UNICEF and their work for children across the world, a share that was adjusted to 100 per cent in 2014. 'Chiquitita' has raised more than an estimated 50 million kronor (about £3.7 million) for UNICEF to date.

During a music convention in Miami in 1978, Stikkan Anderson wanted to know what it would take for Abba to make it big in South America. Stikkan was discussing the matter with his colleague Buddy McCluskey who worked at RCA, Abba's company in Argentina, where he held the title 'Regional Marketing Director for Latin America and the Far East'. Buddy McCluskey explained that the best and perhaps only way would be for Abba to sing in Spanish. Stikkan agreed, they decided to be back in touch when the right song came along.

When he heard 'Chiquitita' for the first time in January 1979, Buddy McCluskey called his friend Stikkan. 'This is the right song!' Things took off from there. Buddy McCluskey wrote Spanish lyrics for the song together with his wife Mary and then flew to Stockholm in February to work on the recording of a new take of that song.

'It was a lot of fun, especially working with Agnetha and Frida,' Buddy McCluskey recalls in the liner notes for a deluxe edition of a CD of Spanish-language Abba songs. 'They were so professional and took on the task with such joy, which made things easier for us. Our coaching was mainly phonetic and we corrected the lyrics so that their pronunciation would sound good even though they didn't speak Spanish.'

The Spanish version of 'Chiquitita' was a bigger success than anyone had dared dream. It made it to number 1 in Argentina, Mexico, Venezuela, El Salvador, Ecuador and the Dominican Republic. In all, 'Chiquitita' was the biggest hit in Latin America for twenty-five years and brought Abba's current album *Voulez-Vous* with it high up on the sales charts.

The McCluskeys returned to Stockholm in August 1979 to record a Spanish follow-up, this time 'I Have a Dream', translated as 'Estoy Soñando'. Abba, who were in the midst of recording new material, didn't really have the time, but managed to find an empty slot in their schedules. The children's chorus, an important part of the song, had to be recorded by the McCluskeys themselves, back in Buenos Aires, with Argentinian children.

When 'Estoy Soñando' made the top five in Latin America the follow-up was obvious: record an entire album in Spanish. 'We decided the songs should be recorded in a "neutral" Spanish, so it would be okay for Mexico, Chile, Venezuela, Argentina, Spain and other countries, avoiding for example certain Argentine or Mexican idioms,' Buddy McCluskey says in an article in the Abba fan club magazine. 'We also had to be careful with the titles of the songs. They had to be clear and catchy.'[16]

The Spanish album was titled *Gracias por la música*, after 'Thank You for the Music'. Posters advertising the album read, 'Abba en Español'. The selection of songs came fairly naturally. There were a surprising number of songs in Abba's catalogue, besides 'Chiquitita', that had Spanish-sounding titles and some kind of Spanish feel: 'Hasta Mañana', 'Fernando', 'Mamma Mia' and even, for example, the somewhat bizarre 'Move On', with a spoken intro by Björn and Peruvian flutes.

Björn and Benny were in the Bahamas writing songs, so the Spanish album was made by Agnetha and Frida together with Michael B. Tretow. To make sure they got the pronunciation right they called in Buenos Aires-born Swedish journalist Ana Martinez, known from programmes on Sveriges Radio as well as for her appearances on Jacob Dahlin's iconic TV show *Jacobs stege*.

Ana Martinez's decision to work with Abba was not popular among her left-leaning colleagues on Sveriges Radio. 'I was called in to an inquisitorial meeting behind closed doors,' says Ana Martinez. She was accused of collaborating with 'that capitalist who is poisoning P3 with treacly repulsive crap, pushing out the righteous songs of the people'.

Abba followed up their Spanish album by translating two songs into Spanish on the Latin American edition of their next album *Super Trouper*, where 'Happy New Year' became 'Felicidad' and 'Andante, Andante' did not need a new title. They also recorded two Spanish-language songs for *The Visitors* in 1981: 'No Hay A Quien Culpar' ('When All Is Said and Done') and 'Se Me Está Escapando' ('Slipping Through My Fingers').

Back home in Argentina, people were proud of Ana Martinez's assignment. When she was interviewed in *Dagens Nyheter* about her long career she said that Argentine newspapers would run articles with headlines such as 'Our girl is teaching Abba Spanish'.

DISCO

Right now, as you read this sentence, Abba is being played in a gay club somewhere in the world. Or at a bar, or a party full of LGBTQ people. If it isn't 'Dancing Queen' it's probably 'Gimme! Gimme! Gimme! (A Man After Midnight)'. These songs might appear full of obvious gay references today, but Björn was completely unaware when he wrote the lyrics almost half a century ago.

The gay community is where you will find Abba's most fiercely loyal fans. After Abba's dissolution in 1982 their music disappeared from the public consciousness for almost ten years. They found themselves out in the cold as far as the media and music business went. It was precisely then that the gay community opened its arms and took them in, and it has stood up to defend Abba as its own ever since.

If you ask why Abba became so big in the gay community, you'll get a range of answers. One theory is that Agnetha and Frida fit the roles as glamorous but ill-fated divas, directly descended from Maria Callas and Judy Garland.

Deeper research, focusing on their music, brings us to two other points of departure. One is the predominantly gay nightclubs in Manhattan. The era is the early 1980s, when a DJ makes his own unofficial remix of what at that time was one of Abba's lesser-known songs, 'Lay All Your Love on Me', twice as long as the original and focused on the beat. That remix became a dance-floor sensation, completely without any involvement from Abba, or even their knowledge.

The other point of departure is Sydney, Australia, in March 1987. If one were to hold a championship of which country in the world loves Abba the most, the finals will always come down to Australia vs the UK. With Australia winning on penalties. The Netherlands will take bronze.

In Australia it started in 1975, when the video for 'I Do, I Do, I Do, I Do, I Do', a single that more or less flopped in England, was shown on the chart show *Countdown*. From that point Abba remained on the singles chart with various songs for thirty-nine consecutive weeks, a streak that culminated with 'Fernando' staying at number 1 for fourteen weeks. The record held until 2017 when 'Shape of You' by Ed Sheeran stayed at number 1 for fifteen weeks.

Many global artists hold off on doing an Australian tour. It is too far; the costs are larger than the revenue. Abba also declined initially, but at the end of February 1977 the group landed at the airport in Sydney. Qantas Airlines had made white bomber jackets for the Abbas. Even at their arrival there was chaos, with thousands of waiting fans. One especially fanatic admirer put a baby down in the road to force Abba's entourage to stop.

For two weeks in March the group played eleven sold-out concerts in Sydney, Melbourne, Adelaide and Perth. Abba's presence completely dominated the nation's news flow. This tour of Australia is documented in Lasse Hallström's feature film *Abba: The Movie*.

In 1987 fans celebrated the ten-year anniversary of Abba's visit to Australia with a large Abba event. Fans recreated the 1977 concerts by miming to scenes from *Abba: The Movie* and bootleg recordings

– four wore Abba oufits while others acted the parts of the backing musicians. Even the audience dressed like they would have done at the old concerts. Today there are similar Abba events across the world, but Australia did it first.

That first Abba event was documented in a segment on Australian morning TV in which fans were interviewed. Two of the people interviewed used the expression 'coming out of the closet', but seemingly only in the sense of coming out as Abba fans. It took a lot of courage to openly say you loved Abba in 1987.

In a country often associated with crocodile hunters and macho culture, the city of Sydney stands out for having a large and vital gay scene. Oxford Street in the neighbourhood of Darlinghurst is known as the main gay hotspot, boasting many bars and clubs as well as events, such as the Sydney Gay and Lesbian Mardi Gras.

The Abba event in 1987 was so popular that bars on Oxford Street began having regular 'Abba nights', an idea that spread to other cities, like Melbourne. Several years of regular Abba nights left their mark on Australian popular culture.

Björn Again was formed in 1988. Initially they were not a cover band but an entire show in Melbourne. (The name is a play on words that only works if Björn's name is pronounced the anglophone way.) Rod Stephen, the brains behind the group, says in the book *We All Love Abba* that he created a satirical parody of Abba in the form of a stage show with choreography and dialogue. A parody that the audience took as a celebration and which thus, in practice, became just that.

When the compilation album *Abba Gold* was released in 1992, Björn Again was invited to promote it. Since then, Björn Again has played all over the world, with more than 2,000 gigs in the UK alone.

The Australian movie *The Adventures of Priscilla, Queen of the Desert* was released in 1994; it is a road movie featuring two drag queens, played by Hugo Weaving and Guy Pearce, and a trans woman played by Terence Stamp. The soundtrack was filled with gay disco favourites and Abba. In one sequence Pearce and Weaving lip synch to 'Mamma Mia', first on the bus and then on stage, dressed as Agnetha and Frida. The song is played in its entirety, not for the half-minute or so that songs in movies typically are.

That same year another Australian film became a big hit across the entire world. *Muriel's Wedding* is a drama comedy about Muriel, who lives in a small town where she dreams of a big wedding to cure her loneliness. Abba songs recur as a central theme throughout the story, including 'Waterloo', 'I Do, I Do, I Do, I Do, I Do', and 'Dancing Queen'. For this movie Abba, who are infamous for saying no to anyone who wants to remake their music, approved the recording of an instrumental orchestral version of 'Dancing Queen'.

The only market that Abba never quite managed to conquer during their original active period was the United States. Abba only had four songs on the Billboard top ten and just one single made it to number 1 – 'Dancing Queen', which reached the top spot in April 1977.

Instead Abba built an American audience from below, through discos and gay clubs.

In the 1970s, Swedish media regarded disco as being music for the upper crust, an upper-class pursuit along the lines of golfing. The rock-loving men who dominated music criticism in the 1970s dismissed disco music as a fad that lived and died with the movie *Saturday Night Fever* and its soundtrack.

On Swedish school playgrounds you might hear the epithet 'disco fag'. The young punk band Glo from Åsam, a small town outside Gothenburg, consisted of four fifteen-year-olds and was one of the best live bands of the first punk wave. Their 1979 debut was a single titled 'Discoäckel' ('Disco creep') on which they sang the word 'disco fag'. The band's pop-punk sound was clearly moulded on that of the Manchester band the Buzzcocks, whose frontman Pete Shelley had yet to come out as bisexual.

In this era, punks, hard-rock fans and raggare in Sweden all had a favourite song in common, '2-4-6-8 Motorway' by the Tom Robinson Band. It was the perfect song to listen to while riding in a car with the windows down and bellowing along to the gasoline-scented guitar riff. Nobody knew that the refrain was inspired by a chant for gay rights: 'Two, four, six, eight, gay is twice as good as straight; three, five, seven, nine, lesbians are mighty fine.'

Tom Robinson was more explicit about his message when he released his follow-up: the EP *Rising Free* featuring the song 'Sing if You're Glad to Be Gay', causing confusion in the ranks. Rock fans went back to worshipping 'masculine' rock singers in leather, such as Rob Halford of Judas Priest.

Disco music so provoked rock audiences across the world that they wanted to ban it completely. There were even organised bonfires at which disco records were burned. 'Disco Demolition Night' at a baseball stadium in Chicago in the summer of 1979 was a ghoulish gathering with racist and homophobic undertones at which the audience was incited to bring disco records, most of them recorded by Black artists, to watch them be blown into the air in the middle of the field.

When Nile Rodgers of Chic spoke of the event in Swedish music magazine *Sonic* many years later he said, 'What would have happened if Donna Summer had stepped into the arena in that moment? Would they have killed her?'

Disco turned out to not be a passing fad; in fact, it survived all declarations of its demise and came to completely change the course of popular music as a whole.

In 1970 Sly Stone sang 'Everybody Is a Star'. Disco gave birth to the revolutionary idea that the audience – not the artist – could be the true star. The idea that the record could be more important than the live performance was also born in the discotheque.

Peter Shapiro's book *Turn the Beat Around: The Secret History of Disco* rewinds the tape all the way to the 1800s, to a place in New Orleans named Congo Square. Classically trained Creole musicians and free, formerly enslaved, people met in musical duels on Sundays, during which marching music was transformed into jazz. The audience that marched behind the victorious band was called 'the second line'. Their clapping and shouting was so active that it helped birth a new type of rhythm.

In the 1940s and 1950s Earl Palmer, a New Orleanian drummer known from records with Fats Domino and Little Richard, further developed these rhythms from Congo Square. Almost all the rhythms we hear in Western dance music today can be traced to him and the cross-pollination between rhythmic marching music and African beats. Earl Palmer is the father of funk and the grandfather of disco.

*

In Europe, disco was associated with money, glamour and a jet-set lifestyle. But disco was born in New York City, in reaction to urban decay, failed infrastructure and a brutal recession.

From 1966 and up until 1973, the year when disco made its breakthrough, the murder rate in New York City increased by 173 per cent and the number of rapes by 112 per cent. A report published in December 1972 didn't just testify to widespread police corruption in Manhattan, but to police officers selling heroin and handing over snitches to the mob.

Movies like *Taxi Driver, Midnight Cowboy, Dog Day Afternoon, Shaft* and *Warriors* captured the claustrophobic atmosphere in the city during this era. *New York Times* film critic Vincent Canby wrote that the New York City of the movies is a metaphor for 'the last days of American civilisation'.

Out of this reality, music was born that could comfort the body and inspire hope in ways that the intellect could no longer muster. This was when African American, Latino and homosexual people created disco culture.

High up on Broadway, on the Upper West Side between 73rd and 74th Streets, lies the magnificent Ansonia, an old apartment hotel where opera singer Enrico Caruso once lived and Igor Stravinsky could be counted among the tenants.

In the late 1960s and early 1970s the basement of the same building housed the Continental Baths, an all-male bathhouse and club. Then-unknown Jewish singer Bette Midler was the house entertainer. The cheers knew no bounds when Bette Midler slid along the edge of the pool singing numbers such as the scandalous 'Marahuana'.

The men in that basement, including Bette Midler's pianist Barry

Manilow, wore nothing but towels wrapped around their waists. Class and economic status were left in the locker rooms, traded for liberating anonymity. The Continental Baths were a symbol of liberation of equal importance to the pill, Woodstock and the Black Panthers. Bette Midler's audience warm-up was followed by a DJ who mixed the music into one single long flow.

The dance floors at the clubs that emerged in New York City were non-hierarchical. A CEO might be dancing next to a humble wage slave. Dancing all night was a way of flipping the bird at conventional society and its narrow moral confines. The movie *Saturday Night Fever* is about a guy in Brooklyn who works at a paint store during the day and is the king of the dance floor at night. Another stretch of street in New York where you might end up lingering if you've read *Turn the Beat Around* is 54th Street between Broadway and 8th Avenue. This was where the lines snaked around the block for Studio 54, the world's most famous discotheque, that opened in April 1977, one year before *Saturday Night Fever* hit the cinemas.

Two of the people in line on New Year's Eve that year were Nile Rodgers and Bernard Edwards, studio musicians who had just released their first album under the name Chic. It had been a good year; they were finally close to a breakthrough. Besides having had a couple of big dance-floor hits, they had been asked to collaborate with Grace Jones, who had invited them to a meeting after her New Year's concert at Studio 54.

It was cold and snowing. Edwards was dressed in a Cerruti blazer, Rodgers was wearing an Armani blazer. They were shivering in the long line on 54th Street but they couldn't get in. It didn't matter that they tried shouting that they were there to meet with Grace Jones. The bouncer ignored them completely.

Finally they gave up. Angry and dejected they waded through the snow to Rodgers' apartment. On the way they bought champagne, marijuana and cocaine and decided to have their own New Year's party – just the two of them. As they often did, they began to jam on bass and guitar. They shouted 'Fuck Studio 54!' over and over again. After a while this battle cry was shortened to 'Fuck off!' And they discovered that they'd written a song.

Thirty minutes later their song was finished. They knew they couldn't call it 'Fuck off!' so they changed the refrain to 'Freak out!' but other than that it was intact. When the song was released on single in 1978 as 'Le Freak', it became the bestselling single in the history of Atlantic Records.

Disco was labelled as superficial music in the 1970s, but the best songs in early disco and its predecessor, Philadelphia soul, are not about escapism at all; they deal with themes such as disappointment and the desire for revenge and have melancholic undertones: 'The Love I Lost'. 'Bad Luck'. 'I Will Survive'.

The streak of melancholia has its counterpart in Abba, who heard these songs played at discotheques in Stockholm, without knowing the cultural context. After 'Dancing Queen' Abba continued to be influenced by disco and travelled to Criteria Studios in Miami to record the title track for *Voulez-Vous*, accompanied by local Latin disco band Foxy.

When Abba landed in New York City during their North American tour in the autumn of 1979, some of their entourage, headed by audio technician and Swedish disco pioneer Claes af Geijerstam, made a beeline for Studio 54.

In *Turn the Beat Around*, Peter Shapiro writes that disco was a party, but also a celebration of a world that was being lost. Much of the ground won by the Black civil rights movement in the 1960s had been lost in the 1970s. The biggest loser during the recession was the Black middle class; its members were starting to realise that they had been had.

Disco was – and is – subversive music. Disco hints that individual liberation on the dance floor might also liberate the world. In fact the connection between disco music, resistance and rebellion is further underscored by the origin of the word itself: the term *discotheque* can be traced back to Nazi-occupied Europe during the Second World War.

An underground movement emerged in Nazi Germany, 'Swing Kids', or *Swing-Jugend*, young people who rebelled against Hitler's directives by dressing in extravagant fashions and listening to American jazz. Since the movement was banned one could not play live music as was customary, but had to dance to records.

When the same movement spread to occupied Paris, secret basement clubs were started, *discothèques*, where one could order the record one wanted to hear alongside a drink. *Disque*, or record, was portmanteaued with *bibliothèque*, library.

When the media declared disco dead in the early 1980s, it moved back underground.

One of New York's most prominent DJs at the time was Raul A. Rodriguez. (Confusingly there is yet another famous disco DJ with the same name, Raul Rodriguez, house DJ at legendary Ushuaïa Beach Hotel on Ibiza.) The New York City Raul A. Rodriguez was one half of producer duo COD (Cash On Delivery) alongside Man Parrish, an electro and hip-hop pioneer. Old-school disco songs with strings were no longer requested at the gay clubs, now people wanted new, futuristic styles with heavier beats and a faster tempo. House and techno were in their infancy, but the road there was being mapped out.

Rodriguez managed to create exactly what the audience wanted when he took his copy of Abba's latest LP, *Super Trouper*, recorded it on his reel-to-reel tape recorder and focused on the penultimate track on the B-side, 'Lay All Your Love on Me'. With analogue tools such as tape and razors he literally cut a new version of the song with looped sequences.

The song he created was twice as long, less sophisticated, and even more effective on the dance floor. One looped instrumental segment in this remix is so rough that the song makes a sort of audible jump and the accompaniment sounds like explosions, or hammer hits.

The DJ Robbie Leslie, the king of New York gay disco, who played at legendary NYC gay clubs such as the Saint as well as the Sandpiper on Fire Island has said of the Abba remix: 'The first time Rodriguez did it was a mistake, then everyone did it on purpose.' The audience, high on poppers, fists raised, loved that effect.

Raul A. Rodriguez's radical eight-minute reworking of 'Lay All Your Love on Me' was released as a twelve-inch single by Disconet under the credit 'a Raul Dance Mix'. It wasn't for sale in record stores: it was only available as a subscription service for DJs.

Disconet was started in New York City in 1977. An ad for the service shows three smiling men; two of them have generous Village People moustaches. Record companies have a long-standing tradition of pressing twelve-inch singles exclusively for DJs – Swedish SweMix, where producer Denniz Pop began his career, was one such service. The advantage of this format lies in the sound quality. The dense engraving on LPs makes it so that there is less pressure when songs are played at a high volume. Seven-inch singles are better than albums, but they too are suboptimal in terms of sound. When you let just one song take up space across twelve inches, with plenty of space between the tracks, the music takes on an entirely different quality. The needle also stays deeper in the groove, which enables the DJ to experiment more with the turntables.

Abba did not consider 'Lay All Your Love on Me' an important song when their album *Super Trouper* was released in November 1980. Five singles were drawn from the album worldwide, and only two of those were mass released: 'The Winner Takes it All' (July 1980) and the title track 'Super Trouper' (November 1980).

Listening to those songs in sequence tells you something about Abba's unlikely musical range and underscores that their albums were never homogenous: they range from sentimental sing-alongs at the grand piano such as 'Happy New Year' and 'Andante, Andante', associated with a middle-aged audience with kids and mortgages, to state-of-the-art pop music and thumping, hedonistic disco.

The Disconet version of 'Lay All Your Love on Me' became a sure-fire way to fill a dance floor in Britain and Sweden too. Alongside his work as Abba's audio technician, Claes af Geijerstam was a travelling DJ in Sweden and made radio shows with dance music. He had a catchphrase on the radio 'Yowsah yowsah yowsah!' which he had borrowed from Chic.

'When I first heard "Lay All Your Love on Me" I immediately thought "it's too short",' says Claes af Geijerstam. 'It has such a great goddamn beat. When that sequence ends you want it to come right back. So I made my own extended version that I played as a disc jockey.'

Dance floors were now anticipating Abba releasing their own remix of 'Lay All Your Love on Me'. But none came.

'Benny and I were skiing somewhere and began talking about it,' Claes af Geijerstam recalls. 'Even back when "Voulez-Vous" was released the record company wanted to release an extended twelve-inch version but Benny thought that was completely unnecessary. "What kind of nonsense is that? You know, the song is what it is. *This is it.*"'

But the unauthorised remixes of 'Lay All Your Love on Me' continued to spread. In the end Claes af Geijerstam felt pressed to bring the topic up again.

'I had to explain why we would do it, since I myself worked as a DJ. While Benny felt that the song was done and of a perfect length, as a DJ you wanted some tarmac on which to gather speed. You didn't want a bridge suddenly interrupting it. You also wanted to be able to use the song to launch into the next one.'

This resulted in a compromise. Benny did not change the production, but in July 1981 they released 'Lay All Your Love on Me' as a twelve-inch single, eight months after the release of the album. It became the bestselling twelve-inch record in the history of the UK, a record that held for two years, until New Order released 'Blue Monday'. Abba releasing a song exclusively on twelve-inch was taken as a clear sign by the world of gay disco that the group affirmed their popularity on their dance floors.

The sound and the thumping energy in 'Lay All Your Love on Me' made an impression on other artists. In 1984 a producer trio was formed in Great Britain, Stock Aitken Waterman who worshipped Abba and Holland-Dozier-Holland (also favourites of Benny's) and fused the same type of tunes with hi-NRG, fast-paced electronic dance music, directly descended from Raul A. Rodriguez and which became a predecessor to today's EDM.

Stock Aitken Waterman productions such as future gay classic 'You Spin Me Round (Like a Record)' by Dead or Alive and their songs featuring a young singer from an Australian soap, Kylie Minogue, took over the charts in the UK and the rest of Europe. When Abba's career was on ice, Kylie Minogue tended the flame of Abba's unfinished legacy. Compare Kylie Minogue's brilliant 'Can't Get You Out of My Head' from 2001 with Abba's swan song 'The Day Before You Came' – the same froideur at twice the speed.

When Erasure released *Abba-esque*, a 1992 EP containing four Abba covers, 'Lay All Your Love on Me' was cemented as one of the high points of Abba's entire catalogue.

Vince Clarke, who was straight, chose two of the songs, 'SOS' and 'Take a Chance on Me'. Andy Bell, who was gay, took the disco tack and chose 'Voulez-Vous' and 'Lay All Your Love on Me'. The latter was the opening track on their EP and its most successful cover.

'I was a huge Abba fan growing up,' says Andy Bell on Zoom from his home in Miami. 'My best friend in school, who would later become my boyfriend, loved Abba, ELO and Kate Bush. There were two kids in his family; there were six in mine. We used to meet and listen to vinyl. I remember when *Voulez-Vous* was released and how much we listened to it and danced to it.'

Vince Clarke was one of the founders of the synth-pop band

Depeche Mode and was the songwriter in the band until he suddenly quit, soon after the group had their breakthrough. Instead he formed the duo Yazoo with Alison Moyet as singer and then later Erasure, with Andy Bell, in 1985.

The Abba influences shone through even before *Abba-esque*: on the group's third single, 'Oh l'Amour', one of the B-side tracks was a cover of 'Gimme! Gimme! Gimme! (A Man After Midnight)'. The plan was that Erasure would call their debut album 'Greatest Hits' – in tribute to Abba's classic compilation record *Greatest Hits* from 1975. 'But we realised nobody would get it.'

The homage to Abba was recorded spontaneously in Amsterdam over the course of five days. For a while there was an idea of doing an entire album. 'No matter how pleased I am with how the songs turned out, I am very glad that didn't happen. *Abba-esque* became so big that people thought of us as a cover band for years afterwards.'

Part of the reason for the success of that EP – it topped the charts in the UK, Sweden and half a dozen other countries – was the fact that music videos were recorded for all four songs.

'In the midst of the recording Vince suddenly decided that he didn't want to be in our videos, or be seen in our visual presentation at all,' Andy Bell recalls. 'So that is why he is only in two of the Abba videos, in the other two it's just me.'

One of these videos in which both members participate has become iconic: 'Take a Chance on Me', where Andy Bell and Vince Clarke create a pastiche of Lasse Hallström's original video, dressed in drag as Agnetha and Frida.

'But we really didn't intend for it to be taken as a statement,' says Andy Bell. 'We really weren't thinking, "We're gonna do Abba drag," we just thought it was fun to copy the original video. I wanted to be

Agnetha and told Vince he could be Frida. Vince answered, '"No, I only agree to this if I can be Agnetha." Which was the correct decision. He looks more like Agnetha than I do, I look better as a redhead.'

Although neither Erasure nor Abba had planned it, Erasure's EP of Abba covers became the perfect pre-promotion for the compilation album *Abba Gold*, which was released three months later and marked the real start of the Abba revival.

The cover band Björn Again released the record *Erasure-ish* that same year in which they did their renditions of two Erasure songs with Abba-inspired arrangements, complete with videos in which they dressed up as Erasure dressed up as Abba.

In Sweden there was already a long tradition of dressing up as Abba that had nothing to do with drag or gay culture. From the 1940s until the 1980s there was something called 'fun hour' on the schedule in Swedish schools, often on Fridays. Successful comics such as Robert Gustafsson and Henrik Dorsin have testified to how important fun hour was for their desire to be on stage.

After Abba's win with 'Waterloo' it was incredibly popular in Swedish classrooms to dress up like Abba during fun hour and lip synch using a skipping rope handle as a microphone. In my class there were girls who would be all four members. The ones who drew the short straw had to be Björn and Benny and would draw beards using magic markers. The famous gay author and comedian Jonas Gardell, who was ten years old when 'Waterloo' hit, writes that he was always Agnetha in his classroom.

The impact of Abba's 1977 Australian tour was linked to Australian heavy metal band AC/DC's breakthrough in Sweden.

Thomas Johansson, the concert booker behind Abba's Australian tour writes in his autobiography, 'The Australian musician's union said they would give Abba permission to tour the country on two conditions: 1. We had to hire as many musicians in Australia as we had musicians on stage. 2. I had to bring an Australian band to Sweden.'[17]

In music industry terms this is called a 'reciprocal exchange of musicians'. The first demand was met by Abba booking twelve Australian string musicians for their tour. The second was taken care of by Thomas Johansson booking a Swedish tour for an Australian band whose debut album he liked.

Thomas Johansson called the agent of the band in question, Richard Griffiths, who would far later go on to be the manager of boy band One Direction, where Harry Styles got his break. There was just one problem: the band Johansson had picked was completely unknown. Who in Sweden would want to buy a ticket to see them?

The solution was that a tour was booked for 1976, in which AC/DC played at dance halls and by the motor racetrack at Anderstorp, alongside *dansbands* that were bigger audience magnets. That is the history of how AC/DC played venues such as the bandshell and out-door dance floor Cortina in Vinberg together with Jigs under the header 'ballroom dancing'. Also *dansbands* like Maths Ronnies and Bert Bennys can boast having played with AC/DC as their opening act. The dance rotunda Nyckehålet in Höllviken in Skåne put a lit-tle pzazz in their ad using the not entirely far-fetched comparison: 'AC/DC is Australia's equivalent of [the band] Status Quo.'

The few Swedes who saw those shows became the foundation of AC/DC's beloved status in Sweden; just as Abba is beloved in Australia to this day.

SID KNEW

John Lydon, better known as Johnny Rotten, has published several memoirs over the course of his career as frontman for the punk band the Sex Pistols and post-punk band Public Image Ltd (PiL). When he released *I Could Be Wrong, I Could Be Right*, Lydon did a book tour in the autumn of 2021, during which he was interviewed on stage.

There is a YouTube clip from a theatre in Bury St Edmunds which starts right as that evening's talk has come to an end. The interviewer leaves the stage, but Lydon lingers in front of the audience.

'Sid constantly comes up in my mind,' he says. When the Sex Pistols fired their bassist and main songwriter Glen Matlock in 1977, ahead of recording their debut album, he was replaced by John's best friend, whose name was also John – John Ritchie – but who was given the stage name Sid Vicious. He couldn't even play the bass, but his style and attitude made him perfect for the role. He was the ultimate punk. Sid Vicious died at twenty-one from an overdose.

'There was a question that was asked about what was my favourite Abba song,' John Lydon continues. 'And Sid, Abba was his favourite band in the whole world. He loved David Bowie, but he adored Abba.'

This is borne out by another anecdote from the time: during the Norwegian leg of the Sex Pistols' Scandinavian tour in the summer of 1977, a sixteen-year-old Norwegian girl was taken on as an interpreter and thus began a short-lived romance with Sid Vicious. In her book *A Vicious Love Story*, Teddie Dahlin writes that Sid Vicious only brought one cassette tape on the bus: Abba's *Greatest Hits*.

In Bury, John Lydon tells the story of when Sid Vicious 'met' Abba on the same tour. The unlikely event occurred at Arlanda Airport in Stockholm: at the other end of the terminal they spotted a group that looked like Abba. Sid Vicious forgot that he'd thrown up on his jacket during the flight and ran towards them, overjoyed, shouting, 'You are my favourite band! I love you!' Abba's security detail did a quick read of the situation: a deathly pale teenage boy with a vomit-encrusted jacket and a dog collar around his neck was headed straight for them. Abba was discreetly hustled away and they never met.

After John Lydon has recounted this story he tells the audience: 'Let's sing a song for Sid. His favourite song was "Fernando".' The camera films him from behind; you can't see his eyes in the video, but you can hear from his voice that he is having a hard time holding back his feelings.

At first John Lydon isn't so sure of the lyrics, but the audience helps him. When they get to the chorus, a few hundred old punks, now in their sixties, unite and sing along emphatically to the song they remember just as well from their youth as anything by the Sex Pistols: 'There was something in the air that night, the stars were bright, Fernando.'

I bought the Sex Pistols' single 'Holidays in the Sun' when I was fourteen, at a record shop on Ågatan in Linköping. That same week I bought 'The Name of the Game' by Abba, so for me Lydon's anecdote feels like something akin to validation.

Punk and Abba might have been seen as opposites in 1977, but there were points of contact. Early punk had turned its back on the rock establishment and macho culture. Punks targeted bands that were regarded as the holy cows of rock music. Johnny Rotten and Paul Cook of the Sex Pistols wore T-shirts that read 'I hate Pink Floyd'. On the B-side of their first single the Clash declared that a new era had arrived: 'No Elvis, Beatles, or the Rolling Stones, in 1977.'

At the end of the 1960s and during the first half of the 1970s, rock songs grew increasingly long, sophisticated and complex. Rock stars considered themselves artists. Punk bands, headed by the Ramones in the United States, went in the opposite direction. Influenced by trash culture, comic books, bubblegum pop and Phil Spector's perfect teenage symphonies, they fired off songs that were never longer than three minutes.

Danny Boyle's 2022 drama series *Pistols* is based on the auto-biography of guitarist Steve Jones. In one scene the Sex Pistols and friends are hanging out in their rehearsal space, and dance and sing along to Bay City Rollers teen hit 'Shang-A-Lang'. Scottish band Bay City Rollers, dressed in tartan, were the Backstreet Boys of their day. Teens worshipped them for their life-affirming choruses and in the mid-1970s they were the epitome of the sort of ultra-commercial disposable pop that rock critics loved to despise.

If one digs a little deeper one might note that 'Shang-A-Lang' was written by masterful pop-artisans Bill Martin and Phil Coulter, the duo behind Sandie Shaw's 'Puppet on a String', Cliff Richard's 'Congratulations' and Slik's 'Forever and Ever'. Slik was a Scottish glam-rock outfit fronted by singer Midge Ure – who would later become better known with Ultravox – that knocked Abba's 'Mamma Mia' from the number 1 spot on the UK chart in February 1976.

The Sex Pistols' manager Malcolm McLaren admired Bay City Rollers so much that for a while he considered recruiting the singer of the group.

Long before the first punk club, the Roxy, opened in London in December 1976 the city's first generation of punks would gather at Louise's, a lesbian club at 61 Poland Street. The first punk rocker to frequent Louise's was Siouxsie Sioux, whose sister was a go-go dancer and knew the gay scene in London, well-hidden in those days.

Siouxsie Sioux, who would later become the queen of goth music, brought others in the Sex Pistols' early circle of fans, which went by the moniker the Bromley Contingent, to the lesbian club.

The fact that they weren't gay themselves didn't matter much. Louise's was a welcoming place for anyone who looked different and didn't fit in. The DJ at Louise's shunned rock and played artists like Doris Day, and disco and Motown. The most popular song at Louise's was 'Love Hangover' by Diana Ross in her biggest disco-diva mode. You can almost hear her flinging her feather boa around as she sings it.

Knowing this, it isn't hard to see why the London punks, openly or secretly, would also embrace Abba, another group that was looked down upon by the male-dominated rock establishment.

Today you'll find the club Heaven in Charing Cross, a ten-minute walk from where Louise's used to be. When Agnetha unexpectedly decided to make one single public appearance for her solo album *A* in 2013 she chose the theme night G-A-Y at Heaven. Agnetha stepped out on stage that night and declared: 'I wanted to see where all the "Dancing Queen" fans were.'

*

'Pretty Vacant', one of punk's immortal classics, written by Glen Matlock, provides another clue that the Sex Pistols listened to Abba. In the book *We All Love Abba* he says, 'It has been written so many times that I stole "Pretty Vacant" from Abba, but that's not entirely true. What happened when I wrote the song was that I had the lyrics and the melody but realised something was missing. The song needed some kind of riff.'

Glen Matlock studied at the prestigious art school Central Saint Martins in London. He tells the *Guardian*, 'Being at art school and being hip to the Dadaists and Marcel Duchamp, you'd nick something and make it your own.'[18]

One night at the pub Cambridge Circus, where all Saint Martins students and their teachers would hang out, Abba's 'SOS' started to play on the jukebox and Glen Matlock understood what he needed to nick: 'That bit in the song that goes "When you're gone, how can I even try to go on" and the bass rises an octave and sounds *boom boom boom*. That was where I got the idea for the riff in "Pretty Vacant".'

But the scene on which Abba made the biggest impression was the musical genre that emerged in the wake of punk itself – post-punk.

Post-punk existed in opposition to the musical establishment just as much as punk had and took the do-it-yourself ethos a step further. DIY is the realisation that you can start a band without knowing how to play an instrument, arrange your own concerts without being part of the business, issue your own records on your own record companies, start fanzines. Ideas are more important than musical aptitude.

The difference lay in the music itself. Post-punk artists felt that the high-speed guitar-driven three-chord rock of punk was starting to feel limiting and moved on by taking influences from disco, funk, electronic music, dub reggae, avant-garde culture. John Lydon's band after the Sex Pistols, Public Image Ltd, became one of the most important and influential post-punk bands.

The two most important independent record companies, which were established as post-punk emerged, were Factory Records in Manchester, home town of Joy Division, and the now lesser-known but equally important Fast Product in Edinburgh, that released the first editions of artists like Human League and Gang of Four.

Fast Product was run by Bob Last. In the 1993 BBC documentary *A Is for Abba*, producer Pete Waterman describes Abba's manager and strategist Stikkan Anderson as 'an incredible record man', totally focused on the final product, the record itself, being optimally good and, if possible, 100 per cent perfect. Bob Last, on the other hand, had a different vision when it came to disseminating records and how they ought to sound. Bob Last wasn't even thinking in terms of chart success. Fast Product called their releases 'difficult fun' and 'mutant pop'. A wall of gold records is depicted on the cover of the Mekons' second single, meant as a sly comment on consumerism.

One of Bob Last's ideas was to develop a new kind of muzak. Not in the style of Brian Eno, who had started making records with background music that became part of its surroundings, perhaps a room, or an airport, and coined the term 'ambient music'; Bob Last's idea of muzak was more energetic and disturbing.

Edinburgh-based band the Fire Engines had made two perfect, fast and fiery post-punk singles and played concerts that lasted no more than fifteen minutes; a controversial idea that was replicated by their clamorous countrymen Jesus and Mary Chain. But those of us who had been waiting for an entire LP by the Fire Engines found ourselves flabbergasted when we bought *Lubricate Your Living Room* in 1981.

There were no fast songs on this concept album directed by Bob Last. Instead, it had loud instrumental music designed to be played in the background while you vacuumed.

Lubricate Your Living Room was the first album to be issued in Bob Last's muzak venture on the imprint Accessory. The company's second and final release, also from 1981, contained Abba songs played on the accordion.

At Home!, by the traditional accordion player Frank Hannaway and the experimental guitarist Michael Barclay, contains instrumental versions of among others 'Thank You for the Music' and 'Fernando'.

However, few shared Bob Last's own feeling that this venture was genius. In the book *Hungry Beat*, which documents Scottish pop history from this time, post-punk drummer Simon Best says: 'A pub accordion player doing cover versions of Abba songs was one art joke too far.'

However, Bob Last's next attempt to integrate Abba into post-punk was a global hit.

One of the first singles to be released on Fast Product was 'Being Boiled' by the Sheffield band the Human League, a radical synth-pop song from 1978 that still sounds as if it has just been discovered on a vessel from outer space.

The quartet the Human League was soon divided into two halves, both of which found great success with Bob Last as their strategist. The two driving musical forces in the original quartet, Martyn Ware and Ian Craig Marsh, both on keyboard, left and started Heaven 17 and British Electric Foundation (B.E.F.). The 1982 single 'Ball of Confusion' by B.E.F. featured Tina Turner and reignited her career.

On Heaven 17's debut album, *Penthouse and Pavement*, Bob Last is listed as 'executive manipulator'.

The two remaining members of the Human League, who retained the rights to the band name, were singer Phil Oakley and Philip Adrian Wright. The latter didn't play any instrument, but had the title 'director of visuals' and was responsible for images and lights at the concerts. How would this new iteration of the Human League manage musically?

Bob Last's strategy was to recruit a new member who could write songs almost as catchy as Abba's: Jo Callis, recruited from the uncommonly melodious Scottish punk band the Rezillos. With Jo Callis, the Human League began writing songs like 'Open Your Heart' and 'Don't You Want Me'.

Next step – which made the band even more of a post-punk version of Abba – was to recruit two female singers, one blonde and one brunette, Joanne Catherall and Susan Ann Sulley, who had impressed Phil Oakley with their dancing at a discotheque.

In the book *Hungry Beat* Jo Callis says that his task as a new member was to unify the influences of the other members, from the Ramones to Abba. 'Phil was a great admirer of the quality of Abba's very honed and commercial production, very pop, which obviously would've influenced getting Joanne and Sue involved. I think the Abba influence was picked up by Bob and he thought, "Let's just have an art Abba with the men wearing make-up."'

'Don't You Want Me' became a gigantic hit across the world and the UK's bestselling single in 1981, the same year that Bob

Last released the accordion album with Abba songs – which almost nobody bought. The Human League's visionary album *Dare* is often listed as one of the best in history.

One passing historiographical detail that may be of interest: Fast Records put out a compilation album to which the goth pioneers Joy Division from rival, but like-minded, Factory Records also lent two songs that were left over from when they recorded their debut album *Unknown Pleasures*. The final track on that album, 'I Remember Nothing', went by the same title as one of Abba's most haunting songs, 'The Visitors', until right before it was released.

Meanwhile in Sweden, eighteen-year-old Klas Lunding started the independent record company Stranded Rekords, inspired by both Bob Last at Fast Product and Tony Wilson at Factory Records.

The first Swedish punk bands were imitations of the Sex Pistols and the Clash and sang in English. But starting in 1978, Swedish punk developed its own niche, with politically conscious lyrics in Swedish. At that point the Swedish progg movement finally took punk rock under its wing – the same progg movement that had initially rejected punk and still hated Abba. Stranded Rekords was not interested in those types of progg-inflected punk bands; they were looking for young people with fresh ideas, a striking number of whom would go on to become prominent artists, directors and authors.

The Swedish post-punk band most typical of that time was named Lustans Lakejer, which over the years came to be called a synth-pop group, although it started out as a band inspired by post-punk bands such as Joy Division and Magazine, as well as by the perennially experimental glam-rock band Roxy Music.

Lustans Lakejer, from the Stockholm suburb of Åkersberga, showed up right as the 1970s were turning into the 1980s and were a perfect band for Stranded. From a pop-cultural point of view Stockholm at this time may as well have been part of the Eastern bloc. There were two state-run TV channels and three state-run radio stations, one of which played pop mixed with accordion music and trad jazz. Music teachers in schools declared folk-music-making progg bands such as Arbete & Fritid and NJA-gruppen to be superior to Donna Summer and Abba. No entertainment venues were given liquor licences unless they also served hot food. All-night shops did not exist. Flying anything other than charter cost the equivalent of one month's salary.

Considering this, it isn't surprising that on their 1980 debut Lustans Lakejer's seventeen-year-old singer and songwriter Johan Kinde recited exotic words and places – champagne, perfume, Rio, Brussels, Zürich, The Hague – as if they were an incantation, a way of smoking out the old days.

Lustans Lakejer's second album from 1981 was called *Uppdrag i Genève* ('Mission in Geneva'), the first with their new keyboardist Tom Wolgers. One of the best tracks was 'Rendez-Vous i Rio'.

'Tom Wolgers and I wrote it in half an hour,' says Johan Kinde. 'I had already written the synth loops and had really envisioned it as a heavy Joy Division song, but its character shifted completely when Tom, who was deeply into Abba's album *Voulez-Vous*, joined the band. It was the first song we wrote together and it completely set the tone for *Uppdrag i Genève*. I had never been to Rio or Geneva. But a lot of it probably came from the settings of James Bond movies.'

An equally influential band in Sweden was Ratata. Originally Ratata was a trio with songwriter and singer Mauro Scocco and two film directors-to-be, Anders Skog and Johan Kling, the latter of whom would also go on to become a novelist. Things truly clicked musically for Ratata when the trio fell apart and was reincarnated as a duo with Mauro Scocco and new member Johan Ekelund, a musician and producer ready to work for however long it might take to create the perfect sound.

Johan Ekelund loved Abba. When he was in the band P3 they printed their own Abba badges to wear on their jackets; a provocation aimed at the more puritanical punk circles that did not approve of Abba's easy-going pop songs. At that time shops in Stockholm sold badges with the names of punk bands such as Incest Brothers, Grisen Skriker and Ebba Grön, but there were none with Abba.

One might say that things came full circle when Stranded Rekords was bought by Abba's Polar Records in the mid-1980s. Stikkan Anderson may not have understood the post-punk ideas, but he could hear gold in Mauro Scocco's tunes: in terms of melodies, songs like 'Doktor Kärlek' and 'Jackie' would not have been out of place on Svensktoppen, back in the days when Stikkan was the king of that chart.

In the years after Stranded was bought by Polar, Ratata ended up rubbing shoulders with Abba at parties at Stikkan's house. When it turned out that Frida liked Ratata, there was talk of collaborating.

The result, in 1987, was the duet 'Så länge vi har varann' ('As long as we have each other'). By the time Frida makes her entrance in the song, which she does after a full one minute and thirty seconds, Johan Ekelund has built up perhaps the grandest of all Swedish 1980s productions. The video by Anders Skog is also an exceptional artefact of its era: slow tracking shots, dead-serious faces and white sheets everywhere.

The album on which that song is included is also distinguished by perhaps the most fastidious record production ever heard in Sweden after Abba. *Mellan dröm och verklighet* ('Between dream and reality') became a Swedish equivalent of Donald Fagen's *The Nightfly*: a standard reference when hi-fi stores wanted to showcase the perfect sound.

The same year that Frida sang with Ratata, Bill Drummond, another one of the sharpest brains in post-punk, set his sights on Abba's music.

Bill Drummond was a key figure in Liverpool's music scene in the wake of punk. He was in the band Big in Japan with, among others, Holly Johnson of Frankie Goes to Hollywood. He also started Zoo Records, which issued the first recordings with Echo & the Bunnymen and The Teardrop Explodes.

Drummond started the duo the KLF together with Jimmy Cauty in 1987. Inspired by hip-hop, they wanted to make pop records consisting of fragments borrowed from other records – samples. The KLF would fundamentally change the world of pop with genre-bending, or genre-destroying, chart-toppers: 'What Time is Love?', '3 a.m. Eternal', 'Last Train to Trancentral' and 'Justified and Ancient' on which country star Tammy Wynette sang lyrics. Bill Drummond and Jimmy Cauty even wrote an instruction manual for the art of making chart-toppers, *The Manual* (*How to Have a Number One the Easy Way*).

But the KLF's beginnings were chaotic. Their debut album *1987* (*What the Fuck Is Going On?*) set the record for number of samples on one record. In the late 1980s, sampling was a new way of creating music and still legally untested. Around the same time hip-hop artists like Public Enemy and De La Soul also put out music consisting of samples that were not approved by those who held the rights.

The KLF's debut album contained everything from recordings of the London Underground, sex sounds and informational films about AIDS, to snippets of music by the Monkees, Dave Brubeck, Jimi Hendrix, the musical *Fiddler on the Roof,* Led Zeppelin, Stevie Wonder and post-punks the Fall, among others.

But it was an Abba sample that caused them problems. The song 'The Queen and I' uses and distorts, without permission, a significant portion of 'Dancing Queen' (as well as a snippet of the Sex Pistols' 'God Save the Queen', which can be heard in the same song). After Abba and the organisation MCPS (Mechanical-Copyright Protection Society) got lawyers involved, the KLF were ordered to take their album off the shelves and to hand over the master tapes along with everything that had been used to produce and manufacture the record.

Abba is known in the business for never approving samples. The group has made two exceptions. When hip-hop trio the Fugees were in Stockholm in 1996 and played two gigs that are still ranked among the best to ever take place in that city, members of the group stayed on and wrote a new song, 'Rumble in the Jungle', for a documentary about Muhammad Ali. It samples the bassline from Abba's 'The Name of the Game', played by Abba's masterful bassist Rutger Gunnarsson. When Abba heard the recording they gave it their approval.

The second time Abba approved a sample of their music was when Madonna and her producer Stuart Price built the 2005 song 'Hung Up' on 'Gimme! Gimme! Gimme! (A Man After Midnight)'.

In an episode of the music podcast *Song Exploder*, Madonna and Stuart Price tell the story of how they wrote the song.

Stuart Price was driving home on the highway one night when the song he didn't know he'd been looking for came on the radio: 'Gimme! Gimme! Gimme!' In the podcast he says that 'there is something almost Bavarian' about the song; a possible influence of Benny's, who listened to German schlager music on the radio growing up.

Madonna recorded the song and then it was sent to Abba for approval. Their answer was no. Madonna wrote a personal letter to Björn and Benny and had an emissary deliver it personally. Once again their answer was no.

What is not obvious from the podcast is that the pair were told 'no' and then 'no' again until they accepted Abba's demand: not just reimbursement for the sample itself, but royalties and credits as songwriters: half to Madonna and Price, half to Björn and Benny – a solution that broke new ground. Four songwriters are listed under the song: Madonna, Price, Andersson, Ulvaeus.

'Hung Up' went on to become one of Madonna's biggest hits of all time and perhaps the most important of her career in the 2000s. The video is directed by Johan Renck, who would later play a key role in the realisation of the 'Abbatars' and *Abba Voyage*.

The KLF did not know what they were in for when they tried to convince Abba to approve their sample. But they weren't the last. Through music industry sources I know that one of Sweden's largest artists in the early 2000s had a song on their album that turned out to be too similar to a song by Andersson-Ulvaeus. The rights had not been cleared ahead of time. The result was that the song was taken off the album and the entire first pressing was secretly burned, without it leaking to the media.

Bill Drummond and Jimmy Cauty of the KLF took their legendary custom-built car – an old American police car, a 1968 Ford Galaxy, christened Ford Timelord – to Sweden via a car ferry across the North Sea. *New Musical Express* journalist James Brown was along for the ride. The goal was to drive to Stockholm, ring the buzzer at Polar Studios and get Abba to change their minds. In the car they had the unsold copies of their pulled album and the gold record they had received.

They had not checked if Abba still existed as a group. Abba did not, and hadn't for several years. Björn had moved to London, Frida had moved to Switzerland, and neither Agnetha nor Benny used Polar Studios any more. There was no meeting.

The 2021 documentary *Who Killed the KLF?* shows how the duo finally burned their records in a field outside of Gothenburg. They gave the gold record to 'a blonde prostitute' whom they thought looked a bit like Agnetha.[19]

IMMIGRANT MUSIC

Christakis from Cyprus and Victoria from Athens got married young. Their dreams were too big to be realised in their small village on Cyprus. When Christakis heard that there were jobs to be had in England he decided to try his luck there. They arrived in the 1960s, without any savings, knowing very little English.

The job that Christakis Paphides had hoped for did not materialise. In order to make a living Mr and Mrs Paphides opened a small restaurant, the Great Western Fish Bar, named after the nearby railway, in a suburb of south-west Birmingham. They served the most English food imaginable: fish and chips. As a purveyor of English food, Christakis shortened his name to Chris.

When the couple arrived in Great Britain they originally did not plan to stay for very long. They were going to work and save money and then move back to Cyprus. Things did not turn out that way for two reasons. In 1974 the 'Cyprus problem' detonated. On 20 July 1974 the Turkish military launched an invasion in response to the Greek military junta's support of a coup d'état on Cyprus. This ended with the division of the island with a UN-monitored buffer zone (the 'Green Line') between. The old Cyprus was no more.

The other reason was their children: they had two sons who had come to feel more at home in English culture than in Greek.

Their youngest child, Panayiotakis Paphides was born in 1969 in Birmingham. His name was shortened to Takis, before he declared that he wanted to be known as Peter.

Pete Paphides grew up and went on to become one of England's best music journalists. In his award-winning book *Broken Greek* he describes his roots and his childhood with pop music.

The family lived above their fish and chip shop. Chris worked constantly. He wanted to serve only the very best. His competitors were satisfied with having frozen fish delivered to their door. Chris would get up at 5 a.m. every morning and go out to the fish market to personally select the best fresh cod, haddock and plaice. The variety of potato they used was more expensive than other potatoes, the starchier and more flavourful Maris Piper.

During his mornings at the market Chris would also buy fresh chicken that was far more succulent than the frozen product used by his competitors. He proudly noted that he sold four times as much chicken as all the rest of Acocks Green.

Pete's mother would work the counter alone on Thursdays, so that Pete's father, who was increasingly cranky and worn down by work, would get at least one free day each week. Word spread among the village retirees who could not afford a large portion of chips that she would add a little extra for free, which her husband would not. So on Thursdays a stream of retirees could be seen slowly approaching the establishment 'like turtles on a moonlit beach', as their son puts it.

Pete was shy and introverted. He could feel the bad mood in the family, even though he did not understand it. After a trip to Cyprus he stopped talking. From age four to seven he was selectively mute. He did not speak a word to anyone but his parents, brother and teachers for three years.

Meanwhile Pete concealed from his surroundings the love he had developed for everything British. Pop music especially. *Broken Greek* is a celebration of pop music and pop singles, not as entertainment, but as life-changing missives that explained the ways of the world.

Above all he loved Abba. Because the members were older than other pop stars in the 1970s they were rejected by other children at school, but Pete says: 'That just made Abba all the more interesting to me.' Abba's sad songs of broken relationships gave him insight into his parents' marriage.

At age seven Pete Paphides had never heard his father comment on any record that didn't have Greek letters on the cover. But in 1976 there was a song that made Chris Paphides realise that, like his son, he too was an Abba fan. A song whose lyrics he could completely identify with. The song that the immigrant who worked around the clock loved was 'Money, Money, Money'.

'I work all night, I work all day, to pay the bills I have to pay; ain't it sad? And still, there never seems to be a single penny left for me,' Agnetha and Frida sing. 'All the things I could do if I had a little money.'

'Immigrants have a very realistic relationship with money,' says Pete Paphides while he cooks us food in his home in North London. 'This is because money was the tool that allowed you to unlock the next phase of your life. So money became a symbol for freedom.'

In Sweden the lyrics for 'Money, Money, Money' were taken to mean that Abba now wanted to show everyone how rich they'd become. A barb thrown at those who derided their music as speculatively commercial. One of the verses mentions Monaco, to which famous Swedes such as Björn Borg moved to escape the tax pressure.

But many in Chris Paphides' situation heard something else. Especially those whose first language wasn't English. There was no code to crack in the lyrics. An English or American songwriter would have used some kind of metaphor to signal that the song is about wealth, but not Björn. Everything is said plainly; 'Money, money, money' is rhymed with 'must be funny'.

'My dad never explicitly said, "I like this song because I myself am an immigrant," but it is interesting that this is the song that made him an Abba fan,' says Pete Paphides. 'It means something. The atmosphere in the song is reminiscent of the tensions in our home. My parents were in a country in which they had not planned to stay, their plans did not work out the way they'd hoped. They couldn't treat themselves to things. Money became a symbol of delayed gratification, the deal they had to make with themselves.'

In *Broken Greek* Pete Paphides compares 'Money, Money, Money' to 'If I Were a Rich Man' from the musical *Fiddler on the Roof*.

'The song is so incredibly catchy. The music is doing the same thing as the lyrics. You are constantly being thrown back to the beginning of the song. There's that piano phrase every time, and then "Money, money, money". It is not possible to write in a more clear or direct manner. No English songwriter would express themself like that. Björn sees the poetry in English words and phrases that the English cannot see themselves. Poetry hidden in plain sight. He does it all the time, with "The Winner Takes It All" or "Take a Chance on Me".'

When Pete Paphides stopped talking as a child he was aware that he was embarrassing his family. No amount of therapy worked, until his brother finally helped him. 'I also felt guilty, because, although we were Greek, I was about to be transformed into a different person. The longer we stayed in England, the more English I felt. Pop music was the engine in that insight. When you as a child feel that your parents aren't getting along, that's devastating, it feels as if the world is ending. Abba songs like "Knowing Me, Knowing You" sounded like exactly that. For me that song was like reportage.'

*

English music offers other examples of children of Greek Cypriot immigrants whose parents came to England and ended up in the restaurant industry. Stavros Georgiou had a son who picked up an acoustic guitar and called himself Cat Stevens. Kyriacos Panayiotou also had a son who began to make music in the early 1980s.

When Pete Paphides' dad came home one day and said that the son of a Greek Cypriot business associate was going to perform on *Top of the Pops* that evening Pete assumed it was a misunderstanding. The son's name was Georgios. How could a Georgios, son of Kyriacos from Patriki, be on the nation's, and the world's, most important pop music programme? Impossible.

His father was right, as it turned out. In front of his sceptical son, he made some phone calls to confirm that the information was correct, and relayed the name of the group: 'It's Juan! It's George Michael and Juan!' On the TV screen a Georgios appeared, albeit one who had changed his name to George and the group name turned out to be spelled, not 'Juan' but 'Wham!' It was clear from the singer's presence that this was another immigrant's kid who had found an identity of his own in pop music.

For Pete, pop artists were a different kind of adult, a kind that he could learn things from. 'If you had asked me as a child to draw a grown-up I would have drawn a grown-up with a beard who looked like Benny. If you had asked me to draw a lady I would have drawn Agnetha.'

When Abba was on British TV, where they would often show up on children's programmes, they appeared to be a bit shy, quiet and reserved, which further strengthened the identification Pete Paphides felt with them. 'It was also clear from those programmes that Agnetha and Frida enjoyed being around children.'

Pete Paphides has been accompanied by Abba throughout his life. When he worked at *Melody Maker* magazine he met his future wife, writer Caitlin Moran, who was recruited as a cocky teenager, known for her brutally funny and fearless turns of phrase.

'The first time I was attracted to Pete was when everyone else at the office was going to go see some cool band that you just had to like back then in the early nineties,' says Caitlin Moran. 'Can it have been Sheep On Drugs? Okay, it was Faust. But Pete said, "No, I'm going to go see Björn Again," which became a standing joke at the office.'

'I was very insecure back then,' says Pete Paphides, 'but there were certain things that I considered non-negotiable. One was that I would not let anyone criticise Abba. I recall that I thought, okay you guys will seem cooler, but I will have a lot more fun.'

Caitlin Moran tagged along and they went to see the Australian cover band Björn Again. 'I cried even before they played "Dancing Queen",' Caitlin says. 'When I got back I had to lay my head against a friend's chest. Afterwards I'd cried all my make-up off and left my face on his shirt.'

They became an item when Pete was twenty-four and Caitlin eighteen. When she came home with him for the first time he knew it would last. On the wall at Pete's house – this was in the midst of the wave of Britpop and grunge – there was a big poster with the helicopter image from Abba's *Arrival*.

When one of their children, Dora, learned to speak one of her first words was Abba. They would point at the poster and ask, 'Dora, what's that?' She would answer, 'Abba!' Dora, at twenty-two years, adds: 'And then every time I saw a helicopter I would point to the sky and say, "Oh my goodness, Abba!"'

AGNETHA

'I know this is considered heresy, but I like it best when it's ice cold,' says Agnetha Fältskog, then looks around before spooning a couple of large ice cubes into her glass of Chablis.

We're in the restaurant at the Corinthia hotel in London. It is May 2013. Agnetha will be living here for ten days while promoting her latest solo album *A*. Every other day she meets with media from all over the world. She has alternate days off, in order to be able to manage her schedule, work out and rest at the hotel spa, or take short walks in the West End and Soho.

What brings Agnetha the most joy on the streets of London isn't all the trendy shops and people, but children and dogs. Her extensive knowledge of 1960s pop music is also in evidence: 'Every time we hear some obscure song on the car radio, or at a restaurant, Agnetha is the one who nails exactly what it is,' says Peter Nordahl, one of her two producers on this album. Corinthia is located in Whitehall, where a large part of the work of the British government is done. Less than a ten-minute walk from here is the entrance to the subterranean bunker in which Winston Churchill led operations when Adolf Hitler was trying to bomb London to bits.

Agnetha has checked into the hotel anonymously, but news has nonetheless spread to some of her fans. The people in charge of hotel guests are highly skilled at being attentive to the presence of a legend, while also acting as if nothing is out of the ordinary.

There is something electric about Agnetha. Everyone who recognises her reacts the same way and pauses in their step, perhaps partly because she has been out of the spotlight for a couple of decades. This trip to London is Agnetha's first stay abroad, as well as her first plane journey in decades. A journalist from one of Germany's largest daily papers is told that his interview slot has been moved due to her packed schedule and that he will have to wait. He answers: 'No worries. I can wait, I have waited thirty years for this.'

Having spent an entire day following Agnetha around, I conclude that there is nothing Garboesque about her behaviour, although she is often portrayed that way. She is social, open ('I'm about to tell you something I've never told anyone before') and curious about everything around her.

Agnetha's best friend, Lolo Murray, is with her at the restaurant table. She works as a personal consultant to some of Sweden's biggest artists, with a hand in everything to do with appearance – hair, make-up, clothes. She has worked with Agnetha ahead of every album and appearance she has done since 1980.

'It began when I did a styling gig with Agnetha and Frida for *Clic* magazine,' says Lolo Murray. 'Then I got an offer on short notice to come to Japan with Abba when they were on tour there. Once, when I was rushing to do a quick costume change on Agnetha during a show, I accidentally put her skirt on upside down. "I'll get fired now," I thought. But you' – here she puts her arm around Agnetha – 'let me stay on. That was an incredibly fun tour.'

Agnetha and Lolo talk memories from Abba's tours. At the time of this meeting the *Abba Voyage* project and the holograms that will be called 'Abbatars' are still nine years in the future.

'Several people who interviewed me here have asked if there was rivalry between me and Frida,' Agnetha says. 'But there was none of that. On the contrary, we helped and supported each other all the time, especially on tour. If one of us had a cold the other would step up and pull a heavier load in terms of singing. We always covered for each other.'

It has been a long day in London, prior to us having wine that evening. It started in the morning, when Agnetha was interviewed at the Abbey Road studio by a reporter from *Today*, the biggest and most prestigious morning TV show in the United States.

'I recognise this; I have been here before,' Agnetha said as she got out of the privately chauffeured car, wearing large black sunglasses, and stepped through the doors to the Beatles' legendary recording studio. 'Paul McCartney invited us over when we were here in the 1970s. We visited the studio, said hi and looked around.'

The Abbey Road studio was chosen as the location for this interview since the TV team wanted a more colourful environment than a hotel. And the connection to the Beatles is not far-fetched. In terms of pop history, that is the company in which Abba belongs. *Q* had recently called Abba 'the most prominent pure pop band in musical history'.

The *Today* reporter, a local hire for the occasion, was so over-excited about getting to interview Agnetha that he talked more than she did. Some of the questions were more akin to lists of facts that emphasise Abba's status as royalty in England. 'How do you feel about Kate and William playing only Abba songs at the reception after their wedding? How does it feel that Queen Elizabeth loves "Dancing Queen" and has quoted the lyrics?'

All of this was news to Agnetha, but she did her best to answer.

When being interviewed in English she spends some extra time thinking, searching for the right words, in a way that makes her appear more reserved than she really is. 'During my time with Abba I was anxious about not being as good at English as the others,' she says.

What foreign reporters tend to know less about is how involved she was in Abba's music. Agnetha is a skilled pianist. When Abba formed she was the only one of the four who could read music.

On her solo albums in the 1960s and early 1970s, Agnetha wrote most of her own songs. Out of a total of twenty songs to make Svensktoppen, eleven were her own compositions. A few weeks ahead of her visit to London she had been given the Swedish composer's and songwriter's guild SKAP's award in the memory of Kai Gullmar. Kai Gullmar was Sweden's first major female composer of popular music.

Björn and Benny encouraged Agnetha to write for Abba, but 'there wasn't much time left over for that'. Instead, she became Abba's crystalline voice. Her style of singing is about so much more than technique. Unlike other great singers, she never shows off at the expense of the lyrics or engages in unnecessary warbling. Her presence alone can transform a song into a drama.

'It is always hard to speak to one's own strengths,' she says of her ability to interpret lyrics. 'I know that I can sing, that I can write. But what I'm really good at is understanding what a lyric is about. I always ask questions about the context of the lyric, enter into it, *become* the lyric.'

A bit like an actor would?

'Yes, more or less. Personally, I do think I became a better singer as I gained more life experience. You have so much you want to share. And my way of sharing is through song. That is where I put my feelings.'

Agnetha Åse Fältskog was born on 5 April 1950. In the parish register her name is written as Agneta, but she added an 'h' when her singing career took off. Agnetha is a common name in Sweden, but a tricky name for an English speaker to pronounce. Since people got it wrong so often she started to go by Anna when Abba tried to make it abroad, a plan that never quite worked out.

In 1975 Abba was on TV legend Dick Clark's show *American Bandstand*. Dick Clark turns to Benny – 'Since your name is easy for me to pronounce' – and asks him to introduce the rest of the band. 'This is Frida,' says Benny in English, 'she is my wi— well, I hope she is going to be my wife; we are engaged right now.' Then Benny points to Agnetha: 'Here we have Anna, married to Björn.'

Dick Clark, who had clearly done his research, reacts: 'You shortened Anna, what's the full name?' Benny: 'It's Agnetha, but Anna is a little easier.'

Agnetha undergoes a complete transformation when she goes from standing next to the stage, to artist on stage. During the interview she is shy and doesn't talk much. When she steps up to the microphone and sings 'SOS', she appears to be the most natural pop star of all time. Her gaze burns a hole through the TV screen. When people voted on the best performances on *American Bandstand* through its thirty-one seasons Abba's 'SOS' was in the top five.

Agnetha grew up outside of Jönköping, known as the centre of the evangelical movement in Sweden. Jönköping has been called 'the Jerusalem of Småland'. Another Swedish pop singer who has found international fame, Nina Persson of the Cardigans, is also from Jönköping.

The Fältskog family was working class and did not have a lot of money; four people all slept in the same room. They didn't have a piano, but a neighbour did.

Agnetha: 'One of the first things I did was write a song of my own. I sat there with one finger and wrote a song called "Two Little Trolls".'

The text went: 'Two little trolls met each other, hi said one, hi said the other, let's go play with each other.' The songwriter was five years old and declared that she would become world-famous.

Agnetha: 'I loved playing the piano. So for three years I would go over to our neighbour's house every day. When I was about eight I finally got one of my own – pianos were expensive. I learned how to play properly when I was nine or ten. Then I studied with various piano teachers. I became good at it. When I was fifteen my last teacher said: "Now I have nothing more to teach you." Then I would sit at the front of the church and play the harpsichord, a fugue by Bach.' Agnetha also sang in the church choir.

Alongside playing classical music on the piano, Agnetha began performing revues with two girlfriends in Jönköping. They called themselves the Cambers. Her father, Ingvar, was an amateur actor and musician. 'My dad was something of a revue king, which inspired us. We did all sorts of things: wrote lyrics, sang, performed a ballet.'

After her last day of school in 1965 Agnetha began working as a switchboard operator at Attevik's car dealership in Jönköping. The following summer Bernt Enghardt's dance orchestra asked her to sing with them. The orchestra had lost their singer, Agneta

Desilva, when she and the guitarist fell in love and left. The fact that the young Fältskog shared her first name was convenient; all they needed to do was paste over the picture of her predecessor on the posters.

Agnetha quickly revealed herself as master of many musical styles, from *dansband* songs to James Brown's 'I Got You (I Feel Good)'. Besides, she was determined. She never complained about schlepping across the country in a car alongside six guys and not being dropped off in front of her parents' house until dawn. From age fifteen to eighteen Agnetha sang with Bernt Enghardt's dance orchestra at evenings and weekends. In the daytime she worked her full-time job at the switchboard. In the long run this proved to be an impossible combination. One day her colleagues at the car dealership heard a thud when Agnetha collapsed across the telephones. She had passed out from exhaustion. Her young body was taking a beating. Agnetha smoked a lot and ate little. Her mum Birgit posed an ultimatum: she could be a switchboard operator or a singer.

'Mum was a pretty good singer herself, but my parents still weren't too happy that I chose to sing,' says Agnetha. 'Besides, I was incredibly shy. I had to make a huge effort to step out on stage. To be sure, that feeling did disappear after a few songs, but it would come back for the next concert. It is hard to explain, but the nervousness felt almost like a punishment for me getting to do what I so deeply wanted. Being an artist was my biggest dream – but at the same time I constantly had this struggle to overcome.'

Bernt Enghardt saw the audience reaction. The focus shifted. The posters were redesigned and now read 'Enghardt's featuring Agnetha Fältskog'.

*

The band recorded demos and sent them to record companies, music publishers and radio and TV shows in Stockholm. Lille Gerhard, one of Sweden's first rock kings, worked at the record company Cupol. He wasn't too impressed by Enghardt's as a band, but turned the cassette over and heard a snippet of a song he didn't recognise.

Lille Gerhard called the car dealership and asked to speak to Agnetha. He said he liked her voice and asked who'd written the song. Agnetha answered, 'I wrote it myself,' and said that she had the whole melody at home on her tape recorder. After listening to it, he booked her time in the studio with Sven-Olof Walldoff's orchestra (the same conductor who would appear dressed as Napoleon when Abba won Eurovision with 'Waterloo' a few years later).

On 16 October 1967 Agnetha recorded four songs in the Philips studio in Stockholm. The best two were her own compositions. In the booklet that comes with the CD box set *De första åren: Agnetha Fältskog 1967–1979*, she says: 'It is one of my fondest memories. When my dad and I entered the Philips building and walked down the stairs, we heard an ensemble sitting down there adding strings to my song. I think that's the best experience I ever had.'

Her life changed. 'It was a fantastically happy feeling. Besides, I was terribly well paid when I signed with Cupol: 75,000 kronor a year. Dad helped me negotiate.'

During a period of love troubles, she sat down at the piano and wrote 'Jag var så kär' ('I was so in love') at seventeen. All that has made up the magic and mythology around Agnetha for almost half a century is already there on her first single. With a voice that sounds both crystal-clear and endlessly sad, she sings about once being happy, but now walking alone.

Meanwhile, she was being promoted as a femme fatale on the

single cover, dressed in leather boots and a short dress: a teenage switchboard operator from Jönköping who would soon ignite hearts all across Sweden and then the world.

And who would acquire the most obsessive fans.

'Jag var så kär' bumped the Beatles off the top spot on the sales chart in Sweden. The follow-up 'Utan dej' ('Without you') was just as successful. 'Both these songs had a pretty characteristic second voice, which made people compare me to Connie Francis,' Agnetha says in the CD booklet. 'She was my big idol in those days, so I was flattered.'

Connie Francis has continued to be a favourite. In 2004 Agnetha recorded the album *My Colouring Book*, on which she did her own interpretations of her favourites from her youth. One of the songs is 'I Can't Reach Your Heart', recorded by Connie Francis in 1963, so obscure today that it is not available on streaming services. But Agnetha hasn't forgotten it.

These days she lives in a modest house within walking distance of her children's homes.

'People wonder what I've been up to for all these years when I haven't been in the media, but I've kept busy,' she says. 'I have a farm with horses to care for and I have grandchildren. When I sit down at the piano nowadays it is usually to teach my grandkids how to play, teach them the names of the notes. They are very musically inclined, which is fun, but honestly they are more interested in horses than in playing music.' Agnetha gives a little laugh. 'I like to go for long walks with the dogs and read books.'

Agnetha was a driven songwriter well into the 1970s. In January 1974 she began working on the outlines of what was supposed to be the most ambitious solo album of her career to date. 'I hope to have time to finish writing the material so that the record can be released soon,' Agnetha said in an interview. 'The songs aren't like anything I've ever written before. It is hard to categorise the style, but I don't think they are Svensktoppen material.'

With her new collaborator Bosse Carlgren she created a concept album that was to be called *Tolv kvinnor i ett hus* ('Twelve women in a house'). The idea was to tell the story of their respective lives. In a building with twelve apartments there live twelve women, 'each with her own face, heartaches and joys', Bosse Carlgren wrote in a note.

For a while all the twelve women were going to be called Agnetha with versions of Fältskog as their last name: Grönskog, Gråtskog, Älskog. They also developed a painted, expandable record cover with pictures of all of the women and texts about their backstories.

None of these ideas survived to the release. While she was working on the record, Abba won the Eurovision Song Contest in Brighton. When the release came up again the following year, the record company felt the album lacked a hit song. A Swedish version of the brand-new Björn and Benny composition 'SOS' was added and two women's lives were deleted. When the album was finally released it was called *Elva kvinnor i ett hus* ('Eleven women in a house'), with an entirely different cover, focused on Agnetha herself, lying on cushions in an empty apartment.

At this time Frida also released a solo album: *Frida ensam*, with a cover that was considered the most sexually provocative to ever be done in Sweden. This album had a brand-new song penned by Björn and Benny with Swedish lyrics that would become an enormous Abba hit once translated to English: 'Fernando'.

Agnetha's solo version of 'SOS' went to number 1 on

Svensktoppen. Two of the songs about women's lives, 'Doktorn!' ('Doctor!') and 'Tack för en underbar, vanlig dag' ('Thank you for a lovely, ordinary day'), also made Svensktoppen.

The lyrics for 'Tack för en underbar, vanlig dag', in which the Lord is thanked for coffee being on sale, were taken out of context and misunderstood. Some groups within the Church of Sweden didn't see the humour in the lyrics at all. They accused Agnetha from Jönköping of 'turning religion into consumer goods' and mounted a campaign against the song. Agnetha was also heavily criticised by representatives of the Church when she participated in the Swedish production of *Jesus Christ Superstar*. For the rest of her life Agnetha would have to get used to reading headlines about herself and being considered public property.

When Abba played six sold-out shows at Wembley Arena in November 1979 Agnetha sat down alone at the grand piano to sing her own 'I'm Still Alive', a ballad she'd written with Björn. The song spread via bootlegs before the album *Live at Wembley Arena* was finally issued in 2014.

'The Winner Takes It All', released in 1980, is probably Abba's most famous portrayal of divorce, but Agnetha's 'I'm Still Alive' was written a year earlier and reflects her divorce from Björn being a reality. Agnetha had got through one of the roughest periods of her life. A new chapter lay ahead of her. You can viscerally feel every word in the lyrics: 'The agony is gone, and my mind is slowly waking, and my heart has ceased its aching; I'm still alive.'

For *Abba: The Photo Book* photographer Anders Hansen found a picture in which Agnetha, a mother of two, was slumped in front of Ola Brunkert's drum kit.

When Agnetha saw the picture she recalled, 'I needed to sit down and meditate for a while. Wembley was fantastic, but it was also hard. I recall how Frida and I saw each other every evening in the limousine from the hotel and asked each other how we were going to manage yet another night. Perhaps we were struggling with colds, too. But then we stepped on stage and met the fans who were ready with their lighters. It was such a great atmosphere. The exhaustion dissipated immediately.'

After Abba, Agnetha went on to record three solo albums with foreign star producers, but when she did interviews nobody asked her about her own music.

In 1985 she was a guest on the interview show *Gäst hos Hagge*. Frida had been on the show in 1983. The interviewer, Hagge Geijert, had the same status in Sweden as Michael Parkinson had in England, but was not as good at his job.

Watching the interview programmes with Agnetha and Frida today it is impossible to ignore the whiff of dirty old man. Hagge Geijert puts his hand on Agnetha's arm and says, 'Have I told you that I love you?' Twice. At the end of the show a visibly frustrated Agnetha sits down and plays a piece by Haydn beautifully on the grand piano. Her father appears and together they sing 'En sommar med dig'.

In 1994 Agnetha was struck by a tragedy that caused her to retreat from music for nearly ten years. Around six o'clock one January morning her mother, Birgit Fältskog, was found on the ground outside the apartment building in Jönköping where she and Agnetha's father Ingvar lived. She had fallen twenty metres from the balcony on the sixth floor. Agnetha and her children refused to answer questions when the press called.

Her father died less than two years later, on New Year's Eve 1995. The first album Agnetha released after the deaths of her parents was the previously mentioned *My Colouring Book* from 2004.

In the summer of 2023 I meet Agnetha again at the home of producer Jörgen Elofsson. We show each other pictures of our dogs. Agnetha has a small pug named Bella and a Prague ratter named Bruno. I scroll to pictures of my shorthaired miniature dachshund. 'I love dogs,' Agnetha says. 'I have had many over the years, but I still find it as hard as ever to be away from them.'

In the minimalist home studio at the top of Jörgen Elofsson's house she has recorded a completely new song, 'Where Do We Go From Here?' set to be released the following autumn.

'It felt like it was 40 degrees centigrade in the room when we recorded it. I was completely drenched afterwards.'

Just like she did on many of Abba's songs, she sat down when she recorded the lyrics.

'I think it sounds better. You might think that singing sitting down wouldn't work too well, considering your lungs, your belly, that you end up sort of compressed. But it relaxes me.'

When Agnetha says that she is unsure how she measures up as a singer, Jörgen Elofsson, who has now joined us on the couch, interrupts her:

'You are one of few singers who can really narrate a lyric. That was something you would learn in the old school. There aren't many young singers who are narrators. They just talk about themselves.'

Agnetha: 'But you can hear that my voice isn't the same as it used to be. I think my voice sounds a bit chesty today. I don't have the force I used to either, it turns out different, but it still works. I like that these new recordings capture an evolution. Not to toot my own horn, but I think it sounds cool.'

Even today Agnetha is constantly listening to music. But she's not walking around in headphones, or adjusting the dials on a stereo. The songs are there, inside her head.

'I have music in my head almost constantly. Songs will just appear and I'll walk around whistling them. It could be new songs like "Flowers" by Miley Cyrus, it's so good. Or it might be some song Dad used to sing, or something we listened to in the 1950s or '60s. He was also like that, Dad was, he would often go around whistling some old earworm.'

If she listens to the radio it is often Radio Viking, an oldies station based in the part of Stockholm where she lives.

'Sometimes songs show up like, "My god, I haven't heard this song in a long time," that's cool. I have had a period now when I've been listening a lot to P.J. Proby. Did you know he sang demo songs intended for Elvis?'

'I understand you and Frida were very involved in the arrangements of the songs. What was your process like?' I ask her.

'We lived with the songs from the time they were written up until the recording was made; we heard them emerge. The boys wrote and produced them, but at the end of the day we would all give our input in the studio. I had a lot of ideas about various details in the song. Small gimmicky things, backing vocals, audible breathing, details you might not hear the first time you listen.'

'Were there discussions about which songs you and Frida would sing solo?'

'No, that was planned even as they were written, depending on the key.'

'How does one become a good singer?'

'One answer is that it is innate, but it is also about technique. It was interesting now, when I started singing again after a long break. I went too hard initially, gave myself a sore throat. You need to use your diaphragm, use that extra power. You can't express yourself fully until you are confident technically.'

'Have you saved your old records?'

'No, I don't keep track of that. I gave a lot of stuff to the Abba museum. I have kept certain LPs and CDs, but they're in boxes. I very rarely listen to my own recordings. One exception is "The Winner Takes It All". I listen to that when I'm not feeling confident. *There* I can give myself some kudos. "You did that well."'

RENAISSANCE

While Sweden was on its knees, Abba got back up.

For Sweden, the economic crisis in the early 1990s was even worse than the global financial crisis of 2007–8. From 1991 to 1995, 85,000 Swedish companies declared bankruptcy. During the worst of it, in 1992, an average of eighty-five Swedish companies went bankrupt each day.

Many nations were hit by recessions, a development driven by the side effects of German reunification, but Sweden and the Swedish krona were especially poorly prepared for the currency turbulence that followed. Sweden's ability to compete on the world market was seriously impaired and the whole financial system was thrown into disarray. The old Swedish coin box began to leak and money gushed out.

'Early in the autumn of 1992, Bengt Dennis, the Riksbank and the Government attempted to stop the outflow of currency to hold the exchange rate steady. It was not enough. On 16 September 1992, following several rate rises over the course of a week, the Riksbank made a final attempt to stop the outflow and raised the marginal rate to 500 per cent.'[20]

When the interest rate was gradually lowered again it was too late: the faith in the value of the Swedish krona could not be repaired. Investors picked other currencies over the Swedish one.

In its documentation of this historic crisis, the Riksbank writes: 'Ultimately, neither the Riksbank nor the government could avoid what they had spent several years trying to prevent. On 19 November, the fixed exchange rate was scrapped and the Swedish krona was allowed to float. It would take many years for Swedish society to recover from this.'

So this was the situation in Sweden when the Abba renaissance began, a chance occurrence that perhaps also tells us something.

Today you'd be forgiven for assuming that Abba has always been popular, but the story of Abba is more of a tale of overcoming adversity than one of success. After their two last, failed singles in the autumn of 1982, Abba disappeared for ten years.

'We thought that we would continue to receive royalties through 1983,' Benny says. 'Possibly that it would continue until 1984, but longer than that? Never. There was even a decision made that shows that we were sure of it.'

'We were completely off the radar during the 1980s,' Björn says. 'The general feeling at the time was that Abba was really *uncool*. If you're predisposed to low self-esteem, like I am, it was hard not to think, "Okay, that's that. It's over now."'

While the Abbas themselves had accepted the fact, a revival started elsewhere, in unexpected places. 'The members of the gay community were the only ones who never stopped loving us,' says Björn.

While Erasure's thumping, synthesiser-infused, club-inspired interpretations of Abba conquered the airwaves in the summer of 1992, U2 came to Stockholm to play a concert at the Globe Arena on 11 June, during their Zoo TV Tour.

With their albums *The Joshua Tree* and *Rattle and Hum*, U2 had become one of the world's largest rock bands during the second half of the 1980s. U2 had travelled far from the punk and post-punk that inspired them when they started out and were sounding increasingly grand and American, incorporating gospel, soul and blues elements. U2 was as far from their teenage roots in Dublin as they were from the audience high up in the stands.

With the album *Achtung Baby*, released in November 1991, U2 pulled the emergency brake, creating a musical year zero. The album was recorded in Berlin. Producer Brian Eno felt that his role was to come to the studio once in a while and 'get rid of anything that sounded like U2'. A new U2 emerged that sounded experimental and European, but also wrote more melodious songs such as 'One'.

The Zoo TV Tour, which went on for nearly two years from February 1992 to December 1993, was inspired by the mass media and the channel-surfing of the cable TV era; the key concept here was *sensory overload*. East German Trabant cars were placed on stage as were Nam June Paik-inspired stacks of television sets. As U2 played on stage, the TVs broadcast scenes of conflict from the Gulf War and the siege of Sarajevo. Singer Bono switched between various alter egos such as MacPhisto, the leather-clad The Fly, a high-energy TV preacher, and himself.

At the concert at the Globe – which has since been renamed Avicii Arena – U2 fans stood, mouths agape, trying to enter this new world, like Dorothy in *The Wizard of Oz*. Rock music was not in Kansas any more. When, in the midst of everything, Bono began to sing 'Dancing Queen' and asked us to sing along, my first thought was that this had to be yet another meta-ironical move.

And so a pair of spotlights lit up and there on a ramp was – completely unannounced – Benny by a keyboard with Björn on acoustic guitar.

Björn says that he for the longest time thought the invitation 'was about U2 planning to make fun of us'.

'It wasn't until we were standing there on stage that we realised it was a celebration.'

For the audience it was as if U2 had begun to play the Swedish national anthem, which in a sense they had. Everybody knows the tune and at least substantial parts of the lyrics.

When the music to 'Dancing Queen' had died down, the audience continued to sing the refrain on its own. U2 and Björn and Benny stood silently, just taking it all in. 'Dancing Queen' at the Globe was like 'You'll Never Walk Alone' on Anfield Road in Liverpool. Bono turned to Björn and Benny, knelt down as if he were in *Wayne's World* and declared, 'We are not worthy, we are not worthy.'

In those days there were no smartphones to document the event. The arrival of the first camera phone lay seven years in the future. Even if there had been one, there was no social media on which to post the clips.

When Bono and guitarist the Edge appeared on BBC Radio 2's Piano Room in the spring of 2023, Bono spoke of the moment with Björn and Benny in the Globe Arena and of his lifelong love for Abba's music. Bono said that when he, as a sixteen-year-old, at the height of the punk wave, felt the need to appear macho, he kept his admiration of Abba quiet.

But during his youth their songs were always there. Bono said that Abba songs in Dublin in the 1970s were like 'the national anthem for young mothers'. Bono: 'At closing time at our local pub, often young women would sing "Thank You for the Music" . . . But I was like, what is this phenomenon? This is before their musicals and all that. What is going on with Abba?'[21]

The only thing that could have been more unexpected in the summer of 1992 than U2 bringing Abba out of the freezer, was that the saviours of alt rock, Nirvana, did the same.

Nothing was cooler than Nirvana that year. Rock music had been in a slump. Hip-hop, house and techno had taken over as the most creative musical genres. There was talk of the electric guitar's last gasp. All such prophecies went out the window when Nirvana appeared on MTV in 1991 with 'Smells Like Teen Spirit'.

Nirvana's frontman, Kurt Cobain, had mixed feelings about their breakthrough. The same loud chorus of macho men he had spent his entire youth trying to avoid were now standing in front of the stage, headbanging to his songs. 'Smells Like Teen Spirit', a song named for an ironic scribble made on Kurt's bedroom wall by feminist punk icon Kathleen Hanna of Bikini Kill, had become music to chug beer to.

Kurt Cobain's way of dealing with his band's new-found popularity was to perform in a dress to remind himself, as well as the audience, of the indie culture that had shaped him. Journalist Charles R. Cross, who wrote the biography *Heavier than Heaven*, has said that Kurt Cobain stayed loyal to his sources of inspiration: 'He had about ten influences that he would always return to.' Kurt Cobain loved obscure, free-thinking bands like the Raincoats and the Vaselines, formed in Britain, and Meat Puppets, from the States. And he loved Abba.

When Nirvana played the last day of the Reading festival in the summer of 1992, Kurt Cobain got to be the curator and choose the artists who would play with them. Among musical kindred spirits with loud guitars, such as L7, Screaming Trees and Mudhoney, he also chose the Abba cover band Björn Again. As Björn Again played their set, pumping out Abba tunes to a grunge audience, Kurt Cobain stood by the side of the stage smiling.

That a band like Nirvana could get so big so fast had to do with a change in the method of measuring and reporting record sales. For several decades, the reporting wasn't done by computers, it was done by staff at a few select record stores.

In 1991 in the United States, it became clear just how lacking and subjective this method was. When the new computerised measuring method Nielsen SoundScan was introduced in March of that year, select record stores no longer estimated which albums sold best; the new instrument measured actual documented sales in the cash registers in every neighbourhood.

The Billboard list transformed completely as a result. Suddenly what rose to the top of the chart was not just mainstream pop, but country, hip-hop and heavy metal.

So-called off-beat genres that had received little attention from TV and daily papers turned out to be the ones that were actually selling the most records. The change in measuring method made it so that Billboard from that spring on could be topped by artists such as the gangsta rappers N.W.A and seven-gallon hat wearer Garth Brooks. That autumn Metallica released their black album and Nirvana released *Nevermind*, two albums that would never have made it as big as they did within the old paradigm of measuring sales.

This new musical climate heralded the death of mainstream culture and an Abba compilation album ought to have flopped, but instead the CD compilation *Abba Gold*, released in September 1992, became the most important album of Abba's career.

The status that Abba enjoys today is built on the revival that was started by the likes of Erasure, U2, Björn Again and Kurt Cobain and cemented by *Abba Gold*, an English record company initiative that was released the same week that the interest rate in Sweden was raised to 500 per cent.

'Greatest hits' albums lost much of their significance with the advent of streaming and playlists in the 2000s, but from the 1960s to the turn of the millennium they were important to both artists and record buyers.

Greatest hits albums were not taken seriously artistically and were never reviewed in the music press, but for a number of artists they became more significant than any of their studio albums. For record buyers, 'greatest hits' meant value-for-money albums without filler tracks.

If you dug back through history in the CD era and discovered the pioneers of 1950s rock 'n' roll like Little Richard, Elvis Presley, Chuck Berry and Fats Domino, you probably did so through compilation albums. Full studio albums by the artists weren't available in regular record stores.

Soul and reggae reached new generations of listeners through cleverly curated compilations. EMI in the UK distributed records for the Tamla Motown label, the non-US arm of Berry Gordy's record companies, which from 1967 to 1982 released albums in the series *Motown Chartbusters*, on which every song was a hit. Trojan Records presented rocksteady and reggae in budget series with names like *Tighten Up* and *Reggae Chartbusters*.

Elton John's bestselling record in the United States is his *Greatest Hits*, released in 1974. On the cover he sits in front of a grand piano in a white suit, white hat and with a white cane. Side A opens with

'Your Song', from the 1970 album *Elton John*; it was only because of the compilation album that this came to be one of his signature songs. The B-side opens with the other, 'Rocket Man', from the 1972 album *Honky Château*. You could argue that *Greatest Hits* is Elton John's most important album.

The album that gave Bob Marley iconic status is not one of his regular albums, but the compilation album *Legend*, which has been on the American Billboard 200 constantly since it was released in 1984; a bestseller for forty years.

The bestselling album of all time in the United States is not *Thriller* by Michael Jackson, but a compilation album: the Eagles' *Their Greatest Hits (1971–1975)*, released in 1976. Nine singles plus an album track, 'Desperado'. The music pours out of the speakers and becomes a perfect soundtrack to life in California (and Arizona) – or rather, for all of the people who are daydreaming of life there. *Their Greatest Hits* can be found in the United States' Library of Congress collection of recordings that are 'culturally, historically, or artistically significant'.

The bestselling album ever in the UK is Queen's *Greatest Hits*, released in October 1981. It opens with 'Bohemian Rhapsody'. The third bestselling album is another British crown jewel, actually not a compilation album, the Beatles' *Sgt. Pepper's Lonely Hearts Club Band*, released in June 1967. *Abba Gold* squeezes into number 2 between them.

Abba Gold was not Abba's first greatest hits record. In 1975 they released two different compilation albums in different regions.

First, *The Best of Abba*, which opens with 'Waterloo'. Originally a Dutch compilation released on Polydor, it spread to West Germany, among other places, and was later released by RCA in Australia and New Zealand. The record sold platinum twenty-four times over in New Zealand (where it shares the top spot for bestselling album of all time with *Brothers in Arms* by Dire Straits) and twenty-two times platinum in Australia.

As imported copies of *The Best of Abba* spread to Sweden and the UK, Stikkan Anderson's company Polar quickly put together its own response, *Greatest Hits*, with the famous painting by Hans Arnold and the picture of the kiss on the bench inside the expandable cover. The kiss picture can now be viewed spread across an entire wall at the Abba museum in Stockholm.

Greatest Hits, which opens with 'SOS', was also an enormous success – the bestselling album in the UK in 1976 – but the selection is more off-beat and includes filler recordings from 1972 that were never hits, like 'Nina, Pretty Ballerina', 'He Is Your Brother' and 'Another Town, Another Train'.

In the 2015 movie *The Martian*, in which Matt Damon plays a marooned astronaut trying to survive on Mars, he draws energy and motivation from listening to Abba's 'Waterloo'.

Author Andy Weir and the film-makers spent hundreds of hours getting all the technical details right. But they missed one thing in terms of Abba. In a video chat in the film, the husband of Commander Lewis (Jessica Chastain) shows her Abba album – the American edition of *Greatest Hits*, with a different cover – and says that it is the first pressing. On the movie site IMDB Abba fans explained to Andy Weir that, no, it is in fact the second pressing of *Greatest Hits*, since 'Fernando' is added as a bonus track on the album shown on screen.

Up until the point when Stikkan sold the Abba catalogue to

PolyGram as the 1980s turned into the 1990s, the rights were spread between a number of different record companies in various countries in a way that sets Abba apart from other world-famous artists. In the United States Abba was signed to Atlantic, in England to Epic, in Australia to RCA, in Germany to Polydor, in Sweden to Polar.

'Stikkan simply took the deals he could get after "Waterloo",' Benny says. 'There wasn't much interest. Stikkan has said that when he travelled around in 1974 a lot of record companies told him that piano is passé in pop music.'

Abba's most ambitious compilation album during the group's active years was *The Singles* from 1982, a double LP with the more hopeful than realistic subtitle, 'The First Ten Years'. That collection presented the group's singles chronologically from 'Ring Ring' to 'Under Attack'.

Some years after PolyGram acquired the rights to the Abba catalogue the company was bought by Universal, which thus became, and still is, the largest record company in the world. PolyGram and Universal cleared up the confusion regarding what companies had rights, retracted all old editions and compilations and bet everything on *Abba Gold*. The opening song was 'Dancing Queen'. That turned out to be the best decision in the history of record publishing.

The task of choosing what songs to include on *Abba Gold* fell to Chris Griffin at PolyGram, whose job title was 'director of catalogue marketing'. Chris Griffin squeezed nineteen songs on to one CD with a total playing time of seventy-seven minutes and ten seconds.

He went by feel when making the selection. Abba has so many strong songs that some will always be missing, no matter how you choose. For example, the *Abba Voyage* show in London contains a full twenty songs, yet 'Super Trouper' and 'Take a Chance on Me' couldn't be fitted in.

Today, *Abba Gold* has the reputation of having collected all key songs on one record, but the fact is that several obvious Abba classics are missing: 'Ring Ring', 'I Do, I Do, I Do, I Do, I Do', 'Hasta Mañana', 'Eagle', 'Summer Night City', 'When All Is Said and Done' and fan favourite 'The Day Before You Came'. But nobody considered any of this when they popped *Abba Gold* into their stereo at home or in their car. Most people in the world today who have a relationship with Abba have heard the songs in the order they are presented on *Abba Gold*.

Chris Griffin, who also compiled monumental collections like Jimi Hendrix's *The Ultimate Experience* and Eric Clapton's *The Cream of Clapton*, didn't bother with chronology. He picked songs that flow well together, like a modern playlist. *Abba Gold* starts with 'Dancing Queen', followed by 'Knowing Me, Knowing You', 'Take a Chance on Me', 'Mamma Mia' – and so on – and when the album is capped with 'Waterloo', the sound of which sets itself apart from the other songs and is harder to fit between two songs, you as a listener are convinced that pop music can't possibly sound any better.

All of the songs on *Abba Gold* were remastered – a process that is hard to grasp for outsiders, but has to do with transferring the studio master tape to a record – by the person in the world who was best positioned to do it: Michael B. Tretow.

PolyGram researched the market before deciding on the cover design. After consulting focus groups, they decided not to have a photo of Abba on the cover, since their 1970s look, as opposed to the music, felt dated. Hence the all-black cover with the gold typography. *Abba Gold* wasn't aimed at old Abba fans, rather the intention was to reach an entirely new generation of record buyers who owned CD players.

Still, PolyGram was hesitant about publishing the compilation in the United States. But after music fans proved themselves willing to pay steep import prices for *Abba Gold*, the company was finally convinced and issued the compilation in the autumn of 1993, an entire year later than the rest of the world.

Rick Dobbis, president of the PolyGram Label Group, said to *Billboard* that the timing was excellent, as they saw a growing interest in both the music and the era. 'Enough time has passed that it is no longer *uncool.*'

In the United States, *Abba Gold* would sell 5.8 million copies; it sold a total of 30 million copies worldwide. Abba turned out to be a significantly stronger currency than the Swedish krona.

The re-evaluation of Abba's place in music history happened slowly but steadily through the 1990s. In 1995 the American rock publication *Spin* published a book called *Alternative Record Guide* in which they listed the most significant artists and records through history. Artists with a lot of cred, like Sun Ra, Fela Kuti, Can and the Fall, are typical of the selection, but not the Beatles, the Beach Boys or the Bee Gees. Abba, however, was allowed in. Among the albums that *Spin* gives a ten out of ten are free jazz classics like *Spiritual Unity* by Albert Ayler and *The Shape of Jazz to Come* by Ornette Coleman, but also two Abba albums, *The Singles* and *Abba Gold*.

In 2003 the book publisher Continuum started a series of essay books, called *33⅓*, in which prominent music journalists and authors get to go on about one single album. The series rarely deviates from what rock critics tend to agree are classic albums. The series includes *Unknown Pleasures* by Joy Division, *Forever Changes* by Love, *Sign 'o the Times* by Prince and *Exile on Main Street* by the Rolling Stones.

However there is one book about an album in this series that stands out: *Abba Gold*, written by French-American music journalist Elisabeth Vincentelli.

In the introduction she writes: 'If only I'd written about Lou Reed, Bob Dylan or the Beach Boys . . . People would have looked at me with a lot more respect if I had said that I was going to spend several months pondering the virtues of *Berlin*, *Blonde on Blonde* or *Pet Sounds*.'

Across 132 pages she then goes on to explain why *Abba Gold* is one of the best and most influential albums in existence.

'Its cross-cultural impact links European drag queens and Midwestern housewives, New York hipsters and Japanese students, bridging the mainstream and its satellite subcultures.'

THE BRAIN SURGEON

Two-year-old Olle wakes up in the middle of the night complaining that he doesn't feel well. This happens several nights in a row. He throws up a couple of times, for no apparent reason. His parents Moa and Måns go to a doctor who tells them, 'Children throw up, don't worry about it, he looks healthy.' But it doesn't stop. Olle keeps waking up in the middle of the night saying, 'Mum, I don't feel well.'

It is 2006. The Alfvén family are Swedish, but live in Sydney where Måns works as the head of the Swedish Trade Council in Australia on a three-year commission. They have been there for two and a half years.

Moa: 'We felt something wasn't right with our little boy, so we went to the doctor again. This time we ended up with a paediatrician who had just diagnosed a brain tumour in another child. The paediatrician said, "Let's rule out the worst by sending you to a specialist who can ascertain that this isn't a brain tumour."'

That day they first dropped off their three-year-old daughter Märtha at daycare and then went to Sydney Children's Hospital. Olle was X-rayed, which requires sedation for a two-year-old.

Moa: 'We waited and waited, but nothing happened. Måns needed to go to work. Finally a doctor appeared and said . . . what did he say, Måns?'

Måns: 'He said, "We have very bad news."'

Olle had a tumour the size of an orange on his cerebellum. The verdict was 'unfortunately there is nothing we can do'. Måns's father is a paediatrician and knew the best surgeons in Sweden. In desperation Olle's parents sent his X-rays home to Sweden. The answer was the same: 'The tumour is in such a bad place, it is too big.' The prognosis was that Olle wouldn't live.

Friends in Sydney had heard of Charlie Teo, a brain surgeon who works at a private hospital in Sydney and was as famous as he was controversial for taking on impossible cases.

'We reached out to him for a second opinion. First we sent the X-ray plates, then we got to see him. Immediately when he saw Olle he said, "Wow, what a beautiful boy." He told us that he had studied the X-rays. "I can't make any promises, but I think it is possible to remove the tumour."'

Moa and Måns Alfvén understood that the surgery was high risk.

Moa: 'We felt we had no choice. We felt that Olle wanted to be here with us and that we wanted to have Olle with us, even if he ended up with serious brain damage.'

Charlie Teo, born in 1957, grew up the son of Chinese Singaporean parents who had emigrated to Australia. There is an episode of *Who Do You Think You Are?* – a genealogy show that has been broadcast across the world, including Sweden – in which Charlie Teo makes an appearance.

The programme starts with Charlie Teo, fit and wearing a T-shirt, walking on the beach in Sydney with his four daughters. The fact that he was born in Australia looking Asian made him a target of racism even as a child. Australians hated him for being Chinese, Chinese people disliked that he didn't behave the way they expected a Chinese person to. When he came home from school and told his parents that he'd been beaten up, his father beat him for not fighting back.

This upbringing shaped him into a person who knew that his road in life would be to become better than everyone else and never take any shit. Charlie Teo could be described as the Zlatan Ibrahimović of brain surgeons. He did indeed become better than everyone else and doesn't hesitate to point this out. 'Surgeons hate me and patients love me,' as he puts it.

Charlie Teo is also known for something else: he listens to Abba while performing surgeries. In Australia this fact is as famous as him taking on cases that other doctors have rejected. Charlie Teo has been on TV many times; among other things he's been on *60 Minutes* twice.

'It's always the same thing,' says a smiling Charlie Teo via Zoom from Sydney. 'Every time I'm on TV they set it to Abba songs.'

A date was set for Olle's surgery. Måns and Moa did not know the detail about Abba when they sought out Charlie Teo. 'But when he heard that we were from Sweden he had to mention it.'

Moa: 'When we understood how much he loves Abba we said, "If you save Olle's life we will make sure that you get to meet Abba."'

Charlie Teo operated on Olle's brain for fourteen hours straight. Normally a person cannot work in a focused manner for more than eight to ten hours. The anaesthesiology team is replaced half-way through the surgery, but Charlie Teo doesn't take a break. He doesn't eat anything during the entire procedure, just drinks water through a straw.

'We learned that once the surgery has begun he cannot stop, since every minute carries a high risk. The surgery entails the surgeon basically standing there, removing the tumour cell by cell under a microscope. If even one cancer cell remains the tumour can come back. And you really only have one chance. The next time there will be lots of scar tissue in the brain, which makes it even more dangerous.'

The tumour was located in the back of the brain. If any of the nerves there were severed, the child could be paralysed for life.

Charlie Teo's method for staying maximally focused for fourteen hours straight is to listen to Abba non-stop. He discovered Abba when he was about seventeen.

'I was a boy full of testosterone and hormones. I am not proud of it, but what initially piqued my interest was that I was attracted to the girls. They're both gorgeous. So that started me watching their videos. Through them I started to seriously listen to the music and discovered how amazingly good and well-made it is.'

'What is it about listening to Abba that helps you perform well at surgeries?' I ask him.

'There are several reasons. One is that music helps the brain activate memories. Abba's music brings me back to good moments in my life and enables me to focus completely. There are moments when things go wrong in the surgical theatre, the patient's brain starts to swell and the stress is extreme. When I hear Abba's music it helps me cope. The longer I need to spend in the operating room, with aching shoulders, the longer I get to listen to Abba. It becomes a reward. I promise, I have said it to myself so many times: the music stops me from rushing, it helps me to keep going as long as necessary to remove every last tumour cell.'

The other reason has to do with the way the music is constructed. 'Abba's songs are so incredibly harmonious, which creates a sense of inner peace. Neurosurgery, with the high risk attached, is emotionally and physically draining. Abba's songs also tell stories. I think that is why the *Mamma Mia!* movie worked so well. And their songs are so varied, I never tire of them.'

Moa describes the day of the surgery as the longest of her life.

'It was an awful surgery, we sat outside the OR for fourteen hours, not knowing how it was going. Then, late at night, Charlie came out and just said, "I took it all out." We were like, "What?"'

Måns: 'We said, "Sit down and tell us what you did." But he responded quickly, "I'm so damn hungry, I have to go eat Chinese food," and then he just left.'

As we sit and talk in the Alfvén family kitchen in Stockholm seventeen years later, Olle wanders in and opens the fridge. I ask if it is okay to tell the story of the surgery and his recovery against all odds. Olle answers, half uninterested, 'Sure,' and then goes to his room like teenagers do.

The whole Alfvén family became lifelong friends of Charlie Teo's and always visit him when they're back in Sydney. And when Charlie Teo came to Stockholm they kept their promise to him: Charlie Teo got to meet Benny.

Charlie Teo showed up in a T-shirt (his standard outfit); but it was a T-shirt with a bikini-clad young girl on a motorbike.

Moa: 'I thought, "Oh that's an interesting choice on this important day," but Charlie told us that he had talked to his daughters on the phone, told them he was nervous and asked what he should wear. They said, "Dad, you like motorbikes and you like girls, so that T-shirt should be great."'

They went out to Benny's studio on Skeppsholmen.

Måns: 'We were there for a couple of hours. It turned out so nicely. Charlie got to tell Benny what Abba's music means to him and how it helps him focus when he operates on severely ill patients. I think it was a special moment for Benny too. I don't think he ever considered that his music could have that effect.'

Charlie Teo: 'Then Benny sat down at the grand piano and played "Thank You for the Music" and we all sang along.'

THE LEGACY

Abba's current standing is not about nostalgia. Many of those evangelising for the group's music today were not even born when Abba was active. New generations of Abba fans have taken over.

After Stikkan Anderson sold the rights to Abba's music, he used the money to create the Polar Music Prize in 1989. He wanted it to become the musical equivalent of the Nobels. The prize was awarded for the first time in 1992.

In 2011 the award went to Patti Smith, who was visibly emotional during the entire ceremony. Patti Smith, who loves crime fiction, was able to stay collected – just barely – when the person who read the motivation for the award turned out to be her favourite Swedish author, Henning Mankell. She was also able to hold back tears – barely – when she received the statue from King Carl XVI Gustaf.

But when two relatively unknown Swedish sisters, ages eighteen and twenty, from the southern suburbs of Stockholm got up on the stage at the Stockholm Concert Hall and performed her song 'Dancing Barefoot', Patti Smith could not contain herself any longer. An artist famous for her glowing eyes and stony face during the punk era sat there with tears streaming down her cheeks.

The same thing happened again during the award ceremony the following year when the Söderberg sisters of the duo First Aid Kit did the honours again. This time the award winner being celebrated was Paul Simon. With their youthfully indefatigable and organically interwoven voices they sang Simon and Garfunkel's 'America', a song about being young and wide-eyed and in search of the American dream, now it was Paul Simon's turn to fumble for the handkerchief in his dinner jacket.

In 2015 it happened a third time, when the award was given to Emmylou Harris. When First Aid Kit sang Emmylou Harris' song 'Red Dirt Girl' at the award ceremony and then followed it up with their own tribute song 'Emmylou' during the banquet at Grand Hotel, yet another American music legend proved unable to hold back her tears.

First Aid Kit's signature is their harmonising. Johanna and Klara Söderberg, born 1990 and 1993, provide an example of what is called blood harmony: harmonising so intuitive it can only happen within families. You can hear that the sisters have been singing together since they learned to talk.

Musically the duo started out inspired by Americana and roots music. First Aid Kit broke through when they posted an interpretation of Fleet Foxes' murder ballad 'Tiger Mountain Peasant Song' on YouTube. Inspired by older country music artists such as the Carter Family and the Louvin Brothers, masters of blood harmony, and perhaps above all the interplay between Gram Parsons and Emmylou Harris in the 1970s, First Aid Kit have claimed their own place in musical history as champions of American-style harmonising. As they themselves sing: 'I'll be your Emmylou and I'll be your June, if you'll be my Gram and my Johnny too,' referring to two country greats and their equally genius muses.

In every interview that First Aid Kit did up until 2022 they emphasised their American role models. When First Aid Kit started out, they had something almost like a rule book for how their music ought to sound. Authenticity is the lodestone within Americana culture. The genre comes out of old country, folk music, blues and gospel, so it was for a long time absolutely unthinkable for First Aid Kit to make music with pop influences, to use synthesisers or even electric guitars. Where did that selectiveness come from?

'Some of it probably had to do with the fact that we were women in a very male-dominated world,' says Klara Söderberg. 'We were constantly encountering record-collector types who knew everything and doubted that we were knowledgeable enough. So it became important to us to show that we knew what we were doing and really knew the genre.'

First Aid Kit's fifth album *Palomino*, released in the autumn of 2022, became a comeback after a period of life changes (children, building a house) and crises (burnout, building a house) that had the sisters re-evaluating their identity and questioning their existence as a duo. When they finally found their way back to each other again and started to record new music they went back to what they had listened to as preschoolers in the 1990s.

A first indication of what music had been playing in the Söderberg sisters' childhood room, before they began listening to the Carter Family, came in the form of two covers. In support of the Swedish Cancer foundation First Aid Kit recorded a version of Ted Gärdestad's 'Come Give Me Love', a song with the unusual arrangement of an English refrain and Swedish verses. Ted Gärdestad recorded it in 1973 for his second album when he was sixteen. As previously mentioned in this book, all of Abba can be heard in the background on the original recording.

When the live music business shut down during the pandemic,

Sveriges Television arranged a televised support gala in January 2021, the proceeds of which went to musicians without income. First Aid Kit stepped on stage wearing outfits that were identical replicas of the kimonos that Owe Sandström designed for Agnetha and Frida and sang Abba's 'Chiquitita'. This, too, is a song that the sisters listened to as children.

'I have a very clear memory of being very young and the two of us dancing and like singing along in our living room,' says Klara Söderberg. 'MTV or VH1 or ZTV is on and what we're hearing is Abba. The song is "Money, Money, Money". I thought it was so cool when we sang along to that *aaaa-aa* part.'

'That's always been my favourite song,' says Johanna Söderberg, turning to her sister. 'As children we experienced music through the TV. Abba was also the first record we bought. Although it wasn't actually Abba, it was A-Teens.'

You often hear people speak of *Abba Gold* or *Mamma Mia!* as gateways to Abba fandom. Equally important to kids born in the 1990s is the teen group A-Teens, or Abba Teens, as they were called before Abba forced them to adjust their name.

On MTV and the media, there suddenly appeared an incarnation of Abba in the shape of four extremely perky and bouncy fifteen-year-olds with perfect white rows of teeth. Two girls, blonde and brunette, and two brown-haired boys in the background, although without beards or instruments. Abba Teens were like a *Back to the Future* version of Abba, events from different decades merged.

The first time you heard Abba Teens and saw their 1999 debut video 'Mamma Mia', it was unclear if it was an advert for fizzy drinks or chewing gum, or a music video. But the kids could sing, they had charisma and they danced far better than Abba ever did.

It was obvious that everything was done completely without any involvement from actual Abba – you don't need permission to do covers. Older generations of Abba fans and music critics condemned the shameless move and the updated sound that they considered plastic, but conceptually it was brilliant and kids loved it.

Abba Teens' version of 'Mamma Mia' was number 1 in the Swedish singles chart for eight weeks straight and spread across the world.

Their debut album *The Abba Generation* sold gold or platinum in more than a dozen countries, including the United States – the only large market where Abba never managed to break through during their active years.

Abba Teens started as an idea on Ola Håkansson's desk.

Ola Håkansson, born in 1945, is a key figure in Swedish music history with a career that runs alongside the Abbas – he had his breakthrough with the pop band Ola and the Janglers around the same time that Benny and Björn travelled the country with the Hep Stars and the Hootenanny Singers. Few if any people in Sweden are as knowledgeable about pop music as Ola Håkansson.

'I started Stockholm Records in 1992; it was a joint venture with PolyGram,' says Ola Håkansson. 'Then PolyGram decided that I should also take over Polar which they had bought. They had to talk me into it – I was completely focused on Stockholm Records – but in the end I agreed. That was how Abba's catalogue ended up on my desk. In those days Abba wasn't so hot. Their comeback hadn't started yet. A marketing guy at PolyGram said that it would be good if we could come up with some way of using the Abba catalogue.'

Stockholm Records was Sweden's most creative record company

in the 1990s and into the 2000s. Ola Håkansson was regarded as an industry veteran even back then, with his glory days behind him. Still he managed to once again place himself in the midst of the zeitgeist and discover the next generation of talent. The biggest band on Stockholm Records in the 1990s was the Cardigans, one of the most sought-after bands in the world for a few years in the mid-1990s – the super hit 'Lovefool' was their crown jewel.

'When we began discussing how we could lead a younger audience to discover Abba's songs there was this idea: "What if we do something called Abba Kids? Let kids sing the songs and breathe some life into them that way?" Okay, that could work. I figured we'd do a Monkees. We find kids who can sing, dance and be entertainers. The answer was Base23.'

Base23 is a dance school on Jungfrugatan in Stockholm. Children ranging from age two up to age twenty-three (hence the name) learn to dance everything from ballet, modern and tap, to what is called 'street'.

The Monkees were a fabricated American pop band. In the 1960s, a young film-maker, Bob Rafelson (who went on to make several movies with Jack Nicholson), and producer Bert Schneider were inspired by the Beatles' two movies *A Hard Day's Night* and *Help!* and wrote a TV series about a fictional American equivalent to the Beatles.

In order to find suitable band members/actors they placed an ad in the industry papers *Daily Variety* and the *Hollywood Reporter* under the heading 'Madness!!' The ad said that they were looking for: '4 insane boys, age 17–21. Want spirited Ben Frank's types. Have courage to work.'

Ben Frank's was a diner at Sunset Strip in West Hollywood that was open around the clock and became a gathering spot for young people on their way to and from parties and concerts. The restaurant is still there, now called Mel's Drive-In.

Out of the 437 applicants, four were chosen to form the band the Monkees. It was almost *too* successful: in 1967 the Monkees sold more records in the United States than the Beatles, and the members began to try to detach themselves from their puppet strings.

'Our auditions at Base23 were done with a movie camera,' Ola Håkansson continues. 'The children sang Abba songs a cappella. But when we looked at the result it didn't feel right – kids only worked on paper. So I reconsidered, raised the age to fourteen to fifteen and went from Abba Kids to Abba Teens. Through new auditions we found Marie, Dhani, Sara and Amit.'

When they stepped into the studio with Abba Teens it took a while for them to find their way in terms of sound. 'I never did feel that we found that freshness.'

Finally they chose an arrangement of the song 'Mamma Mia' by the Norwegian Ole Evenrud, who had been a pop star in his home country under the name Ole i'dole.

'His version followed the original, but there was a freshness to it. He added instruments that didn't exist in Abba's time. We used synths in a different way and slightly more high-pitched voices. When the sound was finally there the rest was easy. Choreography was easy for them and they were accustomed to being on stage.'

Next Ola Håkansson started to use the network he had built since the 1960s to get Abba Teens into the world.

As a child Ola Håkansson sang in the Sveriges Radio boys' choir. In 1962, at age seventeen, he became the lead singer in Ola and the Janglers. On their early records their name reads 'Ola & Janglers', yet another example of how Swedes struggled to get their English right.

When Claes af Geijerstam became a member of Ola and the Janglers in 1965 the band levelled up. He too had his start in the radio boys' choir and became the band's guitarist. More importantly: he could write songs. With songs by 'Clabbe' like 'Alex Is the Man' and Ola Håkansson as their frontman and teen idol, Ola and the Janglers became one of Sweden's three truly big pop bands in the 1960s.

Ola and the Janglers' main rivals were the Hep Stars and Tages, known as 'the Swedish Beatles'. In terms of concert tickets sold and numbers of plays on the radio Björn's band the Hootenanny Singers could also have been in the running for biggest band.

'But they didn't count among us pop bands,' Ola Håkansson smiles. 'They were a Svensktoppen band.'

Compared to other Swedish pop bands in the 1960s Ola and the Janglers were more clever, more sophisticated, and they actually managed to make it beyond the borders of Sweden. They toured the UK with the Kinks and played the Olympia in Paris with Dusty Springfield. But when their version of 'Let's Dance' finally found its way on to the Billboard Hot 100 in the spring of 1969 it was too late: the band had ceased to exist.

A few years later Ola Håkansson left the music industry at age twenty-seven and began studying for his high school diploma, something he'd never had time for as a young pop star. 'I wanted to start a new life.'

He nailed all his grades, applied to medical school and was accepted. But the summer before he was supposed to begin his studies, the CEO of the media group Sonet called and offered him a job as head of the company's music publishing arm. 'I said yes. And it was probably wise of me not to become a doctor – I don't like blood.'

As the head of a music publishing company it was part of Ola Håkansson's job to travel to the music convention Midem in Cannes. Ahead of his trip in 1979 the classically trained composer Tim Norell and songwriter Björn Håkanson had written a song called 'Oh, Susie'. Ola helped them record a demo with the synth-pop sound that had just begun to emerge in the UK; he sang the vocals on the demo himself.

The plan was to sell the song to 'some foreign artist' at Midem. But when he played the song at the convention everyone wanted to release it immediately, exactly as it was. Ola tried to explain: 'No, no, you don't understand, there is no artist behind it.'

When a DJ in France began to play the demo for 'Oh Susie', they finally gave up and put out a record with the song, under the name Secret Service. And so, a reluctant synth-pop star was born. When TV channels across Europe began calling, Ola Håkansson had to travel to sing the song. A band was assembled around the song.

'Oh Susie' made it to number 1 in twenty-one countries. In France, Secret Service shared the award for most innovative band with the English ska band the Specials. In Germany, Secret Service stayed on the chart for three years with various songs. The follow-ups, 'Ten o'Clock Postman' and 'Flash in the Night', were equally big hits.

When the Swedish town of Falun applied to host the Winter Olympics, a campaign song was created in which two of Sweden's hottest artists in the 1980s sang a duet: Ola Håkansson of Secret

Service and Agnetha Fältskog. Everything about the 1986 song 'The Way You Are', from the synthesiser sound to the sunset light on the cover photo, appears influenced by the movie *Top Gun*, which was playing in the cinemas at the time. Falun never did get to host the Olympics, but 'The Way You Are' became a huge hit in Sweden.

'During my years with Secret Service I often toured Europe on my own and sang – the budget did not allow for an entire band,' says Ola Håkansson. 'I had got to know Depeche Mode and their company Mute through Sonet; we often appeared on the same TV shows. When I was alone in Belgium, or the like, the guys in Depeche Mode would take care of me; they were very nice.'

When twenty-five-year-old Vince Clarke formed Erasure, Ola Håkansson came to meet Andy Bell.

'We were at the same festival in Bari, organised by Berlusconi's TV company. Secret Service shared a dressing room with Erasure. Andy Bell was just twenty or so, it was his first gig; he looked so young and rosy. Then Joe Cocker came in and I thought, "Damn, he looks old and wrinkled." I took a look in the mirror and realised that I looked just as old compared to Andy Bell. So I walked down the stairs, called Tim Norell in Stockholm and told him, "This is the last time Secret Service is appearing on TV. It's over."'

These experiences were all in the background when Ola Håkansson helped other Swedish artists to venture out into the world, from the Cardigans, E-Type, Abba Teens and Anna Ternheim on Stockholm Records, to Icona Pop, Zara Larsson, Omar Rudberg (from the Swedish Netflix series *Young Royals*) and Benjamin Ingrosso at his subsequent company Ten Records.

Abba Teens were four teenagers who sang Abba songs, but there was nothing retro about their sound or image: in terms of look they were children of their time. With their clothes and haircuts, Abba Teens looked like other manufactured bands and singers did in the 1990s. Their fashion choices were inspired by hip-hop; they wore tank tops and sneakers.

British and Irish boy bands had dominated the charts, but now the scene was taken over by American equivalents who came to Stockholm to work with Swedish producers and songwriters.

The same year that Ola Håkansson started Stockholm Records, Denniz Pop opened the studio and record company Cheiron. Backstreet Boys and NSYNC, featuring a fourteen-year-old Justin Timberlake, were among the unknown American teen groups that made their way to Cheiron Studios. They were no longer unknown by the time they flew back to the United States with songs credited to Denniz Pop and his apprentice, Max Martin.

Aside from the young Americans who spent many months in Stockholm there was also one Swedish girl: Robin Miriam Carlsson, known as Robyn, was only fifteen when she signed a record contract. A white teenager who sang and sounded like a Black R&B artist, she became a sensation in the United States. Two of Robyn's songs – both of them written and produced with Denniz Pop and Max Martin – rose to the top ten on the American Billboard chart in the mid-1990s. Suddenly everybody in the business wanted their own Robyn.

'It turned into a tug of war between BMG and Jive in the United States, over who would release my first album,' Robyn told me when I interviewed her in the early 2000s. 'Of course, neither one of them was very interested initially. But when "Show Me Love" and "Do You Know (What It Takes)" got top grades at a conference at which radio DJs judge new songs, both companies suddenly wanted me and started to outbid one another. When Jive lost they got super mad and said that they'd go find "their own Robyn".'

Just to be on the safe side, Jive made sure that their Robyn facsimile got to record in the same studio as Robyn (Cheiron), with the same songwriter (Max Martin). The name of their facsimile was Britney Spears.

Around the same time, the Spice Girls formed in England. The video that introduced them to the world, 'Wannabe', was an all-Swedish production, with a Swedish director, Johan Camitz, a Swedish producer, Maria Tamander, and a Swedish stylist, Moa Li Lemhagen Schalin, who contributed to developing the different characters of the members of the band.

When Abba made it big in the 1970s, Stockholm had the pop-cultural cachet of Baku, or Bucharest. In the 1990s, Stockholm became a pop-cultural centre in its own right.

So, in terms of sound and attitude Abba Teens were perfectly attuned to the zeitgeist and Ola Håkansson set his sights on a global launch.

'We started in Germany, but initially things were slow,' he says. 'Abba had been huge in Germany and industry people could not let go of the idea of the original. Radio gatekeepers said no. The opening came when we did an ad campaign on VIVA, German MTV. When young people saw "Mamma Mia", things began to shift.'

When Ola Håkansson travelled to the United States to present the music at an international meeting for managing directors, he realised that he had a serious competitor. 'The English now had S Club 7.'

The Spice Girls' manager Simon Fuller had followed up with a new young band, this time with four girls and three boys, called S Club 7, with the same perky energy and emphasis on melodies as Abba Teens.

'After their presentation I thought, "My god, we've been completely outclassed. We've got nothing on this. They will get all available marketing." That night I lay awake thinking of what I would say at my presentation the next day. I figured it out. At the meeting I opened with, "All these songs are already proven hits." I knew that that was what record companies want to hear, especially ahead of Christmas sales. That was how I got the attention of the Americans.'

Ola Håkansson spoke to old industry acquaintances to take care of the American launch. One had managed symphony rockers Yes and Asia, the other had been road manager for psychedelic rockers Country Joe and the Fish. Swedish teachers were flown over to follow the band on tour, since the members were still in school.

Under the guidance of industry veterans Abba Teens, now renamed A-Teens, got all the way to playing warm-up for Britney Spears on her first tour after 'Baby One More Time'. It was successful, a bit *too* successful; the audience was still shouting 'A-Teens! A-Teens!' when it was time for Britney to come on stage. Thus, the order of the bands was changed so that A-Teens were the first band to play warm-up, instead of the last.

A-Teens had hits with 'Mamma Mia', 'Gimme! Gimme! Gimme! (A Man After Midnight)', 'Super Trouper' and 'Dancing Queen'.

In the United States their debut album *The Abba Generation* sold better than S Club 7's debut album. Their name change – from Abba Teens to A-Teens – wasn't planned, but turned out to be a boon.

'Benny called me,' says Ola. 'We'd talked about it before. The situation became legally untenable when the group got its break. Benny said, "Shit, I'm sorry, but you can't keep calling yourselves Abba Teens." I also think Agnetha and Frida felt it was starting to get uncomfortable and I understood it completely.'

The name change opened up the future for the teens. Just like their predecessors, the Monkees, the four members of A-Teens didn't want to be directed by others, they wanted to take over themselves. Their second album, slyly named *Teen Spirit*, on the cover of which singer Marie Serneholt is wearing a grunge-style beanie, did just as well – it sold gold in the United States again – despite them no longer singing Abba but their own songs.

On their third and fourth albums they also wrote their own songs, but the world's interest faded. After half a retreat where they did an interpretation of a Björn and Benny song that was not an Abba song, 'One Night in Bangkok', from the musical *Chess*, A-Teens split up.

'When things started to go really well for A-Teens in the United States Benny called me. He said, "Hey, it's Benny. Is it going well or is it going well?" He felt that A-Teens was doing them a favour in the States. To him it wasn't a downgrade, rather he appreciated it.'

Abba Teens/A-Teens' debut single, 'Mamma Mia', was released in May 1999. That same spring the musical *Mamma Mia!* opened in London.

Ola Håkansson is uncommonly well-suited to explain what makes Abba's music so unique.

'American music comes from jazz and blues,' he says. 'It is music written on wind instruments and guitar. Our music is based on the piano, or an accordion with keys. There are connections in our way of composing and writing melodies that go back to folk music and even Puccini, Mozart, opera. Tim Norell was the one who taught me how to hear it. Listen to the opera *Samson et Dalila*. I think Benny listened to it a lot.'

Samson et Dalila is a grand opera written by Camille Saint-Saëns. It was originally produced in 1877 in Weimar, in German translation. When you listen to the opera's two most frequently played arias, 'Printemps qui commence' ('Spring begins'), a celebration of spring, and 'Mon cœur s'ouvre à ta voix' (literally 'My heart opens itself to your voice', but better known in English as 'Softly awakes my heart'), you hear the connection. The melodies sound at once ancient and recorded in the moment.

It may as well be Benny sitting at the piano.

THE BJÖRN BORG EFFECT

A pair of garage doors in the town of Södertälje, just south of Stockholm, are emblematic of Swedish success and outsider mentality. These days the dark-green and well-worn artefacts from Torekällgatan have been taken off their hinges and are displayed behind glass at a nearby museum.

During his first years playing the sport, tennis talent Björn Borg did not have access to unlimited playing time on tennis courts, or sparring partners. What he did have was his family's garage doors. Summer, autumn, winter and spring he stood there rain or shine, feeding tens of thousands of straight backhands against his silent but indefatigable opponent. Björn Borg might not have been the greatest talent of his generation, but nobody trained harder than him.

Two months after Abba won the Eurovision Song Contest in Brighton in 1974, Björn Borg beat Spaniard Manuel Orantes in the French Open and took his first Grand Slam title. In 1974 the idea that a Swede might become the best tennis player in the world was as absurd as a Swedish pop band conquering the world.

Björn Borg went on to win eleven Grand Slam titles during his career. He was the only one to accomplish this feat in the twentieth century. His pre-eminent rivals in world tennis, Americans John McEnroe and Jimmy Connors, won seven and eight Grand Slams respectively.

Abba and Björn Borg had other things in common. Alongside Volvo they came to represent Sweden abroad for a couple of decades. They were from working-class backgrounds. They embodied the idea of how a Swede ought to behave: hard-working, of few words, and humble to a fault. In both cases these qualities contributed to their being highly respected and loved in Britain. Author Tim Pears once wrote in the *Guardian* that Björn Borg was embraced by England because he was more knight of the Round Table than he was Viking. Humility appealed to the British.

To some extent Björn Borg and Abba moved in the same Stockholm circles. During his teens, Björn Borg was in a relationship with Helena Anliot, also a Swedish tennis star. When that relationship ended Helena Anliot started dating Ted Gärdestad, another promising tennis player with a Björn Borg haircut. Ted was a friend of both Helena and Björn, but he ultimately chose music over the sport. The 1972 song 'Helena', as usual produced by Björn and Benny with background vocals by Agnetha and Frida, is about Helena Anliot.

Abba and Björn Borg inhabited unique positions in their home country. In the 1970s there were no Swedish tennis players, or pop stars, who even came close to their position at the top of the world.

The effect of their pioneering work arrived a generation later. Young Swedes who had grown up with posters of Björn Borg, Abba and slalom star Ingemar Stenmark tacked to their walls set their goals higher: suddenly it was possible for a Swede to not just become the best in Sweden, but the best in the world.

The Björn Borg effect in Swedish tennis was the result of a conscious strategy.

In 1981 Team Siab was formed, with four teenage tennis talents. Trainer Jonte Sjögren managed to get construction firm Siab to become a long-term sponsor. The idea came from a South American venture, Team Rossignol, with a similar arrangement.

Tennis had long been a sport for the upper class in Sweden. The most successful players came from Stockholm's richest neighbourhoods, like Danderyd and Bromma. But Björn Borg, who was from the considerably less well-to-do town of Södertälje, with a father who worked as a shop clerk, broke that barrier. The four players on Team Siab came from regular families in small towns around the country: Hans Simonsson from Färgaryd, Anders Järryd from Lidköping, Joakim Nyström from Skellefteå and Mats Wilander from Torpsbruk.

Tennis is a sport for lone wolves, but Jonte Sjögren infused it with the cohesion and 'all-for-one' mentality typically associated with team sports. Team Siab travelled to Perth, Australia, to train with left-handed tennis legend Neale Fraser: three months of training eight hours a day, with various ballgames being an important element, as well as discussing and analysing matches together.

Their team spirit permeated everything, as did the idea that skill is built on thoroughness. Jonte Sjögren has told *Göteborgs-Posten*: 'I have always maintained that playing on gravel lays the perfect foundation for a tennis career. On gravel one naturally builds strength and conditioning, players work on balance and patience and when that is done the offensive can be fine-tuned on faster surfaces.'

As the youngest of the quartet, Mats Wilander was the one whom everybody else bossed around. When he unexpectedly won the French Open at seventeen, they all recognised the impact. Jocke Nyström has said that if the youngest of them could win a Grand Slam, then so could the rest of them.

The four players in Team Siab won a total of 139 tournaments. All four took Grand Slam titles in singles or doubles; all four made their way on to the top ten world rankings. The momentum generated by Team Siab even propelled other players, such as the somewhat younger Stefan Edberg.

Team Siab and Jonte Sjögren had their musical equivalent in Denniz Pop and Cheiron Studios.

Like the players on Team Siab, Dag 'Denniz Pop' Volle was born in the early 1960s. In his youth he sat in front of the TV and watched Abba win the Eurovision Song Contest and then saw Björn Borg win his first Grand Slam title.

June 1976 also turned out to be an important month for Swedish self-confidence. Abba played their biggest song, 'Dancing Queen', for the very first time to honour the royal couple; three days later, the Wimbledon tennis tournament began, in which Björn Borg won the first of his five straight victories.

Billboard toppers in the United States are the music industry equivalent of Grand Slam titles. Denniz Pop, whose first number 1 Billboard placement was with a pop reggae band from Gothenburg, Ace of Base, created a non-hierarchical work process that has become the standard for writing and producing modern international pop music: songwriting through teamwork. Many of the biggest hit songs globally in the 2000s were created in Sweden, by Swedes.

It seems an unlikely development. A geographically remote country spanning the Arctic Circle with a language that nobody outside of Scandinavia understands should not be able to become a world leader in mass-appeal pop music.

In the mid-1980s the record store Vinyl Mania on Vasagatan in Stockholm was the centre for those who were curious about new club music from the United States and willing to pay hefty import prices for twelve-inch singles. This was an uncommonly creative period: Minneapolis native Prince was at the forefront. Two new genres emerged around 1985, techno and house music, with new twelve-inch singles appearing every week. Hip-hop had just entered what would come to be called its golden era. Many who hung out at Vinyl Mania were DJs. DJs also ran the store and worked behind the counter.

But the DJs who ran Vinyl Mania did not look like their hip colleagues in London. The Swedes were long-haired and might be mistaken for bassists in some hair metal band. One of them was Denniz Pop.

In 1986 Denniz Pop and five other DJs in Stockholm created a company called SweMix. First as a joint booking company, later as a record company, SweMix Records. One of the five, René Hedemyr says: 'There we were at Vinyl Mania, selling records when suddenly we heard this genius and ridiculously simple song from England, "Pump Up the Volume". We thought, "What the hell, we can do that."'

In 1987 'Pump Up the Volume' detonated, released by a short-lived constellation of musicians and DJs who called themselves M|A|R|R|S. 'Pump Up the Volume' was not a song in any strict sense of the word, but a collage of existing records. The eclectic mix of music – hip-hop, rare grooves, go-go, old-school disco – was the exact same as the one sold at Vinyl Mania and played at the night-club Ritz.

That same year, Ritz, located inside the Medborgarplatsen sub-way station in Stockholm, had arranged concerts with the American groups Trouble Funk and Public Enemy; both were sampled in

'Pump Up the Volume'. Eric B. & Rakim, whose rap lyric 'Pump up the volume, dance' gave the song its title, were supposed to be part of the line-up at Ritz, which also included LL Cool J, but they were stopped at the border as they lacked valid passports. The DJs in SweMix began making their own collage records inspired by 'Pump Up the Volume'. The record company SweMix Records was financed by Tom Talomaa, who also owned and managed Ritz.

Denniz Pop found the most success; he had big hits all over Europe with a Nigerian dental student and nightclub mainstay in Stockholm by the name of Dr Alban, known for hit songs 'Hello Africa', 'No Coke' and 'It's My Life'.

In 1992 Tom Talomaa and Denniz Pop founded Cheiron Studios by Fridhemsplan in Stockholm, far from the centre of the action.

An outwardly grim concrete studio with small windows covered by bars, it was reminiscent of an East German power plant. But up until the studio was shuttered in 2000 – after Denniz Pop died from cancer – this power plant housed the production of more hit songs than any other record studio in the world.

Alongside the dance label SweMix Records, the founders ran Cheiron Records, which was open to all genres. Cheiron Records signed a contract with Swedish heavy metal band It's Alive, whose singer went by the name Martin White at the time. It's Alive released two albums, but both flopped.

The long-haired singer of the band was making ends meet as a cashier at the record store Mega Skivakademien at Sergels Torg in central Stockholm, when he got an offer to write songs with Denniz Pop.

After Ace of Base's 'The Sign', produced by Denniz Pop, made number 1 on the American chart in January 1994, Cheiron had been flooded with offers. Denniz Pop, who was a DJ and a producer rather than a musician, realised that he needed a songwriter who knew melodies to help him write songs. He turned to the singer from It's Alive, who had admitted in confidence that he liked pop ballads like the Bangles' 'Eternal Flame' as much as he liked heavy metal.

When their first collaboration was released on record, Denniz Pop had unilaterally changed his new songwriting partner's name to Max Martin.

Max Martin was born Martin Sandberg in 1971 and grew up in Stenhamra, a company town in Ekerö Municipality, an hour commute from Stockholm. His dad was a police officer and his mum was a middle school teacher. His introduction to the world of music came when he watched the local state-sponsored music school's brass band.

'When I saw the French horn I thought it was the coolest instrument ever and I began to play it. Later I realised that there wasn't much to play on a French horn and switched to the trumpet,' says Max Martin. 'Two important things came out of that. One is that playing brass instruments gave me really good abdominal support when I started to sing seriously. The technique is similar; you use the same breathing. The other was that the space that housed the music school shared a wall with a rehearsal space for heavy metal bands. The sound carried pretty well through that wall. That got me interested in that world.'

Max Martin turned out to be able to play most instruments he picked up. His musical frame of reference consisted of the scant dozen LP records his parents had in their collection: Elton John's *Captain Fantastic and the Brown Dirt Cowboy*, greatest hits compilations of Queen and Creedence Clearwater Revival, 'the Beatles album where they look down from a balcony', Vivaldi's *The Four Seasons*, and Mozart's *Eine kleine Nachtmusik*. In all, a master class in melodies.

Abba was played on the radio during his childhood, even though Max Martin is too young to truly have experienced the songs in real time. From Abba he gained, consciously or unconsciously, the insight that singing is the most important thing of all in pop music.

'My focus will always be on the vocal performance, producing the song,' says Max Martin. 'That was how I started out as a singer. I think it has given me the advantage of understanding singers. I understand what they're going through in the studio and the kind of support they need.'

It was a shock to everyone when Denniz Pop died in August 1998, at the age of thirty-five. But the shuttering of Cheiron Studios two years later was also due to the feeling that the so-called 'Cheiron sound' was becoming a liability.

The Cheiron sound had simply become too successful, so widely disseminated and copied that the audience had inevitably begun to tire of it. Thus the Cheiron gang decided to go their separate ways and make names for themselves as individual songwriters.

Max Martin struck out on his own. One month after Denniz Pop's funeral Max Martin was listed as the lone songwriter on a new release. Britney Spears's first single '. . . Baby One More Time' was soon number 1 in almost every country in which it was issued.

Much like his mentor, Max Martin continued to put together teams in which up-and-coming young talents were given a shot. The sound was constantly evolving. Instead of writing for other artists he began writing collaboratively with the artists.

The typically Swedish, non-hierarchical way of working in the recording studio, where many people are collaborating on the same song, contributing different details, has been compared to fifteenth-century painting in Italy: one person paints hands, another paints feet, a third person paints the background.

Max Martin is beyond question the most successful and listened-to songwriter and producer in the world during the 2000s, with more than eighty top ten hits. He has written or co-written twenty-seven Billboard number 1 singles. Only Paul McCartney (thirty-two) has more. As a producer, Max Martin has now surpassed George Martin, and is with twenty-five Billboard number 1 singles the most successful producer of all time.

Max Martin is a man of few words, humble to a fault; he trains harder than anyone else and continues to improve his game. The results are songs that appear simple on the surface.

'Dagge [Denniz Pop's nickname among those who knew him] always said: "It should only take a second for you to understand what song is playing." He learned that mentality as a DJ. If you want people to stay on the dance floor while you change songs they should never have to wonder; it should be immediately obvious what's going on. But you should also be able to find new details in the composition. Perhaps you like the refrain at first. Then when you've tired a bit of that you might long for the bridge. Abba is a good example. When you play their songs you realise that they are far more complex than you initially thought; sometimes they have very unusual chords. That is why you don't tire of them.'

'And how do you find songs you don't tire of?' I ask.

'Each case is different. The soundscape should not have too much information. Clarity is something I work very hard on. You can't have lots of new elements appearing at the same time. One thing at a time. Kind of like in a movie. You can't introduce ten characters in the first scene. You want to get to know a character before you're ready for the next one.'

That songwriting philosophy may be a contributing factor to why Max Martin's songs work so well in a musical.

The musical *& Juliet* opened on London's West End in 2019 and is now playing on Broadway – it is a feminist remake of Shakespeare's *Romeo & Juliet* in which the action is presented through Max Martin songs.

When the work with *& Juliet* began Max Martin had only ever seen two musicals in his entire life: *Hamilton* and *Mamma Mia!*

MAMMA MIA!

A musical about an artist or a band naturally needs to tell the story of the artist. That is what the audience expects. This has been the case with nearly all productions on the foremost stages – on Broadway in New York and in the West End in London – that have then spread across the world.

Jersey Boys, a musical about the Four Seasons, tells the story of a group of boys from mob-run neighbourhoods in New Jersey who became stars, but never completely free themselves of their origins. Jukebox musicals about Tina Turner, the Temptations, Michael Jackson, Carole King and dozens of others all had the same basic structure: hits layered with the story of the artists' early years, breakthrough, triumphs and failures.

Nobody would have raised an eyebrow if an Abba musical had followed that same template. The respective backstories of the four members would have made for great material on stage. Their individual careers in the 1960s, when they glanced at each other from cars on their way to and from gigs and public parks. The two love stories that gave the group its name, A+B, B+A. The divorces that led the group to fall apart; the masterful song lyrics that reflected what was happening.

Perhaps a number based on the famous kiss photo on the park bench in the inside cover of the *Greatest Hits* album from 1975? A perfect start to the third act. Set against a background of autumn leaves – the scenographer can get creative with the leaf blower – Benny and Frida kiss while Agnetha and Björn distance themselves on the bench. 'The winner takes it all, the loser standing small.'

But Abba said no to doing that type of musical, just like they'd said no to 95 per cent of all the offers they'd had: reunion shows for millions of dollars, documentaries, interviews, an official biography. The door to a musical about the members' lives was nailed shut and a 'do not disturb' sign was hung on it.

But that door was left open a crack. Because Abba did want to make musicals.

In February 1972, half a year before Abba was formed, Agnetha got the role of Mary Magdalene in a Swedish production of *Jesus Christ Superstar*. The person who recommended her for the role was her new boyfriend, Björn, who loved the album of the musical by Andrew Lloyd Webber and Tim Rice. The nine shows at the Scandinavium Arena in Gothenburg marked a Swedish audience record with a total of 74,000 tickets sold, at the same time as religious groups protested the making of a rock opera about Jesus.

The first seed for making a musical of their own was sown during Abba's 1977 tour in Australia and Europe. Abba wanted to do something more with the concert format than simply play their most popular songs. During the concerts they performed a twenty-five-minute mini musical.

Björn and Benny had written *The Girl with the Golden Hair*, a story about a young woman who leaves her home town for the dream of becoming a star. There were clear connections in that story to both Agnetha's and Frida's childhoods, but since few people outside Sweden knew much about the members' backgrounds, nobody made that connection.

Agnetha and Frida shared the lead role as the girl with the golden hair, both of them wearing a blonde wig. The songs in the musical represented aspects of her personality. Concertgoers might not have been effusive, but they showed at least a polite interest. Three of the songs ended up on the group's next album, called *The Album*, where they were listed on the cover as 'Three scenes from a mini-musical': 'I wonder (Departure)', 'I'm a Marionette' and the future classic 'Thank You for the Music'. The fourth song written for the musical, 'Get On the Carousel', was rewritten and became 'Hole in Your Soul', a somewhat forgotten song that has been featured in the *Abba Voyage* show where the Abbatars perform it as their second number.

The Album became an enormous success. The mini musical was perhaps perceived as strange, but it did tap in to something in the zeitgeist. The only two albums that sold more in the UK during 1978 also built on a combination of music and storytelling: *Grease* and *Saturday Night Fever*.

When the Abbas went their separate ways in 1982 Björn and Benny decided to realise their dream and began to work on a musical, which would become the Cold War tale *Chess*. They collaborated with one of their musical role models, Tim Rice, the man behind *Jesus Christ Superstar*.

Chess followed the structure of *Jesus Christ Superstar*. In 1984 they released a double album that showed that the songs were strong enough to stand on their own. It would be another two years before a stage production opened. The 1986 West End production did okay, with mixed reviews. The 1988 Broadway production turned out to be a huge flop and was cancelled after two months.

Not long after the reviews came out, Björn woke up one night in New York with chest pains, terrified that he was having a heart attack. All of his colleagues and friends had gone home. He got himself to the hospital where he ended up staying for three days, alone, staring at the ceiling. It wasn't a heart attack, rather it was, according to Björn himself 'something to do with nerves'.

That was why Björn was very hesitant to agree to begin working on a musical based on Abba. Theatre producer Judy Craymer, who had worked on *Chess*, has said that it took her ten years to convince Björn and Benny to lend her their Abba songs.

Mamma Mia! opened on 6 April 1999 at the Prince Edward Theatre and became one of the biggest successes of all time. In the autumn of 2023 it is still playing in London.

Nothing about *Mamma Mia!* followed the typical template. It was the first West End musical ever to have a female producer (Judy Craymer), a female director (Phyllida Lloyd) and a female writer.

The assignment to write the story went to Catherine Johnson, a relatively unknown playwright from Bristol who could draw on her own experience as a single mother for the plot.

The train ride to Bristol is a trip due west from Paddington Station in London. It takes about one hour and forty-five minutes. Outside the train window green, rolling hilly scenes unfold. Richard Adams's novel about rabbits, *Watership Down*, is set somewhere in this landscape. Once at the train station in Bristol I take a taxi to the restaurant that Catherine Johnson has picked for lunch.

After we've ordered, she tells me that she made the very same trip herself – back and forth in one day, although in the opposite direction – when she accepted the life-altering offer to write *Mamma Mia!* Producer Judy Craymer had read one of her plays, about teenage pregnancy, and had the feeling that Catherine Johnson might be the right person for the job.

'I was in a panic about not making ends meet and called my agent to say that I'd take any job,' says Catherine Johnson. 'He got back to me and gave me two proposals. One was to write a few episodes for a children's TV show. I liked that, since my children watched the show. The other suggestion, which he said I'd laugh at, was that someone needed an author for a musical based on Abba's songs. And I really did laugh.'

But the agent vouched for the producer and encouraged her to at least agree to a meeting. Catherine Johnson took the train from Bristol to Paddington Station.

'Ninety-five per cent of me thought, "This isn't a job for me, I'll leave and take the train straight back to Bristol." I had just got the other commission.'

Judy Craymer's voice sounded deep and hoarse over the phone, thus Catherine Johnson had expected to meet 'a theatre person in their seventies'. Instead she found herself face to face with a woman her own age to whom she took an immediate liking.

When Judy Craymer explained that Björn and Benny absolutely did not want a 'cheesy Abba musical', but rather a free-standing story interwoven with the lyrics of their songs, ideally from a female perspective, she had an idea. 'I didn't think I had a single idea, but suddenly I had one. Should I say it now immediately? Or would I appear more serious if I waited a couple of weeks?'

Catherine Johnson was born in 1957 in Suffolk in East Anglia. When she was eight years old her family moved west to a small village in Gloucestershire, forty kilometres outside Bristol. 'For me,

London wasn't the big city you longed for. It was Bristol.'

She grew up in a home full of books. Her mother was a history teacher. Her dad worked in adult education, with a focus on English literature. 'My father loved the theatre. Ever since I was very young we would regularly go to the theatre.'

When she saw the actors on stage she initially dreamed of becoming an actor herself. Then she dreamed of becoming a writer. She was always writing. When she was about ten she and a friend began to write school plays that were staged at the end of term. They also created their own plays at home, sold tickets and performed them in the friend's garden. But her schooling came to an abrupt end when she was sixteen years old and ended up in a verbal spat with the headteacher.

When the headteacher took issue with her clothes, Catherine Johnson told him where he could go. Her parents got a phone call letting them know that their daughter wasn't welcome back at school. She had been expelled.

'I'd planned to go on to college, but I was also tired of the school environment and wanted to make my own money,' says Catherine Johnson. 'So I took a job at a large department store in Bristol selling clothes.'

Most of her paycheque went back to the department store; she was constantly buying clothes as soon as she was paid.

When she was seventeen she met her husband-to-be at the department store. They got married when she was eighteen. 'Very early? Yes, I know, but I think I wanted to fit in somewhere.' She had no idea that Benny and Frida had become teenage parents each on their own.

After that, Catherine Johnson discovered a culture that celebrated not fitting in: punk. Catherine saw the Clash play an early gig in Bristol. She wrote a spontaneous review, sent it to a pop magazine and was published.

She got a job at the record store in her tiny village. 'It was a small family-run record shop that had to please every kind of customer imaginable. We had pop, soul, country, James Last, everything. The owner would not let me play punk rock in the daytime, but because of my own interests I was able to sell more copies of punk and reggae singles than the two or so copies that the shop normally bought. Through working there I got to know like-minded people who are still my friends.'

Her marriage fell apart. Catherine Johnson moved alone to the big city of Bristol and took various jobs to support herself. She cleaned pubs and worked as a bartender.

'My parents were both university-educated and probably imagined the same for me,' she says. 'But they were understanding and supported me anyway; they knew that I needed time to find myself. Looking back now I can see that I was rebellious in a destructive way – getting married young was rebellious to me – but my parents never made me feel I'd made the wrong choice.'

Catherine met a new man and became pregnant. When her first child was two years old she became pregnant again. Meanwhile, she kept working odd jobs at bars and pubs.

'I wanted to write but I didn't know if I could manage to make a living doing that. I thought, okay, I'll give it a year. Otherwise I need to apply to college and get a real job. I didn't want my children to grow up without financial stability.'

One day she saw an ad announcing that the Bristol Old Vic theatre was holding a contest for unknown playwrights. The contest was arranged in collaboration with the local TV station.

Bristol Old Vic was established in the 1940s as a branch of the Old Vic in London. Daniel Day-Lewis has called it the most beautiful theatre in England. The theatre also runs the Bristol Old Vic Theatre School, the alumni of which include Daniel Day-Lewis, Jeremy Irons, Miranda Richardson, Olivia Colman, Patrick Stewart, Alex Jennings and Mark Strong. Catherine Johnson recalls performances featuring Peter O'Toole and Daniel Day-Lewis.

All she had published up until that point were a few concert reviews, like the one about the Clash. She also sent fake op-eds to newspapers that paid ten pounds per published letter. The closest she'd come to literature were a few stories that she'd sent to women's magazines, one of which had been published.

Around this time, she accompanied her father to the Bristol Old Vic to see Jim Cartwright's 1986 play *Road*, about a badly run-down working-class neighbourhood in Lancashire during the Thatcher era.

'Suddenly I saw something that felt completely authentic. Jim Cartwright seemed to be writing about something he himself knew and had even experienced,' says Catherine Johnson. 'Various characters performed monologues about their lives. There was a humour to the language. It was all anchored by Ian Dury, who played the narrator. The play had an incredible energy, punk energy. It felt like going to a concert.'

High off the experience of *Road* and with punk icon Ian Dury's gaze as her inner screen saver, Catherine Johnson went home and threw out the play she'd been working on for the theatre's playwriting contest. Instead she wrote a completely different play, about child abuse kept secret within a family. The setting was the place where she herself had grown up and which she knew inside out. She named the play *Rag Doll*, after a song by the Four Seasons.

'Six months later, when I'd almost forgotten all of it, I got a call from the local TV station telling me that I'd won. I got 2,000 pounds! For that money I bought my first word processor.'

Rag Doll was staged at the Old Vic in Bristol in 1988 and was also filmed by the local TV channel. The director was Terry Johnson – 'I learned so much from him' – a contact who would be of crucial importance later on.

Catherine Johnson kept writing, but she couldn't live off it. She was still pregnant with her second child at the time that she wrote *Rag Doll*. 'I'd get up at 2 a.m. to write, which gave me four hours before the daily chores began. I wrote by hand, which made it so that I later had to type it all up on a computer.'

She sent an unsolicited script to the Bush Theatre in London which was accepted. The recognition opened a door to the larger theatre world; she got an agent and decided to try writing full time.

Another play that she wrote for the Bristol Old Vic contained a lot of music and dealt with teenage pregnancy, a topic close to her heart. This time she borrowed the title *Too Much Too Young*, from a song by ska group the Specials, a song that also deals with teenage pregnancy and being forced to grow up too soon.

The theatre was transformed into a nightclub where the actors moved among the audience. The lyrics of the songs were integrated into the story. The play found its audience. 'Many people came back several times, it was a bit like a concert,' she says. It was also staged at a London theatre.

But she still didn't have any financial security; everything hinged on her constantly finding new work. Her relationship with the father of her two children fell apart. When she got a job with the BBC, she seized the opportunity to buy a house.

'I worked incredibly hard, supported two children, paid my bills and then the news came in the middle of the winter that the BBC project was being cancelled. It was January, tax payments were due at the end of the month. That's when I called my manager and said that I'll take any job at all.'

Terry Johnson, who had directed her first play, was now working with the producer Judy Craymer. When she told him that she was looking for a playwright for a musical based on Abba's lyrics he said: 'Have you heard of Catherine Johnson?'

Judy Craymer read the script for *Too Much Too Young*. There was a lot of Catherine Johnson's own story in the play. Several characters contained aspects of her. She too had done *too much too young*. One character works at a record store and dreams of becoming a writer. The play contained seriousness, humour and an understanding of the significance of music as identity.

Catherine Johnson's idea for how the musical with Abba songs might be designed – a radical idea – was inspired by her habit of watching daytime TV.

In the 1990s there was a wave of daytime talk shows. Evening talk shows typically feature celebrity interviews. By contrast the daytime shows were structured around ordinary people coming on and revealing their private secrets.

Jerry Springer and Ricki Lake's American daytime talk shows became genre-defining and inspired many imitations across the world. The UK had its own counterparts.

'And every single morning, there would be something like "I

don't know who my dad is". I watched them, they did amuse me, although at the same time, I was like, this is so cruel to do this. But it was very much in the public psyche of, "This is the working class, they go around, they have sex, they don't know who the dad is."'

Fights would erupt on screen. Loud reactions from the studio audience were encouraged.

In England around this time, Catherine Johnson says, the Conservative government 'was condemning single mothers. They were saying, "Women get pregnant just so they can get themselves somewhere to live, and then they don't take care of their kids, and those kids grow up in the street."' The government's slogan was, '"We need to get back to the proper traditional nuclear family." And as a single parent, this upset me a great deal.' It motivated her to write a story about a single mother who might have made some mistakes in her past, but to show her in a positive light.

The idea of a daughter, a mother and three possible fathers was what came to Catherine Johnson, and what she subsequently suggested to Judy Craymer, at their very first meeting at Paddington Station.

The lead-up to *Mamma Mia!* is that a young Englishwoman, Sophie, is getting married. She lives on a Greek island with her mother, Donna. Package holidays in the Mediterranean are as popular in the United Kingdom as they are in Sweden. It is also a type of holiday that even the working class could afford. Some people who go on package tours find a favourite place, return to it, and perhaps even stay there.

Donna in the musical got hooked on this Greek island, a fictionalised amalgamation of Skiathos, Skopelos and Alonnissos, and runs a small hotel there. She has never figured out who the father of her daughter is. During a wild summer twenty-one years ago when she became pregnant, she had relationships with three different men. The daughter has figured out who these men are through her mum's stories. She secretly tracks them down and invites them all to her own wedding, since she wants her father to walk her down the aisle. Her mother is shocked when her youthful loves suddenly show up on the island.

And so a cavalcade of Abba songs are unleashed and woven into the story.

'I gave Catherine our hundred songs,' Björn says. 'There aren't more than that, about one hundred. She was given carte blanche to choose which to use, without any conditions, but she was given some directives. One was that the story is the important part; the songs are subordinate to that. The other was not to change any of the lyrics.'

Catherine Johnson grew up with punk, but Abba's music had always been there in the background. 'I remember selling the single "Mamma Mia", the edition without the picture cover, in the record store where I worked. For a time it sold better than anything else.'

When she was given the print-outs of the lyrics by Björn she found love songs for every phase of life. From being young and in love ('Honey, Honey') and wanting to get married ('I Do, I Do, I Do, I Do, I Do') to grown-up songs about growing apart, breaking up, regret, reconciliation, joint custody. When she cracked the riddle of where the story should be set, in the Mediterranean, an obscure track, 'Our Last Summer', became an important song.

'What makes it work is Björn's way of writing song lyrics. He works very instinctively, he paints a picture, especially in the more reflective songs. The lyrics sound like somebody's thoughts. "Walking through an empty house, tears in my eyes.'"

The stage production of *Mamma Mia!* begins with the daughter, Sophie, mailing letters to her three possible fathers. Then she sings 'Honey, Honey', together with her friends Ali and Lisa. For Swedes 'Honey, Honey' is an unexpected main opener, fairly peripheral to the history of the group. It was released as a B-side on the 'Waterloo' single, it was also the last song that Abba recorded in both Swedish and English.

But that wasn't how the musical was supposed to begin. Up until the first preview for the grand opening in the West End, the musical was kicked off with the high-energy party anthem 'Summer Night City', which was also the original title of the musical.

'It was a very lavish production number, perhaps ten minutes long,' says Catherine Johnson. 'All characters talked a bit about themselves, there were lots of chairs on the stage.'

Then came a last-minute change of heart. 'We decided to scrap it completely and dive straight into the story instead,' says Björn. '"Summer Night City" was part of it. Other ideas, like a waiter by the name of Fernando, disappeared early on.'

The song 'Mamma Mia' itself, recorded at the Metronome studio at Karlbergsvägen in Stockholm in March 1975, is also an example of something that finds its form only when a few building blocks have been removed. 'We struggled with the production so that it could grow and become powerful,' Benny says. 'The chorus was supposed to pack even more of a punch than the verse. But then we tried doing the exact opposite. When the chorus came, we dialled the music down to zero so that only the voices remained.'

'I went home and rewrote something after each rehearsal,' says Catherine Johnson. 'For a long time, the musical didn't take place on an island. For quite a while there was a sheriff on the island, he also disappeared along the way. But the basic story remained intact.'

'I did so much promotion ahead of the grand opening,' says Björn. 'It was all about explaining that this was not the story of Abba. Still half the audience probably thought they were about to see "The Abba Story".'

Mamma Mia! has moved between three different theatres in the West End in London and is still playing there after a quarter century, which puts it in seventh place for longest-running stage production. (Number one is Agatha Christie's *The Mousetrap*, which has played since 1952, second is *Les Misérables*.) On Broadway in New York City *Mamma Mia!* played for fourteen years, which puts it first among the longest-running jukebox musicals and ninth for shows in total. *The Phantom of the Opera* is the longest-running Broadway musical of all time – it played from January 1988 to April 2023. *Mamma Mia!* has sold more than 65 million tickets to productions around the world.

The same all-female team that made the musical was tasked with making the 2008 feature film. Phyllida Lloyd had never directed a movie before, Catherine Johnson had never written a script for a feature film. They decided to stay true to the feel of the musical.

The Swedish premiere screening was held in 2008 at Hotel Rival, which is owned by Benny, in Stockholm. It was the first time in twenty-two years that the four members of Abba had been photo-graphed together.

When the Abba museum was created in the early 2010s Catherine Johnson travelled to Stockholm several times to do interviews with

Abba. 'What we learned from making the musical is that the story is everything,' says Björn. 'She wrote a script, the story of Abba, based on the long interviews she did with the four of us, featuring select quotes that were then re-recorded.'

The last time Catherine Johnson was in Stockholm was during the creation of *Abba Voyage*. Benny wanted her to help him with the script for the greeting his Abbatar gives from stage – about three sentences in all. Rattling off record numbers says something about the impact that the musical and the film have had on pop culture, but there is one statistical detail that stands out: in Great Britain *Mamma Mia!* became the bestselling DVD ever, knocking *Titanic* from the top spot. This is clearly a story that bears revisiting. The fact that 5 million Brits bought it means that the *Mamma Mia!* movie can be found in one of every four British households.

THANK YOU FOR THE MUSIC

The Rock and Roll Hall of Fame was established in 1983 and is based in Cleveland, Ohio. Its purpose is to celebrate those who have had the greatest influence on music. The term rock 'n' roll is broadly defined and includes blues, pop, soul, doo-wop, rhythm and blues, punk, metal and hip-hop. About a thousand different experts vote on who will be inducted each year. Since 2012 regular music fans also get a say.

The artists or music personalities who are chosen are celebrated at an annual gala dinner where their fellow artists induct them with celebratory speeches that are often long and personal. Among the first cohort of inductees to the Rock and Roll Hall of Fame in 1986 was Chuck Berry, who was honoured in a speech by Keith Richards; Ray Charles by Quincy Jones; James Brown by Steve Winwood; Buddy Holly by John Fogerty; Little Richard by Roberta Flack.

The purview is primarily American. The first non-American artists to be inducted were the Beatles (1988) and the Rolling Stones (1989). The first artist to be inducted who was not from the United States, the UK or Australia, was the Jamaican Bob Marley in 1994, the same year as Elton John and Rod Stewart were inducted. The inductions do not take place in chronological order, but for the first twenty years they did follow an approximate timeline along which decade after decade was checked off.

On 15 March 2010, the first artist from a non-English-speaking nation was inducted to the Rock and Roll Hall of Fame: Abba from

Sweden. The induction speech was made by the Bee Gees, who were inducted in 1997.

Barry Gibb and Robin Gibb got up on the stage. The third brother in the band, Maurice Gibb, had died in 2003. At the time Robin Gibb would only live for another two years.

Robin Gibb emphasised the timeless quality of Abba's music: 'They are as perennial as the grass.' Barry Gibb mentioned the quality of their songs, lyrics and production and said: 'In 1982, Abba ended their incredible voyage.' At that time there were no signs whatsoever that Abba's career might continue. It was noteworthy enough that Benny and Frida, who were there to represent the group, sat next to each other at the dinner party, surrounded by the other inductees that year, among them Genesis, Jimmy Cliff, and Iggy Pop and the Stooges.

The Gibb brothers' induction speech lasts four minutes. Robin Gibb wraps it up: 'But Abba has remained a vital part of our lives. Their music will live for ever. [. . .] In fact 200 years from now, people will still be singing Abba songs, hopefully along with ours.'

Benny and Frida are welcomed on to the stage to the sound of 'Dancing Queen'. The Gibb brothers hug them and they receive their statuettes. Both are dressed sombrely in black. Their acceptance speeches turn out to be the longest and most planned that the Abbas have ever made. Frida unfolds a note and begins, using her print-out only for support and looking at the audience more than at the note. The speech is worth relaying in full here:

'Good evening, everybody. It's been an absolutely fantastic evening. It is also a very emotional evening for me, for us. We haven't been a group, we haven't performed or sung together for twenty-eight years. We broke up in 1982. And I don't think we will ever reunite again; it is a bit too late for that. I must also say, being a grandmother, I have felt like a teenager tonight. I have had such fun. It's like being at a private rock 'n' roll party, you know, seeing all your favourites, being inspired by them again, it has been absolutely fantastic. I am so thrilled by this evening. And we are of course very honoured and happy and grateful to have been inducted into the Rock and Roll Hall of Fame. To be a part of this illustrious group of very talented people, many of them being our inspiration and our role models. This is beyond anything you can ever dream of. As we haven't played together for such a long time, I actually want to give my thanks to the fellow members of the band: Benny, Björn and Agnetha. Agnetha and Björn are very sorry that they cannot be here tonight, but they send their love and are very grateful, very honoured to be a part of this and they are here in spirit. I spoke to Agnetha today, actually, because I wanted to hear how she was and how she felt about this, and she was very emotional and very proud to be inducted in the Rock and Roll Hall of Fame. I also want to say thank you to Stikkan Anderson, our late manager, he was also called the fifth member of our band. He was a great guy and without him I don't think we would have been standing where we are today, or standing here tonight.'

Here the audience applauds.

'And I am truly very touched by what once started as partnerships, a long time ago, and has brought us here tonight. I also wish to say thank you to all our fans, our very loyal fans all around the world. I know some of them are here today. One, for example, has travelled all the way from Australia to be here just for this and to meet us in person which I think is so moving. I also want to say thanks to one of our biggest fans, and that is my grandson Jonathan, sitting over there. He has always loved our music although he is a heavy metal musician. He loves our music and he loves his grandmother. I am very proud of you, darling, I love you.'

What she does not tell the audience is that Jonathan's mother, Frida's daughter Ann Lise-Lotte, died in a car crash in the United States in 1998, shortly before her thirty-first birthday. Ann Lise-Lotte was one of the two children Frida had in the early 1960s, when she sang in a *dansband* and married the band's trombonist, Ragnar Fredriksson.

The subtitle with Frida's name on the TV screen reads Anni-Frid Reuss. The year after her daughter passed away, her husband, Prince Heinrich Ruzzo Reuss von Plauen – whom she married in 1992 – died suddenly from cancer aged just forty-nine.

The first time Frida spoke publicly about her daughter's and husband's deaths was in 2016, on the TV show *Vänligen Lars Lerin* in which artist Lars Lerin, the pre-eminent watercolourist of his generation, visited her in her home on Majorca. Frida says that it was very hard to find her way back to joy. 'It took a very long time. It took many years of incomprehensible grief. I haven't spoken about this in a very long time.'

At the end of her Rock and Roll Hall of Fame acceptance speech, when Frida turns to her grandchild, the camera pans to Jonathan. He is wearing an earring and tattoos are visible under the rolled-up sleeves of his tuxedo shirt; he gives his grandmother a big smile. (In the autumn of 2023, Jonathan died of cancer.) Right after that, the camera switches to a shot of a serious-looking Phil Collins, chewing gum, with whom Frida made a solo album after Abba's dissolution.

*

Next, Frida makes space for Benny, who walks up to the microphone and unfolds his note.

'You know this is so absolutely incredible. To stand here. You should know that Sweden is a great country, but when I grew up in the 1950s, when all of us grew up in Sweden in the 1950s, we had no radio. So therefore we couldn't hear rhythm and blues, or rock 'n' roll. There was a radio, there was one channel, a public service channel, and they would play maybe one hour or two hours of music per day. "Whistle while you work" kind of programmes. And they would start with a classical number and then go on to all sorts of music. And if we were lucky, they would play one popular song at the end of that show. That's what we had. So we were fed with Swedish folk music, Italian arias, French chansons, German schmaltz and John Philip Sousa.'

The audience laughs.

'Not so bad, actually. Because if you put that all together, it becomes what you can hear, well some of it, on the Abba records. So even if we didn't have any blues, or what you would call blues, in Sweden, we had some kind of blues. Because above the fifty-ninth latitude from eastern Russia, through Finland, into Scandinavia, there is this melancholy belt, sometimes mistaken for the vodka belt.'

The audience laughs again.

'And if you live in a country like Sweden with five, six months of snow and the sun disappears totally for two months, that would be reflected in the work of artists. I believe so. It is definitely in the Swedish folk music. You can hear it in the Russian folk songs, you can hear it in the music from Jean Sibelius [Finnish], or Edvard Grieg from Norway. You can see it in the eyes of Greta Garbo and you can hear it in the voice of Jussi Björling; actually you can hear it in the sound of Frida and Agnetha, on some of our songs too. For those who are observant enough, they might even spot it in the odd Ingmar Bergman movie. So no radio, but there were record shops. So I bought my first record in 1957, "Jailhouse Rock" with Elvis Presley. With the great B-side "Treat me Nice". And from there on there was really no turning back. And if it wasn't for those songs, by Lieber/Stoller, Goffin/King, the Beach Boys, Lennon/McCartney, Ray Davies, the Motown catalogue, Joni Mitchell, Chuck Berry and all the others, we would not be here tonight. I think Abba is a mix of all this European stuff that we heard when we were young and also what came after that. And I was thinking the other day, just before we came here to New York: if all the members of the Rock and Roll Hall of Fame never existed, what would the world be like? You could think about that for a while, I think it would be pretty dull. So the inspiration that we've had from all those wonderful songwriters and performers, combined with this European thing is what made it possible for us in Abba to reach out with music to the rest of the world, in a time when all pop or rock acts were either American or English. And now finally, these songs have brought us all the way in to the great Rock and Roll Hall of Fame, where all our heroes already are. And for that, and I speak for all four of us – Agnetha, Frida, Björn and myself – for that we are deeply, deeply honoured. Thank you.'

METAVERSE REVERSED

'I don't want any ordinary goddamn building!' This was the instruction of the founder of the Swedish Film Institute, Harry Schein, to the architect who was designing Filmhuset ('the Film House') in Stockholm. Harry Schein got his way, as he often did.

Filmhuset, which opened in January 1971, was built to be the headquarters of Swedish cinema. Architect Peter Celsing's edifice in Gärdet has at times been likened to an overgrown bunker in the Eastern bloc, at times to a brutalist masterpiece.

A first-time visitor may recoil before the grey-grey concrete colossus. Not light grey or dark grey – grey-grey. If you take a closer look you might notice the architect's subtle celebration of cinema in the midst of all the grey-grey. The lines of windows along the facade are supposed to bring to mind an analogue film strip. The shiny elevator doors are said to be designed to look like typical make-up mirrors in a dressing room.

Harry Schein was a prominent name in Swedish culture and business. He was born in Austria and arrived in Sweden in 1939 as an unaccompanied minor on a *Kindertransport*, organised by the Jewish community in Stockholm. He learned Swedish, married Bergman favourite, actor Ingrid Thulin and regularly played tennis with Prime Minister Olof Palme. He also drank at least half a bottle of whisky a day. Harry Schein was the one who paved the way for the director Ingmar Bergman to shoot his most viewed and celebrated movie in Filmhuset.

Since the mid-1940s, Ingmar Bergman had been the most prominent player by far in cultural life in the small country of Sweden – as well as the most celebrated abroad. This did not preclude him being arrested, in 1976 – in the middle of rehearsals at the Royal Dramatic Theatre – on suspicion of tax evasion. Ingmar Bergman was eventually cleared completely, but the arrest was humiliating. He felt persecuted and left Sweden. For six years Ingmar Bergman lived in exile in Munich, a big loss of prestige for the Social Democratic government.

Ingmar Bergman was drawn back to his home country by the promise of being granted the biggest budget in Swedish cinematic history for his semi-autobiographical film *Fanny and Alexander*. Harry Schein's successor as the head of Svenska Filminstitutet, heavyweight Jörn Donner, had read the script during a visit with Ingmar Bergman in Munich. After having stayed up all night to read it, he made Bergman the promise, without checking with anyone else in the industry: 'Make the movie!' Meanwhile Jörn Donner had unofficial backing from both Harry Schein and Olof Palme.

Production for *Fanny and Alexander* began in the studios at Filmhuset on 7 September 1981. The cast numbered fifty-four, a scale that no other Swedish movie had even approached. The film is set in Uppsala between 1907 and 1909, but the interior sets were built, and the scenes shot, in the concrete bunker on Gärdet.

The investment in Filmhuset was controversial for a number of reasons. The building ended up next to the Swedish Defence University and the latter opposed any windows facing them for security reasons. This angered the architect, Peter Celsing, who took revenge by putting a giant eye on the windowless short side facing the school, which stares unblinkingly at the military night and day. The eye is still there, though its pupil has rusted.

Forty years later another spectacularly expensive project began at Filmhuset, launched by one of few in Swedish cultural history to make it as big internationally as Ingmar Bergman. It was a project as secret as the matters discussed inside the Swedish Defence University.

In February 2020, the studios where the Ekdahl family celebrated Christmas and danced around their home in *Fanny and Alexander* were taken over by Abba and the special effects company Industrial Light & Magic, founded by *Star Wars* creator George Lucas. Actor Pernilla August, who played the Ekdahl family's limping nanny in *Fanny and Alexander*, later played the mother of Anakin Skywalker in *Star Wars*. Anakin, who as an adult goes to the dark side and becomes Darth Vader.

But nobody on the outside had any idea what was going on inside Filmhuset. Not a single news item was published in Swedish, or international, papers about Abba reuniting for an entire month to play ultra secret shows with electrodes attached to their bodies. The fact that the production was planned for February and not March was a lucky accident. Shortly after the shoot wrapped, Covid-19 shut down the world.

There is a famous scene in the first *Star Wars* movie from 1977, in which the *Millennium Falcon*, Han Solo's spaceship, pulls away from its pursuer by switching into hyperdrive. The Abba project that emerged at Filmhuset took on the music industry equivalent of this faster-than-light speed. Everyone else found themselves left behind.

At that point the idea of creating holographic versions of Abba had been thoroughly mulled over for years. Simon Fuller is an English pop entrepreneur who created the *Idol* concept and was the Spice Girls' manager. In 2016 Simon Fuller made public his visionary idea of reuniting Abba as holograms.

The idea did not appear out of thin air; there were precedents.

Tupac Shakur, who was killed in 1996, was resurrected as a hologram at the Coachella festival in the United States in 2012. Michael Jackson was born again as a hologram at the *Billboard* Music Awards in 2014. Several years earlier, Céline Dion sang a duet with a projection of Elvis Presley in *American Idol*.

A delegation from Abba, headed by Benny's son Ludvig Andersson, travelled to San Francisco to meet the person who, according to Simon Fuller would be able to see the project through. Upon closer inspection it all turned out to be more of an idea than reality. The technology just was not there yet. Making a hologram of a person to be shown on screen for three minutes is not the same thing as creating a whole show with a holographic band. The project was shelved.

A few years later, the idea resurfaced. 'Johan Renck and Svana Gisla came onboard and we started from scratch,' says Ludvig Andersson.

The Icelandic producer Svana Gisla and Swedish director Johan Renck had considerable experience making music videos with some of the world's biggest artists. When Johan Renck made the TV series *The Last Panthers*, Svana Gisla managed to get David Bowie to write the theme song. The collaboration worked out so well that David Bowie asked Johan Renck to direct what turned out to be his two final videos, for 'Blackstar' and 'Lazarus'.

The fact that David Bowie was dying from cancer was kept secret from the rest of the world, but it is quite obvious in the music videos, which were not released until after his death in January 2016. The experience of working closely with David Bowie was so emotional for Svana Gisla that she decided never to work on another music project again; nothing could draw her back in. 'Then Johan Renck called and asked, "How about Abba?"' This was in 2017.

The *Abba Voyage* project started with Björn and Benny making a playlist for the show. Which songs would Abba play if they went on tour in the twenty-first century? After testing more than a dozen different versions, they established a set list that opened with 'The Visitors', a song that they had never previously played live. After twenty songs from Abba's entire career, the concert was capped with an encore, 'The Winner Takes It All', and an instrumental coda, 'I Wonder (Departure)'.

They decided that the avatar versions – which soon came to be called Abbatars – would be based visually on what Abba looked like in 1977 – this was the year in which the four members agreed that they had been at their peak in terms of looks. The idea was that the show would tour the world.

Meanwhile, a hot topic in the media was the metaverse – a virtual space where people could hang out and live. Mark Zuckerberg's obsession with the metaverse began in 2014 when his creation Facebook acquired the virtual reality company Oculus. Every player in the media and entertainment industry began to talk about how they would establish themselves in the metaverse; nobody wanted to miss the train.

The Abbatar project took the idea in the opposite direction. Johan Renck used the expression 'metaverse reversed'. What if, instead of focusing on entering the digital world, you turn the process around and bring the digital into the real world?

As the vision became clearer, the technical aspects dragged. Creating a digital show that could be sent on tour, and thus moved and transported between different stadiums across the world, turned out to be impossible technically, unless you were willing to compromise on quality. During this time Johan Renck left the project to make the TV series *Chernobyl*.

Ludvig Andersson and Svana Gisla stayed on as producers. They formulated questions: 'What will make this project unique? How big a role can we allow technology to play? How far can we push technology without losing the correct feeling?' They decided that the emphasis must be not on technology, but on the emotional aspect.

'Abba's music is very emotional,' says Svana Gisla. 'It means a lot to a lot of people. The music touches them and contains a lot of memories. You hear an Abba song and remember a wedding, or who you were when you first heard it. The problem with technology today is that it is used to take us out of real life. We are not meant to live in front of a screen. We are meant to be with other people.'

The solution they hit upon was to build a custom Abba Arena in East London. This way one could solve the visual issues by adapting the entire construction of the arena to the projections. This would also provide a space for Abba fans to meet.

'We had so many offers to do a digital concert. "If you do it online you'll get untold millions,"' says Svana Gisla. 'But we felt, "No, this is not the way." You need to be there with other people by your side. The arena is designed so that you can see the faces of all the other visitors.'

They tried various digital companies, but nothing worked. In the end the question of solving the whole thing went to the number-one player in the field globally, Industrial Light & Magic, the company that does special effects for the very biggest movies. Even getting a meeting with them was far from a given, but as Svana Gisla says, 'The name Abba opens a lot of doors.'

The Abba team went to California and showed their storyboards. Says Ludvig Andersson: 'We asked: "Can you actually do this?" They answered, "Hell yeah, we can." None of us grasped until far later that *Abba Voyage* far exceeds what they've done for feature films. It is one thing to create believable characters such as Yoda and Gollum in minute-long movie scenes. It is something else entirely to create a whole evening with avatars singing with a real live band in front of an audience. I think the challenge for ILM was that they'd never worked with music before and they wanted to try it.'

So, in February 2020, a hundred or so people from Industrial Light & Magic's offices around the world arrived in Stockholm and checked into various hotels. Then they gathered at Filmhuset to shoot shows with the members of Abba, now in their seventies, dressed in tight motion-capture leotards and helmets.

'It was very important that the show feel like something that is happening *right now*,' says Ludvig Andersson. 'That this is something Abba is doing in the twenty-first century. If these had been real shows – which they actually are – they would be based on the present. It would be pointless to pretend that it is the 1970s. Besides, Abba was never that kind of band. They are constantly evolving.'

The set-up was a sort of *Groundhog Day* in which the same Abba concert was performed day after day, from every possible angle. The focus was primarily on Agnetha and Frida, the group's two front figures and lodestars.

'Over the course of a month we put on our space suits and helmets to perform our songs,' Agnetha says. 'An amazing team sat behind hundreds of monitors and followed it all to catch our movements and facial expressions. It was a bit warm with the lights and spotlights . . . but there was nothing to do but keep going. At times we probably wondered what we had got ourselves into, but we had a lot of good laughs looking at each other.'

'It would not be an exaggeration to say it took a few days to get used to it,' Frida says. 'Both looking oneself in the mirror and seeing the others in that strange get-up. Besides we had black dots painted on our faces to mark muscle movements when we sang our songs. Those in the production crew who weren't busy with something stood in front of us on the stage floor, dancing and clapping their hands.'

Aside from all the music videos and shows that Abba made during their active period, both Agnetha and Frida have experience acting in feature films. After all, Agnetha was in *Raskenstam* with Gunnar Hellström in 1983.

Frida's movie role is less well-known. In 1979 she was in Stig Björkman's film *Gå på vattnet om du kan* ('Walk on water if you can'), written by author Sun Axelsson. Frida played a divorced woman who is visiting her ex-husband (Tomas Pontén) and his new wife (Lena Nyman). There are connections to Ingmar Bergman here too. Both Tomas Pontén and Lena Nyman did theatre and film with Ingmar Bergman. Director Stig Björkman is known for his book of interviews with Ingmar Bergman.

To keep things interesting for the five weeks during which Abba played themselves, a Camp Abba was built inside Filmhuset, where two studios had been merged. When the members of Abba came to the studio at 10 a.m. every day, they had their own little tents and a large dining table for lunches.

'We also made sure to change something every day to mix things up,' says Svana Gisla. 'One day we had Eurovision Day – the entire crew dressed like Napoleon and in the Eurovision costumes. We had a Fernando day and so on.'

Due to the top-secret nature of the movie project, inviting outside audiences was out of the question. Meanwhile an actual audience was needed for the shows to feel real. The offer went out to young people working as servers at the restaurant in Filmhuset. 'Would you like to see Abba?' None of them said one word about their unique experience to the media.

Baillie Walsh, from England, was hired to direct *Abba Voyage*, he too had a long experience of music videos. He was the person behind Massive Attack's iconic video for 'Unfinished Sympathy'.

Baillie Walsh tells me that his whole life has been set to the tunes of Abba. He saw Abba win the Eurovision Song Contest in 1974. Living in the West End in London, he hears Abba's music every day, streaming out from tuk-tuks, bikes and cars.

'My job as a director was to problem-solve. What would I like to see? I want to see a real concert. So how can human-sized avatars become believable on screen? The audience will understand that they are not seeing real Abba live, but through the live band on stage they get to see a live concert with the Abbatars.'

When asked how he would describe Abba to someone who has never heard them, Baillie Walsh asks for time to think about it. One day later he replies by email: 'Like a folk music group from Mars.'

TO OLD FRIENDS

t is pretty modest, even for a bench.

There isn't even a backrest.

But in June 2016, this little wooden bench was unveiled outside of Rally Hotel in Linköping, a work of art commissioned by the municipality, to mark that this is where the friendship between Björn and Benny started fifty years earlier.

That same weekend their respective bands had played by the Ålleberg table mountain outside of Falköping. The fact that the joint afterparty happened in Linköping had to do with the Hootenanny Singers having booked rooms at Rally Hotel – the members were supposed to enlist for their military service in that town the next day. Linköping was a major military town at the time.

Rally Hotel, which was Clarion Collection Hotel Slottsparken at the time this book was written, opened in 1960 advertising itself as 'Sweden's first car hotel'. Across the entire facade, facing a round-about, it loudly declared its offerings: restaurant, bar, bank, travel service, garage and motel where 'travellers as well as their cars are taken care of'.

The Hootenanny Singers checked in along with their friends and girlfriends, as well as Björn's sister Eva. The afterparty got a late start due to the Hep Stars taking a major wrong turn and other hotel guests began to complain about all the noise.

It was a warm and light night of the kind that characterises Swedish summers, so Björn and Benny went over to the park across the street, sat down on a bench under a large oak and began to sing and play songs by the Beatles on their acoustic guitars. They stayed half the night, and enjoyed talking about music to the extent that they decided to try to make something together in the future.

On the commemorative bench their initials B and B are carved into the seat, the backs of the letters facing each other.

In the summer of 2016, as the fiftieth anniversary drew close, Björn and Benny decided to celebrate it in Stockholm. They rented Berns Salonger for a private party.

Berns Salonger is a classic entertainment venue, which opened in 1863. August Strindberg's 1879 novel *Röda Rummet* ('The red room'), generally considered the first modern Swedish novel, is named for one of the rooms at Berns. Louis Armstrong, Frank Sinatra and the Supremes have all performed at Berns, in addition to the entire Swedish entertainment establishment over the past 150 years.

Björn and Benny invited people from all over the world with whom they had worked during their fifty years together. 'They found everyone, dug up every old roadie who had schlepped stuff for them,' says Claes af Geijerstam. Everyone in the Swedish entertainment world who had crossed paths with them in any way was there, from erstwhile nightclub queen Alexandra Charles, whose eponymous club the Abbas used to frequent, to actor Jan Malmsjö for whom Benny had written a contribution to the Melodifestival. Even a few journalists from TV, radio and newspapers who had followed their career were invited.

When we arrived at Berns at 6.15 p.m. that evening, nobody knew what would happen. Not even Björn and Benny. They had delegated the entire party to Claes af Geijerstam. 'The idea was that

Björn and Benny would know as little as possible,' he says. 'I had put mics by their table so that they could be like the old guys on *The Muppet Show* and interject or comment whenever they felt like it.'

My favourite Abba image is a photo of Agnetha and Frida sitting close together on a private jet during their tour of the United States in the autumn of 1979, drinking champagne from paper cups. The photo is taken by Anders Hansen, the photographer who took the best photos of Abba. The image shows Agnetha and Frida's close friendship as well as the salt-of-the-earth sensibility that Abba has always combined with the glamour.

When I look through books with photographs taken by Anders Hansen I find another picture, taken at the same time, that I have never seen before. The picture shows the people in the aeroplane seats across from Agnetha and Frida, who were likely very much part of their moment of laughter: Benny and Claes af Geijerstam. And if anything might accurately describe 'Clabbe' it is that any context will be just a little bit more fun when he shows up.

Claes af Geijerstam can even boast that he defeated Abba in the Melodifestival, a barb he did not neglect to throw at them during the fiftieth anniversary gala.

It was when the group that was not yet called Abba competed with 'Ring Ring' in 1973 and lost to 'Sommar'n som aldrig säger nej' by the duo Malta, consisting of Claes af Geijerstam and Göran Fristorp, who both played acoustic guitar and were inspired by Crosby, Stills & Nash.

They placed fifth in the Eurovision finals. The duo had to change their name to Nova in order not to be confused with the island nation of Malta, although that country did not compete that year.

In English, the chorus ended up being the anything but poetic: 'You're summer, you never tell me no.'

Claes af Geijerstam structured the anniversary evening at Berns like a classic fiftieth birthday with a slide show, movie clips and fun anecdotes, although a fiftieth birthday about friendship and with a level of music that the rest of us can only dream of. On stage there was a sign reading *Baldalstalken*, a reference to the eccentric prank-caller Kalle Sändare, beloved by Björn, Benny, Claes af Geijerstam and everyone else in Abba's entourage. Björn even supported Kalle Sändare financially once his career waned.

The evening starts with Claes af Geijerstam himself, backed by Benny Anderssons Orkester, BAO, performing 'Down By the Riverside' on a washboard, a reference to Björn's first skiffle group in Västervik.

The language on stage shifts between Swedish and English that night, so that foreign guests won't feel excluded. Benny, who already appears visibly moved, raises his wine glass – filled with water – and tells everyone assembled: 'If you wonder why you are here . . . Your talent makes our lives easier.'

Björn continues: 'Most songwriters die with their boots on. Some slow down. That never happened to us.' He presents himself and Benny as entertainers: 'You can book us. We are pretty expensive.'

Claes af Geijerstam tells the story of Rally Hotel in Linköping and has even dug up some new facts – such as the news that the popular French chanson singer Charles Aznavour lived there and married the receptionist, Ulla Thorsell.

'Björn and Benny wrote their first song, "Isn't It Easy to Say", at the paper mill in Västervik where Björn's dad worked,' he tells me.

Then Svenne Hedlund, the Hep Stars singer (who died in 2022), gets on stage and performs that exact song.

The story of Björn and the Hootenanny Singers is summed up: their first number 1 on Tio i topp. The band's inadequate English. How they were discovered by Stikkan Anderson and began singing in Swedish. The recording of an album with lyrics by Dan Andersson.

A trio unique to this evening consisting of Tomas Ledin, Anders Glenmark and Claes af Geijerstam gets up and sings 'Jag väntar vid min Mila', one of the Dan Andersson poems that Hootenanny Singers set to music. They nail the harmonies perfectly.

Claes af Geijerstam goes on to show pictures and video clips while talking about Benny's youth. How Benny played boogie-woogie piano at the youth club in the suburb of Vällingby, where he grew up. How he would lift the organ up and play it like an accordion when he was with the Hep Stars.

Jerry Williams, king of Swedish rock 'n' roll (who passed in 2018), walks on from the side of the stage, wearing a yellow blazer, and heaves and sweats his way through 'Cadillac' in his inimitable manner. This is the moment at which many small paths of Swedish musical history converge into one great highway. Benny cannot contain himself; he gets up on the stage and plays the solo for 'Cadillac' on the organ.

Pictures from 1970. The Abbas' catastrophic appearance as 'Festfolket' – a revue show that everyone involved did their best to forget. The TV appearance with Björn as a fisherman in Smögen, when he gets to meet Agnetha for the first time. Claes af Geijerstam has dragged one of Björn and Benny's more embarrassing songs out of storage: 'Det kan ingen doktor hjälpa' ('No doctor can help with that'), from 1971, the time during which they performed as a duo and their wives sang background vocals.

The song is now performed as a duet by two of Sweden's most prominent entertainers of all time, albeit from different generations, Lill-Babs (who passed away in 2018) and Peter Jöback (born in 1971).

Then there is the story of how Abba was formed. Lots of inside jokes. Recorded greetings from a few people who couldn't make it in person. Lasse Hallström and Lena Olin film themselves walking on a beach somewhere in the world singing 'Knowing Me, Knowing You'. The glasses on the tables have been refilled a number of times, which is beginning to affect the noise level.

Benny's two sons, Peter Grönvall on the piano and Ludvig Andersson on the electric guitar, join up with BAO to squeeze every last drop out of one of Abba's most high-energy songs, 'Rock Me'.

Claes af Geijerstam lets those assembled know that the price tag for booking Abba for a show in Sweden in 1973 was 4,900 kronor. 'Are you worth that much?' Björn and Benny are sitting at the table with their long-time secretary Görel Hanser. Right next to them are Agnetha and Frida with their guests.

Then it is time for *Chess*. Björn and Benny's court singer in contemporary times, Helen Sjöholm, who was not part of *Chess*, sings one of Tommy Körberg's showstoppers from the musical, 'Where I Want to

Be'. Later Tommy Körberg comes on to sing Helen Sjöholm's biggest song with BAO, 'Du är min man' ('You are my man').

Benny's sons remain on stage. The ceiling lifts and the ghost of August Strindberg begins to disco dance when Pernilla Wahlgren and Lena Philipsson do a rendition of 'Hole in Your Soul', an unexpected choice to many. Perhaps this reminder of how well the song works live is the reason why 'Hole in Your Soul' got such a prominent place in the *Voyage* show six years later.

A segment about Swedish working-class author Vilhelm Moberg. Seeds from astrakhan apples, brought from Småland to America, that grow into new trees. The story of how Björn and Benny created the musical *Kristina från Duvemåla* from Moberg's *The Emigrants* series of novels. Singer Frida Hyvönen, from a younger generation of artists and songwriters connected to Benny's studio Riksmixningsverket, sits down at the piano and sings a vulnerable, stripped-down rendition of 'Min astrakhan'.

Niklas Strömstedt translated the songs for the Swedish production of *Mamma Mia!* With 'Kan man ha en solkatt i en bur' he nearly outdid the original lyrics for 'Slipping Through My Fingers'. Now he performs his version.

The grand finale that night comes when the Swedish Dynamos, the three singers who were in the Swedish production of *Mamma Mia!* – Gunilla Backman, Charlott Strandberg and Sussie Eriksson – sing 'Kisses of Fire'.

But one last video greeting remains: Paul McCartney appears on screen. 'Hi Björn and Benny,' he says, 'congratulations. None of us knew anything when we started out. We started writing songs and it ended with people all over the world knowing them. That is a beautiful thing. Your songs are wonderful, you have done fantastic things. I know that everyone "thanks you for the music" and so do I. Fifty years! What an incredible feat! Love you, sending lots of love from England. Keep it up.'

Björn and Benny, visibly overcome by the evening, get up on stage and make their way through 'Does Your Mother Know'. They maintain eye contact with one another the entire time, except for when Björn needs to glance at a note to remember the lyrics.

Claes af Geijerstam thanks everyone present and says that he remembers a song that would end Abba's concerts at Wembley Arena in 1979. 'Welcome on stage, Frida and Agnetha.'

Frida takes the microphone. 'It's not easy to come after Björn and Benny. All our love for everything that has been and everything that is. We have had good times, bad times, love you, we dedicate this song to you.'

And then Frida and Agnetha sing 'The Way Old Friends Do' and not one single eye in the room is dry.

The four Abbas are all on stage now. 'Do you want us to sing together?' Björn asks with tears in his eyes.

Benny: 'But this party was for you, not for us.'

Benny says that dancing will start soon, with BAO as the house band. 'Five quid to the first couple up on the dance floor.'

It is fifty years to the day since Abba's songwriters met for the first time. Frida gets the last word: 'It brings to mind when we were young and partied and sang drinking songs. We'd always sing "Alla goda vänners skål" ['A toast to good friends']. Let's sing it now together.'

To the lines of the traditional song, centuries old, written down by folk musician Knut Håkansson (1887–1929) and as melancholy

as it is life-affirming, the glasses are now raised to the chandeliers
at Berns.

Nu alla goda vänners skål, gutår!
Ja, alla goda vänners skål, gutår!
Närvarande, frånvarande
och de som komma farande, gutår!

(Now to toast all good friends, cheers!
Yes, to toast all good friends, cheers!
Present, absent and those to come, cheers!)

HERRING AND AQUAVIT

A different start to the story of Abba takes place in Kungshamn on the Swedish west coast. Deep below the ground in the province of Bohuslän, the bedrock has been blasted to make room for a gigantic warehouse.

The space is the size of the submarine caves where megalomaniac villains like to hole up in James Bond movies. On a total of 16,000 square metres, the equivalent of two football fields inside the bedrock, there are eight large refrigerated rooms, perfect for storing herring. The storage capacity is 100,000 barrels. The temperature of this natural refrigerator is 5 °C to 8 °C, no insulation necessary.

The caverns were excavated by the Swedish Civil Contingencies Agency in the early 1950s, during the Cold War. After that they were taken over by a herring company by the name of Abba.

In 1972 Abba blasted out even more space; four caverns became six. The rubble that was carted away was so voluminous that it was used to build out the harbour in Kungshamn.

When yet another two caverns were excavated in 1995 the rubble was used for the foundation of the Öresund Bridge between Sweden and Denmark, which had just begun to be built and would open in 2000. There is something beautiful about the name Abba also being linked to a bridge from Sweden to the continent.

The herring company took their name from an abbreviation of AB Bröderna Ameln (Ameln Brothers Limited). The brothers who had taken over the family business in the early 1900s realised that the acronym looked better and was easier to read on the packaging.

The company was founded in 1838 by the brothers' father, Christian Gerhard Ameln, of a Norwegian family who had been in the herring, salt and seafaring trade for generations in Bergen. He began focusing on Sweden and in 1850 moved his headquarters to Stockholm. When his two eldest sons, Johan Gerhard and Carl Henrik Adolf, took over the family business in 1906 it was restructured and relaunched as AB Bröderna Ameln.

In the decades that followed, the family business grew into a modern grocery business whose products are part of the standard assortment at any Swedish grocery store today. Around 1967–8 the colourful original label was replaced by a restrained logo, defiantly modern, four black letters on a white background, in the Futura font: Abba.

Christian Ameln, who was the CEO at the time, grandson of Christian Gerhard Ameln, realised that the road ahead for Abba lay in the export business, but also that this would necessitate different ownership. 'Export demands a strong mother,' said Christian Ameln, a line of thinking that was not entirely different from that of Stikkan Anderson.

In 1969 the herring company was sold to Pripps, mainly known as a beer brewery. For most of the 1980s the majority owner of Pripps was the Volvo car conglomerate. Sweden seems like a very small country at times.

Just as every Swede has heard Abba's songs, every Swede has eaten herring and other fish products from Abba: fish balls, mussels, sauces, tuna, caviar.

Christian Ameln's son Carl, who was five at the time, is the face reproduced on the Kalle's Kaviar tube, Abba's bestselling item – their equivalent of 'Dancing Queen', as it were. The recipe for lightly smoked cod roe paste was bought from a travelling salesman in the early 1950s.

Inevitably Abba the company was sometimes confused with Abba the band. During the 1970s the herring company's phone reception had to field calls from Abba fans across the world who wanted to speak to one of the members of the group. They had to make do with signed photos of their idols.

When Anni-Frid Lyngstad, Benny Andersson, Björn Ulvaeus and Agnetha Fältskog began making music as Björn & Benny, Agnetha & Anni-Frid, the name worked reasonably well in Sweden, since the four of them were already well-known individually. From a Swedish point of view, Abba was formed as a supergroup. All four members had been big pop stars in their own right in their home country during the 1960s. But an international band name consisting of hard-to-pronounce Swedish first names was unworkable. When the members stared at their initials they saw another possibility. A solution that also made for a logotype that would look perfect on a record cover.

When the quartet announced, ahead of the 1974 Melodifestival, that they were changing their name to Abba, they realised they would need to clear it with the herring company first. It stood to reason that they'd get a 'no'. What would a successful food business possibly gain from this? But Per Bolund, head of staff at the Abba herring company at that time, gave his permission – without asking anything in return – on one condition: 'that the young people behave well and not tarnish Abba's good reputation'.

This promise wasn't hard to keep. The Abbas were hardly young any more – they were parents of young children, their wildest party days behind them. As opposed to other bands in the 1970s with whom they competed in the charts, they did no drugs and weren't in the habit of trashing hotel rooms.

For instance, during the same era, the band Kiss, with their provocative choice of typography for the letters SS, were accused of spreading Nazi propaganda to Swedish youth, as the media had no idea that the frontmen were from Jewish backgrounds. Bassist Gene Simmons was even born in Israel.

Sweet, another band who wrote distinctive pop songs, were accused by the press of defecating in their dressing room at Gröna Lund, an amusement park in Stockholm where many great artists have played. After a fight with Ove Hahn, the principled head of Gröna Lund, famous for pulling the plug on Jimi Hendrix when he exceeded his allotted time slot, Sweet (who have denied being involved) allegedly took revenge by smearing ketchup on the windows in the dressing room, urinating in the champagne cooler and – yes – taking a dump on a table cloth.

Everyone knew Abba would never do anything like that.

Herring is a cornerstone of the culture that shaped Abba's music.

Sweden is a country with a long coastline and tens of thousands of islands. Until industrialisation Sweden was a nation of poor peasants, which shaped the food supply.

Swedish food culture is based on potatoes, grain and fish, herring in particular. As opposed to beef and pork, herring was often abundant, even for the very poorest. People would catch as much fish as possible when it was available and store it for future use. This was done by salting, drying or smoking the fish.

'Herring is part of our cultural core,' writes Richard Tellström, associate professor of food and meal science at Stockholm University. In 2017 when the radio show *Morgonpasset* held a call-in vote on the unofficial national dish of Sweden, herring and potatoes won.

Herring is eaten primarily at midsummer and Christmas. The version of smörgåsbord that is typically served during these holidays can be traced back to the 1600s and was called 'aquavit table' at the time. Drinking aquavit with herring and singing drinking songs is an immortal Swedish custom.

The members of Abba have lived their entire lives with herring, potatoes and aquavit. That was what was served in their homes when they were kids. That was what they continued to eat and drink as adults, including when they started working as musicians.

In ad campaigns for herring, the photos are pretty much always taken by docks, or with the sea as background. Herring and potato culture is closely associated with life in the archipelago, or at least with the dream of life in the archipelago. Beer brands have also been marketed in the same way. Even if you're sitting in a one-room apartment in the city your mind will go to sun, wind and water (and consequently also a song by Ted Gärdestad) when glasses are being filled.

A striking number of photos of Abba, especially from their early years, are taken on the Swedish coast, where they are sitting in sailing boats, or standing on docks.

The coastal island of Viggsö is central to the history of Abba. It is a small island, just slightly more than one kilometre long, situated between Grinda and Värmdö. The only way to get there is by boat. Waxholmsbolaget, the venerable ferry company of the Stockholm archipelago, runs ferries to the island, but the boats only stop there if waiting passengers have hoisted the semaphore signal by the dock.

Abba and their families used to spend all their summers out on Viggsö. Stikkan had his own summer house on the island, as did Agnetha and Björn, and Frida and Benny. The melodies for many of Abba's classics were written on Viggsö as the waves lapped the shore and the potatoes boiled.

Björn and Benny worked in a small boathouse. All they had to hand were a simple piano, an acoustic guitar and a notebook.

'The way we worked in the songwriting shack on Viggsö emphasises what it is all about,' says Björn. 'Work, work, work. And time. If you don't spend an extreme amount of time you will never sharpen your skills. We were also good at editing, throwing out a bunch of shit. We couldn't hide anything. Two guys sitting out on an island with an acoustic guitar and a piano, then the song really needs to work.'

There was plenty of alcohol on Viggsö. After fruitful songwriting sessions there was always reason to celebrate.

Alcohol is as integrated into Swedish culture as herring. The strict Swedish alcohol laws stem from the fact that Swedes were literally drinking themselves to death, well into the twentieth century. Over time society's view of alcohol shifted, but in the Swedish music industry the romance with alcohol lingered for a long time.

In a 2020 interview with *Dagens Nyheter* Björn said: 'Once upon a time, when Benny and I celebrated our triumphs with whisky and other things, then we could really celebrate. Then it was: "Yeah, number 1! We got it!" But nowadays, how the hell am I supposed to celebrate?'

He quit drinking entirely in the late 1990s.

'It was affecting my life too much. Yes, I was a sober alcoholic, or rather: you *are*, I *am* a sober alcoholic. I wish I'd done it sooner. But this is a very permissive business; that is why so many artists and musicians develop problems.'

Benny quit drinking around the same time as Björn. He talks about it for the first time in the TV show *Skavlan*.

'I did not want my life to become a black hole. I realised that if I were to continue drinking I would lose everything.'

In the TV interview Benny says that he has had a fantastic life, but that alcohol was always close at hand. Out of fear of 'becoming an outcast, losing my driving licence, wife and job' he decided to become a teetotaller.

Benny was sixty-five years old at the time of that interview. His son, Ludvig Andersson, had accompanied him to the studio and shared that he too had been a sober alcoholic for the past seven years.

'If it's in your family, you are predisposed to it,' Ludvig told the host Fredrik Skavlan. 'It is hereditary.'

The TV interview was done in the autumn of 2011. Three years earlier Abba's unbeatable drummer Ola Brunkert had died in tragic circumstances after a hard life.

In 2015 Abba's bassist Rutger Gunnarsson was found dead in his apartment. He had been checked into a treatment centre for his alcoholism.

In her book about her father, Stikkan's daughter Marie Ledin describes how she found him dead on the kitchen floor in September 1997, in a home full of empty bottles. He was sixty-six years old.

'The last few years you could only talk to Dad before lunch,' says

Marie Ledin. 'Then the alcohol took over. He chugged at least one bottle of whisky a day.'

The drinking culture is different in northern Europe than it is in southern Europe. While wine dominates in the sunny south, pure liquor is the name of the game in the dark north. In southern and central Sweden it is dark eighteen hours a day during the winter months.

Benny returns to the idea of what is sometimes called the vodka belt – which includes the Nordic countries, the Baltic nations, Russia, Ukraine, Greenland and Iceland – when he tries to explain the origin of the melancholia in his melodies: 'I think it has to do with the vodka belt. The darkness. It emerges when you play.'

BENNY

So, where does Abba's melancholia originate?

The answer is obvious to Frida; she doesn't need more than a few seconds to answer: 'From Benny and his grandfather's accordion. I remember when we were together and would walk around Mjölkö, the island in the archipelago where he spent his summers as a child. He would show me places, narrate and explain. I understood then how much of Abba came out of those memories and the folk music he grew up with.'

Benny is sitting in his office at Skeppsholmen in Stockholm. He is doing what he has always done, what he always makes time for: he is playing the piano. The sun makes its way through the windows. Every workday, no matter if he is actively working on a project or not, he will sit here and play to himself for a couple of hours.

'I do it to keep myself limber and to see if anything comes. Through the years I have learned that the most distinctive thing about writing music is that it takes time. Why it takes so much time, I can't really understand. I know what I've been looking for when I hear it. Four beats that I can take somewhere. "This I can work with." You need to be patient.'

Benny has calculated that he averages twenty minutes of useable new music a year. Yet he is, by far, the one of the Abbas who has been the most musically active after Abba was put on ice in 1982. In the early 2000s he and a total of sixteen musician friends formed

Benny Anderssons Orkester, known by the acronym BAO. Since then the orchestra has regularly toured and recorded new albums.

Parallel to their musical projects Björn and Benny have also collaborated under the BAO banner, without making a big deal of it. Björn is not part of the orchestra, but has written lyrics in Swedish for at least a couple of songs on each album. Thus every BAO album contains new material with the credit Andersson-Ulvaeus – world news if they bothered to promote it.

The most successful song by Andersson-Ulvaeus in Sweden is not an Abba song, but 'Du är min man' by BAO, released in 2004. It stayed on Svensktoppen for five years and eighteen weeks. Abba's close ties to *dansband* culture got its final confirmation when 'Du är min man' was announced as *dansband* song of the year at the annual *dansband* week in Malung.

When BAO toured Sweden by bus in 2019, the band had a dance floor built in front of the stage, decorated with leafy branches. Among the dancers was Sweden's prime minister at the time, Stefan Löfven. I saw a fantastic concert at the outdoor museum Skansen in Stockholm, where BAO played fifty songs over the course of four hours, among them deep cuts from the Abba catalogue, such as 'Lovers (Live a Little Longer)' and 'Put On Your White Sombrero'. The *New York Times* was on the scene and wrote the apt headline 'A Bus Journey to a Time before Abba'.

Benny keeps playing his piano as he talks. Sometimes I get the impression that he is better able to express feelings through his playing than through words.

The useable beats that emerge might be something for BAO, they might be film music, perhaps a score for theatre. It *might* even be something new for Abba. The songs that Benny has written during his life as a composer are quite varied, but they do have one common denominator: even the lightest, most life-affirming melodies have something dark about them. That is true of the music he writes now and that was true of the music he wrote with Abba.

'That was definitely the case. Take "Honey, Honey", for example. A happy song, right? But listen to what it sounds like when I play the basic melody.'

Benny starts playing 'Honey, Honey' – a song that I danced to when I was ten years old in the Bergström sisters' basement den – and now it suddenly sounds heartrendingly sad.

'I wonder if the music one makes reflects oneself?' Benny says, thinking out loud: 'Maybe that's what it is. If you're not true to yourself, the music has no signatory, no sender. When we made music with Abba we had no idea things would go so well. We were just true to ourselves, did what we liked.'

Göran Bror Benny Andersson was born on 16 December 1946 in Stockholm. His first musical memory is of accordion music. When he turned six he was given his own accordion. His grandfather taught him how to play 'Där näckrosen blommar' ('Where the water lilies bloom'), a song written in 1928 that has surfaced in many versions throughout the twentieth century.

Benny: 'The idea behind choosing that particular song was mostly, "Pick something that's not too fast." Dad had a button accordion; mine had keys and was easier to play. It also provided a good base for learning to play the piano, although I didn't think about that at the time. I especially liked playing with my grandfather. He didn't mind much if I didn't play exactly right.'

Benny's grandfather was a house carpenter. His father was also in the construction business; he worked his way up and eventually become operations manager at the housing company Svenska Bostäder.

The Andersson family moved frequently when Benny was little; they lived in different places in Stockholm and in Eskilstuna. His father worked a lot. One stable point were the long summer holidays with his grandparents on a small island in the Stockholm archipelago with only about 150 houses.

The music Benny heard growing up helped shape the melodies he wrote for Abba. The radio played everything from classical music and operettas to folk music and European schlager. The radio station for popular music, P3, was not launched until 1964, in response to the popularity of the pirate radio stations Radio Nord and Radio Syd that broadcast pop music from boats off the coast of Sweden.

But more than anything else, Benny was shaped by the folk music that his grandfather played on his accordion. At times, three generations of Anderssons – his grandfather Efraim, his father Gösta, and Benny himself – would play the accordion together at dances on Mjölkö, calling themselves 'Bennys'.

The accordion first appeared in various forms in the 1820s in Germany and Austria. By the 1860s hundreds of thousands of accordions were produced in Germany alone. Around the same time the accordion also became big in Sweden. In the nineteenth century poor European immigrants brought the accordion to America. The accordion also became a crucial part of Tex-Mex music through German and Czech emigrants who ended up in Texas.

The big breakthrough for the accordion in Sweden happened in the 1920s, when Swedish accordion manufacturing began on a larger scale. The accordion became the instrument of the working class in Sweden. It was cheap to mass produce, sold at a relatively low price, easy to learn, and, not least, easy to carry with you. Svenskt Visarkiv, the national Swedish song archive writes: 'It was the perfect instrument for entertainment and distraction in charcoal-burners' huts, lumberjack barracks and railway workers' quarters.'

When Abba became Abba in the early 1970s, more than half of the Swedish population would watch accordion kings and accordion orchestras on primetime TV. The programme *Nygammalt* was broadcast from 1971 to 1989 and had 4.6 million viewers at its peak, significantly more than half the population at the time.

Anyone who grew up in Sweden in those years will remember the show's host Bosse Larsson, who was described by local paper *Göteborgs-Posten* as 'having hambo [a Swedish folk dance] in his gaze and a "whoo-hoo" on his lips'. At his side were his constant wingman Kjell Wigren and his house band Bröderna Lindqvist with two accordionists in their line-up. From the start *Nygammalt* was strictly folk dancers and accordions, but Bosse Larsson was a pragmatist and after a few years he allowed some pop and even Christian music on the show. 'We decided to include some hallelujahs and that worked out quite nicely,' he says in the book *TV! Nedslag i Sveriges televisions historia*. Such were the musical offerings in Sweden during the 1970s and 1980s while hip-hop was being born in the South Bronx.

Accordion culture did not carry much clout with experts at musical institutions and on the culture pages. The conductor, music teacher and TV host Sten Broman made a name for himself as Sweden's pre-eminent hater of accordions.

In one radio interview Sten Broman said that the instrument was not worth playing 'as it lacks overtones'. He added: 'Besides, the existing repertoire for this instrument is of terribly low standing. It is so low from a musical point of view that there is hardly any other music in the history of the world, anywhere on earth, that is so low.'

One person who stood up in defence of the accordion, and always has, was Benny. During the 1979 Abba tour, Benny would pull out his accordion at the end of each show. And so the Abbas stood at the front edge of the stage and sang 'The Way Old Friends Do', a song that did not exist on record at the time but was released in a live version the following year on *Super Trouper*.

Abba also kicked off their concerts on the same tour with Swedish folk music. Audiences in cities across the world, standing in front of the stage eager to hear Abba, were first greeted by the choral psalm 'Gammal fäbodpsalm från Dalarna' ('Old farm hymn from Dalarna'), arranged by folk musician Oskar Lindberg in 1936 but with roots in the 1880s, performed on Benny's modern synthesiser. The psalm is a strong candidate for the most beautiful and saddest piece of music to come out of Sweden and is often played at funerals.

'I played the *fäbodpsalm* back then so that the audience would know where we came from,' Benny said in an interview with author Jerker Virdborg in *Dagens Nyheter*. 'That we grew up with Swedish folk music.'[22] Benny also noted that the melancholia in Abba's music is 'incredibly well hidden behind all the choruses and arrangements'.

The accordion appears on most albums Benny has been involved in, from Björn's and Benny's 1971 duo album *Lycka*, through the Abba records and on to his solo albums and BAO. In

The Complete Recording Sessions by Carl Magnus Palm, Michael B. Tretow says that Benny in his eagerness to always try every option even tried the accordion on 'Dancing Queen', although that idea was eventually scrapped.

When Benny was eight years old, his family moved to Vällingby, a suburban neighbourhood in Stockholm that was long considered the epitome of the Swedish social democratic project. Prime Minister Olof Palme lived in a semi-detached house in Vällingby with his family, a symbol of social democracy's deep rootedness in society.

Benny spent most of his school years at Grimstaskolan. In a reportage in local paper *Mitt I*, former classmates are interviewed and testify that he would seize any opportunity to play the organ or the piano. A classmate says: 'When it was break time and the others would go out into the playground, Benny went inside to play the piano.'

After finishing school at fifteen, Benny got a job as a trainee at Svenska Bostäder through his father's connections there. ('I worked on building the police headquarters as well as the Åhlens department store in Vällingby.') One thing led to another. A stair cleaner at Svenska Bostäder, a city-run property development and management company, heard that he played the accordion. 'Do you play the organ too, kid? I heard they need someone for the Electric Company orchestra.'

Ahead of a gig with that orchestra, Elverkets Spelmanslag, Benny ran into Svenne Hedlund who played with the band the Clifftones. 'We had a gig, but no car. Svenne agreed to drive us. At the gig he got up and sang a few songs.'

Svenne Hedlund would later become the singer in every raggare's favourite band, the Hep Stars. When the band's first organist Hans Östlund quit, Benny was asked if he would replace him. The rest is Swedish, and international, music history.

We are seated on opposite sides of Benny's desk. His grand piano is behind him. When I ask questions and he wants to explain something he turns to the grand piano and shows me the notes and fingering.

Fragments of melodies that I have heard a thousand times fill the room. Beats from 'Thank You for the Music', 'The Winner Takes It All', 'Mamma Mia', and 'Honey, Honey'. Hearing them this way, from a lone piano, reminds me of the primordial force inherent in these melodies.

To the right of the grand piano is a Synclavier, an instrument of mythological reputation in musician circles. The Synclavier is an early digital synth and sound module with a sampler that showed up long before either the concept 'sampler' or 'sound module' were in use. The gong sound at the beginning of Michael Jackson's 'Beat It' comes from a Synclavier.

'How is a melody born?' I ask him.

'That is a very good question. I don't really know. But my process involves sitting here at the grand piano and just playing, without any preconceived notions.' Benny plays a few notes. 'Was that music? Was that worth anything? Perhaps. It's not about improvisation. What I am looking for is to arrive at what I think is worth something.'

'How do you know that you've found it?'

'I can hear it. I trust myself. I don't know why I end up choosing this over that, but I keep working until the melodies are solid.

When the lyrics are created they always help, they elevate the song further. I don't get involved in the lyrics. Björn can write whatever he likes. I'm happy if there's substance to the lyrics, there always is nowadays. All my focus is on where the syllables will go.'

'Do you record yourself to remember melodies?'

'No, never. When I have something I go over to the Synclavier. Add a drum beat, perhaps some strings, a clarinet. I need songs to have an identity of their own. You can make a song by taking a Beatles phrase here, a Beach Boys phrase there, and stitching them together to create something new. Many people in this country work that way. Nothing wrong with that, it works. But for me the whole point is to find a melody that nobody has heard before, but that still sounds accessible.'

'Much has been written about Abba, but remarkably little about the music itself.'

'That is where it is at, if you ask me. The sound. Who the girls are. How it is mixed, edited and arranged. That is what makes Abba Abba. Everything else is just window-dressing. The only thing we did for those ten years was write and record music. Björn and I were constantly working. Micke B. Tretow also had a big part in the work. We were never satisfied until we all thought it was good. It was understood that it wasn't enough for just one of us to like it.

'The girls also had a unique capacity. The fact that one is a soprano and another is a mezzo gives you a span from low D to high D. That is quite a lot,' says Benny, and demonstrates on the piano, his hands far apart. 'Unfortunately I still tend to think in terms of that span when I write. The notes spread out too much and it becomes impossible for one person to sing. But it was possible to write that way when both the girls sang together.'

*

In 1987 Benny and Görel Hanser started Mono Music, the music publishing and record company that publishes the music that he writes. Görel Hanser worked as Stikkan's secretary. Everything in Benny's and Abba's world runs through her. If anyone can be called the fifth member of Abba, it is, strictly speaking, not Stikkan, but Görel Hanser.

In the house next to the office building with Benny's own room there is an entire recording studio, Riksmixningsverket. The young British musicians who make up the live band in *Abba Voyage* were flown over to Stockholm in 2021 and rehearsed here together under the supervision of Benny's son Ludvig Andersson and Benny himself.

'It is important to us that they be young, hungry musicians,' Benny told me as I got to listen in on the rehearsals for a bit. 'And that there is an equal number of women and men in the band.'

In the 2000s, Benny has emerged as one of Sweden's leading feminists. When the Feminist Party (Fi) was founded in 2005, they received significant financial support from Benny, among others. Ahead of the 2014 Swedish general election a campaign film was made for the party in which Benny participated.

'Hi, my name is Benny Andersson and I am a feminist,' Benny says in the film. 'It seems there is some kind of uncertainty and confusion regarding the concept of feminism, but for me it means being aware of the existence of structural gender inequalities and not accepting them, but rather doing something about it. This is what makes one a feminist.'

Fi got more than 3 per cent of the vote in the 2014 election and thus came very close to securing seats in parliament.

*

'Which Abba album are you happiest with?' I ask.

'Oh that's a difficult question. But I'll say *Super Trouper*. There aren't really any misses on it. On some of the earlier albums there were. Björn and I had some notion that it was cooler to do rock 'n' roll and insisted on writing rock songs. We shouldn't have.'

'What kind of music do you personally listen to?'

'I have stopped listening to pop. I stopped around the time we made *Chess*. I've only really listened to folk and classical music since then. But during the years with Abba I kept up. It was fun and interesting to follow what others were doing. What does the Eagles' new single sound like? What's Rod Stewart up to? How did Donna Summer create that sound?'

Benny walks around the room, sits down at the grand piano, plays some more. This time it is 'Thank You for the Music', an evergreen hit that sounds as if it could have been written by Irving Berlin in the 1940s.

'This one was an exception,' Benny says. 'I wrote it in half an hour at Stikkan's house during a party. He had a piano under the stairs in his living room. I went over to it, started to play and the song was just there. Those are the moments you're waiting for. I'm not religious, but if I was, I would describe it as divine intervention. "Okay, he's been sitting here for four and a half months, he can have a few minutes now." When those minutes finally arrive, that's a high I can ride for days. It's a euphoric feeling. You never know when it will end. There might be a day when it all dries up. But the fact that I get to sit here every day and try; it is a pretty wonderful job.'

The music that Benny has recorded on his own has occasionally made its way into Abba's world. *Abba Voyage* in London starts with the folk tune from the instrumental song 'Skallgång' from the solo album *November 1989* (with cover artwork by Swedish artist and feminist icon Marie-Louise Ekman). Abba's comeback song 'I Still Have Faith In You', which foreshadowed their 2021 album *Voyage*, is built on a melodic fragment from Benny's score for the movie *The Circle*.

In 2017 Benny recorded a solo piano album for the pre-eminent record company for classical music, Deutsche Grammophon. The fact that the opening track ended up being 'I Let the Music Speak', a lesser-known song from *The Visitors*, does not feel like an accident. It was a title that hinted at an autobiography written in musical notes.

When I floated that thought in a music podcast for Sveriges Radio Benny said, 'Well you know, that's interesting. I didn't really have any kind of thoughts of anything, I just wanted to make a piano album, nothing else, with old songs. But when I'd recorded this record, and listened to it all the way through, I was struck by how much content there was in the music, even though everything was stripped away.'

'You must have been asked so many times to write your autobiography?'

'Well, it happens. The answer to that question is "no thanks".'

'An autobiography in musical notes might be better?'

'Yes, very convenient. That way you don't have to write anything or tell anyone about how things have been, which is good.'

THE SONG OF THE BLACK-THROATED LOON

A record company must never give up hope. When work on the follow-up to *The Visitors* appeared to have stalled, Abba's record company issued the compilation album *The Singles* at the end of 1982 and went big with the subtitle 'The First Ten Years'.

There was never any official notice of Abba's dissolution, but even then it was obvious to everyone what was happening. The first ten years? More like the only ten years.

The group made one of their last joint TV appearances at the end of 1982 on the BBC's *The Late Late Breakfast Show*. Their professional smiles and the cheery studio decor do little to hide the tensions between the members. Watching the clip today with the sound down, you don't hear Abba's music, but rather 'Mental istid' ('Mental ice age'), a contemporary and extremely dystopian song by Swedish punk band Ebba Grön. Mentally the Abbas had already grown apart and were setting off in their respective directions.

Frida and Agnetha were now recording albums with foreign star producers.

Frida's solo album had been released that September, a collaboration with Genesis drummer Phil Collins. He had just become a major pop star in his own right, with his first solo album on which he'd created a new sound with the divorce drums on 'In the Air Tonight'.

Agnetha chose producer and songwriter Mike Chapman who had recently completed a suite of effervescent hits for artists like Sweet,

Suzi Quatro, Mud and Smokie – bands that had competed with Abba in the charts – as well as the smash hits 'Heart of Glass' by Blondie, and 'Mickey' by Toni Basil, which both topped the Billboard chart.

At the end of the 1980s these activities had petered out. Frida and Agnetha had one big solo hit each, but despite the star producers and the massive studio budgets their solo albums did not become the international successes one might have hoped.

Meanwhile Björn and Benny were living out their dreams of doing musical theatre.

The *Chess* duet 'I Know Him So Well', sung by Elaine Paige and Barbara Dickson, topped the charts in the UK, but did not become a hit in the rest of the world. 'One Night in Bangkok', performed by Murray Head (who had played Judas in *Jesus Christ Superstar*) reached a surprising number 3 on the Billboard chart in the United States, making the song Björn and Benny's biggest single hit in the United States after 'Dancing Queen' and 'Take a Chance on Me'.

The album was a success, but the stage production was largely a flop.

Abba was enveloped in radio silence. The band name disappeared from lists and magazines. The lid was put on. The silence bred speculation. There were rumours that Benny had retreated to his studio in Stockholm. What secret project was he working on?

The answer came in 1990. It was not what the music business had been hoping for. Rather than writing new hits, one of the most brilliant and sought-after composers in the history of pop music opted to spend a couple of years recording and documenting: birdsong.

The album was given the name *Fågelsång i Sverige* with the subtitle *90 välkända fåglars läten* ('Birdsong in Sweden: The calls of 90 well-known birds'). It came with a 200-page companion book with watercolour illustrations of all the birds, along with descriptive texts about their lives and sounds.

The text about the common swift, bird no. 33, reads 'What would Swedish summer be without the screeching call of the common swift? Poorer! No sound is more intimately connected with warm, still, sunny nights at the end of July or early August. Listen to the recording, close your eyes and imagine an entire flock of swifts swishing above the roofs at dizzying speed, or flocking high in the blue sky, screeching their sharp *srrih, srrih, srrih, srrih*. Can you feel the summer heat, the taste of bilberries in your mouth, the melancholia?'

Srrih, srrih, srrih, srrih. No it's not exactly 'Knowing Me Knowing You'.

In the prologue to *Fågelsång i Sverige* Benny writes, 'I have long been interested in birds, and over time I have learned what various species look like, aided by field guides. But not how they sound! To correct this I decided to make a bird record of "my own", or rather, I asked Lars Svensson and Dan Zetterström for help in making one.'

Ornithologist Lars Svensson had been collecting bird sounds for twenty years and is among the top experts in the world in this area. Field ornithologist Dan Zetterström is known as one of the best bird artists.

Like everything else Benny Andersson has taken on out of pure enthusiasm and curiosity, from Abba to BAO, *Fågelsång i Sverige* turned out to be successful against all odds in his native Sweden and ended up in the charts. The album went gold at 64,000 copies, a number that few Swedish pop artists of that era could match.

The first bird you hear on *Fågelsång i Sverige* is a black-throated loon. It may be a coincidence that this particular bird is on the first

15

track on this record, but if you dig a bit deeper into Benny's discography it doesn't feel like a coincidence.

In 1966 the Hep Stars released their third and eponymous album – this is the album that contains the very first Andersson-Ulvaeus composition, 'Isn't it Easy to Say'. The last track on side A, 'Sound of Eve' isn't like the Hep Stars' rock 'n' roll at all, rather it is reminiscent of baroque music and is totally dominated by Benny's billowy piano playing. After that there is something as unexpected as it is fitting – the song of a black-throated loon. A pop group incorporating birdsong into their music was not common in 1966.

The song of the black-throated loon is heartrendingly beautiful, even as there is something fated about it. The text in *Fågelsång i Sverige* points out that the black-throated loon 'is often used as background in radio thrillers and film with suspenseful content, even when the environment depicted is completely out of the question for the black-throated loon!'

The working title of Abba's 'The Day Before You Came' was 'The Suffering Bird'. When Benny played the same song on his 2017 solo piano album, the piano melody portrays the black-throated loon's portent that something terrible is about to happen.

The black-throated loon's habitat is the same as that of the folk music and culture that has marked Benny's melodies: the dark, northern hemisphere. The black-throated loon is a water bird that nests along the latitudes spanned by the vodka belt.

In 1991 Swedish folk musician Kalle Moraeus released an eponymous solo album. Kalle Moraeus has played frequently with Benny and is a member of BAO. On the album, Benny plays the piano and Björn plays a twelve-string acoustic guitar. It's all produced by

Michael B. Tretow. Ted Gärdestad, who took his own life six years later, plays the grand piano on several songs. He also penned one of them. Track number four on the album, titled 'Schottis from Lima', starts with the song of the black-throated loon.

If you listen your way through all of the sounds on Benny's birdsong album you will find yourself transported out into Swedish nature. As a songwriter Benny has often captured urban environments, as in 'Summer Night City', and 'Voulez-Vous', but nature is never far off in his melodies. Even a neon-lit metropolis has green trees along its boulevards.

Taking influences from birdsong is something Benny and Paul McCartney have in common. The Beatles' song 'Blackbird' from 1968 began as a poem written by Paul, titled 'Blackbird Singing'. He borrowed the melody from a Bach piece for the lute. Paul McCartney recalled that 'bird' was also English slang for 'girl' (lending 'blackbird' the dual meaning of 'Black girl'). This had him associating to the American civil rights movement.

The song of the blackbird is beloved in many countries. In *Fågelsång i Sverige* it is noted that 'if one were to arrange a singing contest among all the birds of Sweden, the blackbird would be one of the favourites for the final title'. The blackbird may be the only creature on earth that is more musically inclined than both Paul McCartney and Benny Andersson. There is that combination of euphoria and melancholy in its call.

Birdsong influences can also be found in the Beatles' song 'Mother Nature's Son', from the same album as 'Blackbird', the double album titled *The Beatles*, but which more commonly goes by 'the White Album'.

In his book *The Lyrics: 1956 to the Present*, Paul McCartney writes about how an encounter with a skylark inspired him to write the song:

> There was that strong sense of the countryside, and I was very lucky to access it so easily. I had the privilege – the joy, really – of watching a skylark rising. In the middle of a field there's a bird that just rises, vertically, singing as if its life depends on it, and it goes up this column of air till it gets to the top, and then it stops singing and just glides down. That's how it leads you away from the nest, fluttering like the solo violin in *The Lark Ascending*, that lovely piece of music by Ralph Vaughan Williams. It's now a golden memory. Most people I meet these days haven't seen this behaviour of the skylark, but it was very powerful for me, the sheer glory of nature.

In his excellent work of pop history, *Let's Do It: The Birth of Pop*, musician and journalist Bob Stanley promotes the thesis that pop history does not start in 1963 with the Beatles, in 1956 with Elvis Presley, or even in 1949 with the vinyl single format. Bob Stanley demonstrates that pop history has roots that stretch all the way back to the dawn of the twentieth century. Irving Berlin, born in 1888 in Siberia, has written more immortal pop songs than most.

But perhaps the history of pop starts far earlier than that. Approximately 100 million years earlier.

Birdsong is about the same things as pop music: sex and identity. Birds sing to attract a mate and mark their territory. If you take a walk across fields, or along beaches, you will hear the most timeless melodies.

THANK YOU

I would not have written this book if my publisher Daniel Sandström had not convinced me by sending me Craig Brown's book on the Beatles: *One Two Three Four*. That was when I understood that the story of a band need not be told in a linear way. It is perfectly fine to skip the linking passages included in a traditional biography and just focus on what you – I – find most interesting.

Thanks to my editor Johan Söderbäck who has been the Michael B. Tretow of this book.

Thanks to those of you who have read it at various stages, without you I would never have crossed the finishing line: Malin Cumzelius, Johanna Lindborg, Christine Edhäll, Kajsa Harrysson, Kaisa Palo, Astri von Arbin Ahlander, Jenny Stjernströmer Björk, Niklas Elmér, Erika Palmquist, Christian Manfred, Charlotta Magnusson, Hugo Solding, Chris Carter, Ian Hallard, Sam Matthews and Hannah Knowles.

Thanks to Andy Bell of Erasure who reminded me that a book about Abba should not sound like the silence at the National Library.

Thanks to Claes af Geijerstam who has been so generous with his time and made me aware of details in the music, such as Benny's piano sound being built around his heavy use of the sustain pedal.

Many people have participated in interviews or shared their knowledge with me and opened doors during the ten-year journey that led to this book. A thousand thanks to: Catherine Johnson,

Bengt Palmers, Ola Håkansson, Pete Paphides, Caitlin Moran, Ulf Andersson (rest in peace), David Thyrén, Moa Alfvén, Måns Alfvén, Olle Alfvén, Charlie Theo, Marie Ledin, Michael B. Tretow, Görel Hanser, Mia Segolsson, Ludvig Andersson, Johan Renck, Svana Gisla, Baillie Walsh, Anders Hanser, Helga van de Kar, Max Martin, Jörgen Elofsson, Peter Nordahl, Lolo Murray, Elisabeth Vincentelli, Hasse Huss, Johanna Söderberg, Klara Söderberg, Ahmad Sarmast, Larsåke Thuresson, Björn Nordström, Thomas Johansson, Christofer Fredriksson, Tanja Määttä Berg, Jonas Holst, Rebecca Edwards, Bruno Glenmark, Klas Lunding, John Seabrook, Nik Cohn, Nick Tosches, Andreas Johansson, Maria Lindholm, Peter Fellman, Jeppe Wikström, Bengt Wanselius, Petter Karlsson, Anna Sanner, Michael Nystås, Mark Wood, Zoe Miller, Anna-Karin Korpi.

And the biggest thanks of all to Benny Andersson, Agnetha Fältskog, Anni-Frid Lyngstad Reuss and Björn Ulvaeus for making the world a more beautiful place.

SOURCES

Unless otherwise indicated, all quotes in this book are from my own interviews with Benny Andersson, Agnetha Fältskog, Anni-Frid Lyngstad Reuss and Björn Ulvaeus, as well as interviews I've done for the book with other people who have insight into Abba.

In 2013 I did a report on Abba for the *Dagens Industri* weekend magazine *Di Weekend*, the first in thirty years in which all four members participated in an interview.

The next year, *Abba: The Photo Book* was published (Bokförlaget Max Ström) in which I and my fellow journalist Petter Karlsson conducted new interviews with all four members of the band and wrote the text for the book. I was with Björn and Frida in London when the book was launched at Tate Modern.

Since then I have interviewed the Abbas in various contexts. I have written liner notes for the album *Live at Wembley Arena* and for new editions of *Arrival* and *Abba Gold*, interviewed Benny for my own podcast on Sveriges Radio, Björn in his capacity as chair of CISAC, which works to protect the rights of creators, and Agnetha in the context of the release of her 2013 solo album *A* and ahead of the release of her album *A+* in the summer of 2023.

For *Abba Voyage 2022* I once again did new interviews with all four for the playbill.

This is not an authorised biography of Abba – the group has never been interested in doing one of those – rather this is *my* book about Abba, based on a lifetime of listening to Abba's music and insights from more than four decades of working as a music journalist.

Another source that has been of great use to me is the member publication issued by the Official International Abba Fanclub in Roosendaal, Netherlands – one of the best and most trusted fan clubs in the world. The magazine, published since 1990 with more than 150 issues to date, is a goldmine for information on Abba.

Carl Magnus Palm is one of the world's pre-eminent Abba experts and has published many books on the band, their music and members. His book *The Complete Recording Sessions*, especially, is indispensable for detailed facts.

NEWSPAPERS

Dagens Industri, Dagens Nyheter, Expressen, Svenska Dagbladet, Aftonbladet, Eskilstuna-Kuriren, Östgöta Correspondenten, Göteborgs-Posten, Västerviks-Tidningen, Sydsvenska Dagbladet, News55, Guardian, Sunday Times, Financial Times, Daily Mail, Evening Standard, Sydney Morning Herald, New York Times, New York Post, Daily Mail, Washington Post, Los Angeles Times, Vecko-Revyn, Månadsjournalen, Okej, QX, New Musical Express, Melody Maker, Q, Smash Hits, Variety, Billboard, Entertainment Weekly, Rolling Stone, Bomp, Uncut, Mojo, Sonic, VnExpress, The Times Magazine, Smithsonian Magazine, Das Freizeit-Magasin, Pop Foto, Mikro Gids, Culture Poland, Svensk Damtidning, Classic Pop Magazine, Tidningen Extrakt, Berendsen Safety, LGBTQ Nation, Norrköpings Tidningar, Abba Omnibus Blog, Världens historia, Bass Player.

BOOKS

Benny Andersson, Lars Svensson and Dan Zetterström, *Fågelsång i Sverige: 90 välkända fåglars läten* (Mono Music)

SOURCES

Michael Bracewell, *Re-make/Re-model: Becoming Roxy Music* (Da Capo)

Fred Bronson, *The Billboard Book of Number One Hits* (Billboard)

Craig Brown, *One Two Three Four: The Beatles in Time* (Fourth Estate)

David Byrne, *How Music Works* (Canongate)

Jimmy Cauty and Bill Drummond, *The Manual (How to Have a Number One the Easy Way)* (Ellipsis)

David Cheal and Jan Dalley, *The Life of a Song* (Brewer's)

Ian Cole, *Abba Song by Song* (Fonthill)

Elvis Costello, *Unfaithful Music and Disappearing Ink* (Penguin)

Charles R. Cross, *Heavier than Heaven: The Biography of Kurt Cobain* (Sceptre)

Remko van Drongelen, *Frida beyond Abba* (Remko van Drongelen)

Leif Eriksson and Martin Bogren, *Livets band: Den svenska dans-bandskulturens historia* (Prisma)

Agnetha Fältskog, *Som jag är: Livsbilder berättade för Brita Åhman* (Norstedts)

Connie Francis, *Who's Sorry Now?* (Star)

Jan Gradvall, *Nyponbuskar, nyponbuskar, hela vägen nyponbuskar* (Albert Bonniers Förlag)

Jan Gradvall, *TV! Nedslag i Sveriges Televisions historia* (Sveriges Radios Förlag)

Jan Gradvall, Petter Karlsson, Bengt Wanselius, Jeppe Wikström, *Abba: The Photo Book* (Bokförlaget Max Ström)

Jan Gradvall, Björn Nordström, Ulf Nordström and Annina Rabe, *Tusen svenska klassiker* (Norstedts)

Peter Guralnick, *Last Train to Memphis* (Abacus)

Lars Gurell, *Svensktoppen i våra hjärtan* (Premium)

Klas Gustafson, *Schlagerkungens krig: Abba och Hoola Bandoola på Stikkan Andersons slagfält* (Alfabeta)

Ingmarie Halling, *Abba: The Backstage Stories* (Bonnier Fakta)

Will Hermes, *Love Goes to Building on Fire: Five Years in New York that Changed Music Forever* (Farrar, Straus and Giroux)

Gerri Hirshey, *Nowhere to Run: The Story of Soul Music* (Pan)

Taylor Jenkins Reid, *Daisy Jones and the Six* (Penguin)

Thomas Johansson and Mats Olsson, *Rock 'n' Roll Circus: The Performers, the Music, the Meetings* (Bonnier Facts)

Dylan Jones, *Sweet Dreams: The Story of the New Romantics* (Faber & Faber)

Eva Kjellander Hellqvist and Karin Hallgren, *Kultur och kommersialism – några exempel från svenskt 1970-tal* (Linnéuniversitetet)

Håkan Lahger, *Proggen* (Atlas)

Marie Ledin, *Min pappa hette Stikkan: Nedtecknat av Petter Karlsson* (Anderson Pocket)

Douglas MacIntyre and Grant McPhee, *Hungry Beat: The Scottish Independent Pop Underground Movement 1977–1984* (White Rabbit)

Paul McCartney, *The Lyrics: 1956 to the Present* (Norton)

Barry Miles, *London Calling: A Countercultural History of London since 1945* (Atlantic Books)

Paul Morley, *From Manchester with Love: The Life and Opinions of Tony Wilson* (Faber & Faber)

Hans Olofsson, *Stora Schlagerboken vol. 1* (Premium)

Carl Magnus Palm, *Abba: The Complete Recording Sessions* (CMP Text)

Carl Magnus Palm, *Benny's Road to Abba* (Premium Publishing)

SOURCES

Carl Magnus Palm, *Bright Lights, Dark Shadows: The Real Story of Abba* (Omnibus)

Carl Magnus Palm and Anders Hanser, *From Abba to Mamma Mia!* (Premium Publishing)

Bengt Palmers, *Slumpens skördar* (Anderson Pocket)

Pete Paphides, *Broken Greek* (Quercus)

Simon Reynolds, *Rip It Up and Start Again: Postpunk 1978–1984* (Faber & Faber)

Thomas Jerome Seabrook, *Bowie in Berlin: A New Career in a New Town* (Jawbone)

Peter Shapiro, *Turn the Beat Around: The Secret History of Disco* (Faber & Faber)

Rob Sheffield, *Turn Around Bright Eyes* (It Books)

Bob Stanley, *Yeah Yeah Yeah: The Story of Modern Pop* (Faber & Faber)

Anders Tengner, *Turnéliv* (Premium Publishing)

Larsåke Thuresson, *Ikoner* (Thuresson's Photo Collection)

David Thyrén, *Musikhus i centrum: Två lokala praktiker inom den svenska progressiva musikrörelsen: Uppsala Musikforum och Sprängkullen i Göteborg* (Stockholms Universitet)

Peter Torsén and Rolf Hammarlund, *Popåret 1967* (Vaktel)

Elisabeth Vincentelli, *Abba Gold 33⅓* (Continuum)

Elisabeth Vincentelli, *Abba Treasures: A Celebration of the Ultimate Pop Group* (Omnibus Press)

Carl Wilson, *Let's Talk About Love* (Bloomsbury)

Stany Van Wymeersch, *We all Love Abba* (Stany Van Wymeersch)

PHOTO CREDITS

NOTES

1 Kurt Loder, 'Pete Townshend: The Who's Final Days', *Rolling Stone*, 24 June 1982.

2 John Clarkson, 'Blancmange: Interview', *Pennyblackmusic*, 24 July 2012.

3 'Hep Stars i Afrika!', *Musikbyrån*, SVT, 2004.

4 'France Finally Acknowledges Its War Children', *Independent*, 7 March 2010.

5 Per Sinding-Larsen, 'Fotograf dokumenterar dansband efter black metal', *SVT Nyheter*, 15 April 2009.

6 'Stikkan Anderson is dangerous'; 'Stikkan Anderson represents unscrupulous speculation'; 'Of course what I write is shit', quoted in Klas Gustafson, *Schlagerkungens krig: Abba och Hoola Bandoola på Stikkan Andersons slagfält* (Alfabeta).

7 *Myggans nöjeslexikon.*

8 Leif Schulman, 'Sveriges Radio: 90 år och 100 procent dubbelmoral', *News55*, 25 Aug. 2015. Schulman's article has been a primary source for this section.

9 'Titiyo: "Pappa fick inte åka på ABBA:s turné för mamma"', P4 Extra, 11 Oct. 2018.

10 'It's Gibberish, but Italian Pop Song Still Means Something', NPR [website], 4 Nov. 2012.

11 A. O. Scott, '*Mamma Mia!* May Be Mindless but It's a Lot of Fun, Too', *New York Times*, 18 July 2008.

12 'Björn Ulvaeus' episode of *Sommar*, P1, 13 July 2008, https://sverigesradio.se/avsnitt/369369.

13 Kjell Ekholm, 'Han var basen i Dancing queen', Yle, 11 May 2015.

14 Tammy Lovett, 'ABBA, Fireworks and Feasting: Ringing in the New Year in Vietnam' [blog],19 Feb. 2015, tammylovett.wordpress.com/2015/02/19/abba-fireworks-and-feasting-ringing-in-the-new-year-in-vietnam.

15 Martin Rama, '"Happy New Year!", with a Bittersweet Smile', *VnExpress International*, 19 Feb. 2018.

16 Oscar Alejo Smirnov, 'The Spanish Lyrics', *Abba Fan Club* magazine, issue 100, Sept. 2009.

17 Thomas Johansson and Mats Olsson, *Rock 'n' Roll Circus: The Performers, the Music, the Meetings* (Bonnier Facts).

18 Dave Simpson, 'Glen Matlock: "No matter what we do, nothing will equate to the Sex Pistols"', *Guardian*, 11 April 2014.

19 'The Abba Incident', KLF Online, [n.d.], klf.de/home/the-abba-incident.

20 '1992: Interest Rate 500%: The Krona Floats', Riksbank, [n.d.], www.riksbank.se/en-gb/about-the-riksbank/history/historical-timeline/1900-1999/interest-rate-500--the-krona-floats.

21 Kevin Rawlinson, 'Bono Says Pressure to Look "Macho" Made Him Hide His Love of Abba', *Guardian*, 16 March 2023.

22 Jerker Virdborg, 'Med vemodet som ständig följeslagare', *Dagens Nyheter*, 26 July 2009.